The Life of Lotus Flower

by

Nalini Johal

CREATEASPACE
BY AMAZON

IN DEDICATION TO MY DECEASED SON, EDWIN

MY DECEASED MOTHER, HARPARSHAN

MY DECEASED FATHER, KISHAN

MY DECEASED NIECE, DIMPLE

MY DECEASED CAT, KIKKU

THE BEST THINGS IN LIFE CANNOT BE SEEN OR HEARD BUT FELT BY THE HEART.

Life is a journey, whether it exudes with happiness or is filled with sorrow. God's Will, is for each of us to complete it, as He planned for us. My son Edwin, died eight years ago, and I am still here on earth surviving from day to day. Not a day goes by when I don't think of him and my deceased parents and my niece Dimple. This all seems so long ago. I started writing this book in July of 2008 as self-therapy, after I got laid off from my temporary job with the social services in Hercules on May 27th, 2008. We struggle all our lives working, paying bills and making money. In the end we do not take anything with us. Only the love we give others will remain with them. Death does not discriminate against anyone, whether we are rich and famous or poor and unknown. This year of 2009 has taken away so many famous people, like Michael Jackson and Ted Kennedy, just to name a few. This has taught me that I must live each day to its fullest, as tomorrow is not guaranteed. My motto is that "everything in life happens for a reason". It might not be so obvious at the moment, but in the long run you will realize WHY. I have my younger son Billy and my husband Marco to live for. I also have my two cats Yoda and Patchee, who are ten and a half years old, who depend on me and I love very much. Billy and his wife Xandra gave me a beautiful granddaughter, Isabella, who was born this year, on March 30th. Of course, I will never get to see my grandchildren Elleona and Efrem, children of my deceased son Edwin; since their mother Kenya is the reason my son is dead now.

The year 2008 was a very long and difficult, and full of disappointments for me, as I could not find work. With the nomination of Barack Obama to run for President of the United States for the Democratic Party, brought some hope for some of us, who were looking for work. He finally became our President in the November elections. This is a man whose father was from another country, and yet the people of the United States trusted him enough to choose him for our President. I supported his campaign by a small donation and I get emails from his office, the most recent one being on his Nobel Peace Prize, which he fully deserves for working diplomatically to repair the trust, we as a nation, have lost in the world with previous administrations. I was finally working at the credit union in San Francisco, for the city and county employees on a temporary basis. My friend Sandra finally came through for me as she recommended me to her bosses in the beginning of February of 2009; they hired me as a temporary employee in the "service/ call center" and I began working on February 17th and am still working now, in mid December, 2009 and we are almost upon 2010. My last day here is December 31, 2009. Now I have to look for work again. I know, I was discriminated against because of my age, as I definitely know a lot more than the twenty something person who replaced me. I will never understand these office politics and will move on. Everything in life happens for a reason, and maybe it would be in favor of me in the long run, who knows. I am going to miss all the people with whom I worked there; and specially my boss Warren, who was one of best bosses I have ever had.

President Obama came to the bay area October 15th for a Democratic Party fund raiser at the Sir Frances Drake Hotel, for the first time since he became the President. I wish I could have met him and Michelle, as they are a lovely family and so down to earth and so helpful to common people like me and you.

I had made a lot of friends at my place of employment. Our department, the Call Center; I also have friends in the EPC Department, Accounting Department, Member Services, Collections, Marketing, and Financial Services; also the executive assistant to our CEO. They were all great people to work with and I will always miss them.

Of course I left good friends at the Appeals Unit in the Social Services department in Concord, where I worked as a temporary Senior Level Clerk for five years, with whom I keep in touch via telephone and email. I was laid off along with hundreds of temps that worked for the Contra Costa County, due to California's budget cuts by our governor, Arnold Schwartznagger on February 15, 2008. For the year I was not working, I would meet them for lunches occasionally. Gris is a permanent Senior Level Clerk with the County and she is the one who taught me every aspect of my job there. When I started working with them in March of 2003, our Supervisor was Scot, who finally retired in January of 2006, and was replaced by Yrma, who was one of the Appeals Officer then; another great boss. The other Appeal Officers were Chris, Blanca, Janie and Carl. Carl quit in November of 2003 and moved to Atlanta, in Georgia, where he found a job with the Social Services there. He was replaced by Eleanor in January of 2004. In July of 2005 I had to pick another temporary agency, as the agency I was working for, did not get their contract renewed by the County. I knew I was going to miss my friend Noel there; we promised to keep in touch even though I was not working for her agency anymore. Noel moved to Oregon, with her family to a branch of her company there and we do keep in touch. By 2006 we had two more Appeals Officers, Mitch and Denise and Laura in 2007. Carl also came back to our unit in 2007 from Georgia. Our senior Officer was Ralph.

CHAPTER 1 – THE CHILDHOOD YEARS

This is the story of LOTUS FLOWER, who was born in Poona in India on May 19th, in the late forties. India was in the grips of civil unrest and turmoil prevailed all over the country. The British Raaj had ended, and English had practically taken all of India's valuables with them. But even then, the Indian people fought amongst each other over their Hindu and Muslim religions. It was a very unsafe environment. After a couple of years of fighting and bloodshed, India was finally divided into two countries – INDIA & PAKISTAN. Mr. Jawaharlal Nehru was named the first Prime Minister of India by Mahatma Gandhi. Mr. Jinah, the Prime Minister of Pakistan. India's independence came at a steep price, of human sacrifice on August 15th, 1947.

On the other side, the birth of Lotus Flower, brought jubilation and celebration in the house of her parents, Kishan and Harparshan. She was the second child of Kishan, and an only and first child of Harparshan. Lotus Flower had an older brother, Harbhajan, from Kishan's first marriage, in which his first wife died, and an arranged marriage of Kishan and Harparshan took place. There was a big age difference between Kishan, an Indian Army Officer, and Harparshan, who was born in Lahore, now in Pakistan.

Lotus Flower grew up in a very loving environment. Harparshan was adamant in giving her husband, a boy next. So, a year and three months later Lotus Flower's sister Goodi was born on August 15, in Madras, India. Since Kishan was in the army, the family moved around the country a lot, along with their pack of servants. Two more sisters, Lali in Jullunder (January 26th, India's Republic day); and Meera in Ranchi (August 15th India's Independence day) were born, adding to Kishan and Harparshan's household. Harparshan had given birth to four girls and no boy, within a short period of time. There was the usual horseplay and interaction between the four girls who were all so close in age. Lotus Flower being the oldest was the leader of the pack. Mind you this was an era with no modern amenities like the television to keep the children occupied in their leisure time, after school. Yet, there was never a dull moment in the invention of games by the four girls and their imagination had no bounds. When one girl got in trouble, all four were punished, by taking away their playtime and having to stand in the corner for an hour or so. That was a big punishment for them. No one could lay an abusive hand on them.

As Lotus Flower and Goodi got to school age, they were left with their maternal grandmother, Chachijee and maternal uncle, Rajinder, in Jullunder and were enrolled in school there. This brought about big separations for the girls and their parents. The girls missed their parents a lot. When Lotus Flower was three years old she was enrolled in a nursery school, where her maternal aunt Harprastish was the school principal. Every morning she was walked to the school bus by the servant and picked up at school by her aunt. In the afternoon she was put on the school bus and dropped off at a corner, where the servant was waiting to pick her up after school. This was a happy time in Lotus Flower's life, as she got to play with children her own age with the toys at school.

Until one afternoon, the school bus dropped off the little three- year- old at one corner before hers. When she got off the bus, there was no servant to take her home. The more she walked around, calling the servant's name over and over again, the more lost she got. She walked and walked in the scary streets to no avail, she finally ended up in the courtyard of a nice family, who tried to feed her. She would not eat, even though she was hungry and thirsty. She was taught not to take anything from strangers. She finally did take a drink of water and lay down on a cot under the tree offered by the nice family, and fell asleep. When she awoke, she still could not find a familiar face. The nice family, who took her in, arranged a search of her family. They put her on a bicycle and walked the bazaar, by beating drums and saying "this little girl is lost and who does she belong to". Lotus Flower's brother Harbhajan's friend saw her and led them to her house. In the meantime, there was a big search going on at her grandmother's house too. When she saw the servant, Lotus Flower started to cry and kick him saying "Why did you not come to pick me up". The day after this incident, her mother Harparshan, made a solemn promise to herself, to build a big house in New Delhi, India and stay in one place with her children. She was tired of moving around the country with her husband who was in the Army. She wanted to keep all her children together.

Lotus flower's maternal aunt got an arranged marriage with an Army Captain Brar. The marriage was arranged by her father and mother. The wedding was a big affair at the Army house in Jullunder. That whole week was party time. All of Kishan's and Brar's Army bigwig associates participated in the affair. Lotus Flower and her sisters had a great time. This marriage of her aunt produced their only daughter named Bubbles, who was the girls' cousin now.

Harparshan's wish came true, when her husband, Kishan, was transferred to New Delhi, India. Harparshan bought some land there and started to build her dream home. She learned how to drive the family car "Hillman" (an English car with stick shift), by herself. Kishan went on army maneuvers every now and then, but Harparshan stayed with her daughters, whom she enrolled in the local private convent school there. This worked out very well for the family.

Days turned into weeks, and weeks into years. Here come the adolescent years for Lotus Flower and her sisters which should have been happy times for them. But, there came this time when Kishan and Harparshan could not see eye to eye. Harparshan had built the house in Chanakya Puri, a very high end suburb and worth a lot of money, and Kishan's relatives egged him on saying "How come your wife owns the house. You, as a man must force your wife to transfer the house to your name". This is a typical response in a male-dominated country like India. Unknown to Harparshan, who could not read or write English, Kishan, had her sign over the house to his name. Harparshan had built the house with her sweat and tears and she was not ready to give up the fight for her house. Their children (including their step- brother Harbhajan) were affected with the negative feeling between their parents. This brought a great deal of sorrow in their young lives. Lotus Flower looked up to her brother Harbhajan, who was about twelve years older. To her, her brother was cool and could drive almost anything. He could drive a motorcycle, car, big rigs and fly an aircraft. She said she wanted to be like her brother when she grew up.

Lotus Flower had to accompany her mother to lawyers and judges chambers and act as her mother's translator, while in her early teens. She had to miss school in order to do this. There was always a threatened danger from Kishan's retaliation towards his wife. He would beat his wife up for no reason, when he came home, drunk from Army parties. One night, with her father at another party, Lotus Flower asked her mother if she could sleep with her, as she had a nightmare. In the middle of the night, she heard her mother screaming and someone beating her up and when the light was turned on, she found it was her father who was beating her mother. She screamed at her father to stop it and that she hated him. Later that day when her brother Harbhajan came home Harparshan took her anger out on him. Beaten and bruised, threw him out. Where was he to go? Lotus Flower was very sad as she did not want her brother to leave and she cried when he did. This brought about Harparshan going into hiding with her friend's and relative's houses, along with her oldest daughter, Lotus Flower. There were long separations from her brother and younger sisters. It was terrible as her family life was being torn apart due to a court case between her parents.

One night Lotus Flower fell sick with influenza virus and her temperature reached to very high level and had to be taken to the emergency room at the army hospital. After a few days stay there and with the help of medication she was able to return home. That night when she fell asleep outside on a cot, as it was too hot to sleep indoors, she awoke in the middle of the night, looked up at the sky, and amidst the twinkling stars she saw the image of her "Guru Nanak". She tried to yell to the other family members asleep but lost her voice. She wanted everyone to see what she was looking at but could not. A total calm and love for her religion came over her. It was as if god was telling the thirteen year old that life was about to turn around for the better for her and her family. She did not want her parents to split up as she loved them both dearly. The next day when she awoke she told her mother this and everyone thought that she must have hallucinated. But as god told her that night, her father and mother settled their differences and Kishan signed over the house back to Harparshan's name in the coming weeks. This was the start of a deep faith in god embedded in Lotus Flower's Life, one that would stay with her the rest of her life. This faith in god is what would carry her through all the difficult times about to come in the future.

CHAPTER 2 – LOTUS FLOWER'S STORY IN HER OWN WORDS

 I, Lotus Flower (Nalini), was born in a Sikh household. My maternal grandfather had fought for the freedom of India from the British rule, along with Mahatma Gandhi. The British government would imprison all who retaliated against them. Both my mother's parents would be imprisoned for a day or two and released when the prisons got too full, along with other protesters. My mother and aunt were very young when their father, who came from a wealthy family, passed away at an early age. He got very sick from the prison food. As soon as he passed away, my grandfather's mother and older brothers and their families kicked my grandmother out along with my mother and aunt. When my mother's grandmother died they found a chest of gold buried under their house. My maternal grandmother had to go through a very hard time trying to provide for her children. She had to take a job as guard at the mentally ill patient hospital, which was unheard of in those days. My mother dropped out of school to clean and cook for the family, and to see that my aunt would get her education, which she did. She eventually completed her Bachelors degree, which was unusual for a woman to accomplish in India in that time and age. My grandmother would tell us stories about the crazy patients in the hospital and how one of them tried to kill her, after an altercation. As my mother got a little older, my grandmother arranged a marriage for her with my father, an Indian army officer. Soon after the marriage, I was born.

On the other hand I knew very little about my father's family. My father was the youngest of four brothers and had two sisters. When I was very little I remember seeing an old lady in white clothes carrying and walking with a stick and all hunched over. I remember screaming and crying of terror when I saw her. Someone was saying 'Meet your grandmother, your dad's mom'. That woman looked so old and scary to me and I would not go near her. My father's families were all farmers. They produced corn, wheat, mustard and vegetables, which were later sold at the markets in town.

 I remember my mother telling me, that when I was a baby and would cry, she would move my Pram (stroller) in a flowerbed. That would stop me from crying and I would baby-talk to the flowers. I guess that is why I have a great love and respect for nature. Growing up in a big household, we had no shortage of imagination. Our parents would put us down for an afternoon nap, as it was too hot to venture out in the heat in the afternoons. As soon as my parents took their nap, Goodi and I would wake our younger sisters Lali and Meera and drag them out on the veranda to play. I remember one instance, when we were playing doctor, nurse and patients. Of course, I was the doctor and Goodi was my nurse and Lali and Meera (three and a year and a half old), our younger sisters were the patients, together with the five young puppies, that were born recently. I would run down to our bathtub, fill a syringe, I found, with water and gave enema to my sisters and the puppies. I put my little sisters on their potties, but the puppies were crying and going all over the veranda. All this commotion woke my parents up and I was in deep doodoo. I was told that I was punished and no more play for me for the rest of day and I had to stand in a corner. This drama was played out as this actually happened to me. A nurse had come by our house one time and gave me an enema behind a screen door. My sister Goodi thought that she was being left behind, that I was getting candy and she was not. She yelled "I want the same thing as Lotus Flower is getting" and would not take no for an answer. My father chuckled and told the nurse to take Goodi next. When the water started to fill up in her stomach she yelled "that's enough. I don't want this anymore. Where is my candy"?

When my father was stationed in Ranchi, where my youngest sister Mina was born, we actually lived in an old castle, which was built by a Muslim king for his American wife. When the king died his American wife returned to her country, leaving the castle deserted. It was overgrown with vegetation inside and out, but my father's army regiment cleaned all that out and made it habitable. My father's regiment," the 1ST SIKH L I", all moved in this castle, along with us. The grounds had about two hundred guava and mango trees and some banana and Lychee trees. The hot and dry weather of Ranchi was also home to poisonous snakes, like the king cobra. There was an old well on the property, and I remember seeing snakes fall from an overhanging tree branch, into the old well. I used to think that the snakes climbed up the tree branches to eat the fruit, until one day I saw a snake swallow a bird on the tree branch. That was so gruesome to watch, for a six year old.

I remember one evening my friends (twenty army families were living there) and I were playing games on the veranda. Someone said let's find a jump rope, and I yelled "I found one" and went running to pick it up and it turned out to be a coral snake. One of my friend pulled me away, as the snake reared its head up. All the children started yelling "snake, snake". Our parents, who were having their evening tea in the garden, thought we were all playing "snake". Finally one of the servants saw the snake and brought out a big stick to kill it, by squashing its head. He said that he could feel the poison travel up the stick and burn his hands. There were also rumors of ghosts in the castle, among the servants. One of the servants peed on the grave of the king that was buried there. The other servants said that they heard him yelling and could hear someone slapping him. This was all very scary to me, except in the daytime we would climb the four towers of the castle and play hide and seek. We would all stay indoors after dark, so, one evening after my sister, Meera was born my mother asked me to go get an extra blanket for the baby from her bedroom. I thought, how she could ask me to do that. I would have to cross the front veranda from the living room to her bedroom. I used to see two shiny eyes in the dark (maybe a cat). I braced myself, and ran as fast as I could, and slammed straight into a big lock hanging off the closed bedroom door. I must have passed out, as the next thing I remember was, that I was lying in the bed and my parents and the house doctor and nurse were all hovering over me. My head hurt and mom said that the doctor had put stitches on my wound on the forehead. I still have this scar, to this day. My beautiful white dress was all red with my blood.

We had a little dog named "Bum Bum". Ever since I remember we always had a dog or two in our household. My father's army papers came for his transfer. My parents were discussing about "Bum Bum" one evening and what to do with him, as we were all flying to New Delhi this time and not taking the train. The next day our dog started to froth at the mouth. The servants said that a snake had bit him. He had to be put to sleep. I remember my sister Goodi and I cried a lot at his loss.

In the months before our departure from Ranchi, a woman who worked for us as a maid brought her oldest daughter, Sudan. Our maid discussed with our mother if we could take Sudan with us as she could work for us. She said she had eight kids and she could not afford to take care of them all. After a lot of hesitation, my mother finally agreed. Sudan was about seven years older than I, and instead of being our maid, Sudan became my buddy, even though she was a teenager and older than I. My mother treated Sudan as one of her daughters. When time came for us to leave, Sudan came along with us to New Delhi. I had a special bond with Sudan, not only as an older sister but a bond strong enough to last forever. Later on my mother changed her name from 'Sudan' to 'Darshan', which was more of a Punjabi name.

My father was stationed at New Delhi, the capital city of India. Here we adopted a dog named Rita, a German Sheppard. She was a fierce dog and chased after anyone who came near us. We loved her a lot, and after she died, we were devastated again. We kept one of her pup, named him Johnny. Johnny lived with us for fourteen years, and practically grew up with us. Johnny was a mellow personality compared to his mother Rita. He protected us fiercely too.

After residing in the Army houses for a few years, here is where my mother put down roots and started to build us a house in Chanakya Puri, which was a mile and a half from the "Rashtri Bhavan" (Presidential palace) and within walking distance to all the embassies, including the American Embassy and Hotel Ashok. When the annex of the house was completed, we moved in it, while the rest of the house was still being built. We had to move in there, as my father got stationed to Darjeeling, Assam, after a three year stay in New Delhi. One evening Johnny was hit by a car on the main road, and broke his hind leg. My parents took him to the emergency room at the army's veterinarian hospital. His leg was bandaged and he was admitted to the hospital for a few days. The next morning we received a telephone call from the hospital that Johnny had escaped, with his leg still in a bandage and his bones not set yet. My father called his old regiment at the army base, to see if Johnny had come by there, as that is the only place my father used to take him occasionally. They said he did come by there and then left. He still did not know our new home in Chanakya Puri yet. We were all shaken up by this and put out posters of him but to no avail. Two days later Johnny found us. He had traveled about six or seven miles on his broken leg. The minute he saw us he started to wail and cry. He jumped on us, and I actually saw tears in his eyes. It is as though he was saying "why did you leave me so far away". We all were so happy to have him back and so was he. From then on he would follow us to school every day and sit outside the fence of the school. When school was over he would follow us home. This went on for a couple of weeks, until the school principal, Mother Blanda, called my mother and complained about our dog outside the school fence and that finally had to come to an end.

Our widowed grandmother and her son, Rajinder, my mother and aunt's half brother, came to live with us. My grandmother was getting old and senile and could not take care of herself anymore. It could have been Alzheimer's disease, as back then no one knew anything about it. My mother sold her house in Jullunder and my grandmother and uncle were permanent fixtures in our house. So, when our house was finally built, my mother leased the whole house to the royal family of Indochina for three years, to recuperate some extra money to pay off her building debts. We all moved into a big rented house in another superb of New Delhi. Here we were enrolled in another school, Delhi Public. Darshan helped my mother run the household.

When my mother and I were hiding from my father, in my mom's friends homes, I would have to pull out of school for several weeks to accompany my mother to her lawyer's office and finally before the judge. I was my mother's translator, as my mother could not speak, read or write in English. My mother was trying to take back the house she had built, from my father who had tricked her into signing it off to him. This went on for several months and finally my parents realized their folly. They were tearing the family apart. They both settled their differences and we finally became a family again.

In the meantime, unknown to my mother, her brother Rajinder had gotten Darshan pregnant. My mother was furious at them, and forced them to get married. Now Darshan became our aunt. She had two daughters with Rajinder, Pinky and Neelu. As number of people in our household grew we needed to move back to my mother's house in Chanakya Puri. So, when the three year lease was up, we all moved back to our old house, which was large enough for all of us.

In the meantime my brother had an arranged marriage, when I was in my teens. His wife, Amarjeet was from a village neighboring ours. His wedding was a very big occasion in our village, near Jullunder. There was a big celebration which last about a week. We all went to Jullunder, Punjab for this occasion. We all liked our new sister-in-law, Amarjeet. My brother and his new wife rented a house in Jullunder, in order for his wife to finish her college at the University in Jullunder. My brother had applied for a position in the Indian air force, which was rejected, as he did not pass the physical of a twenty/twenty hearing and eyesight test. He then got a job flying planes and delivering goods from one city to another, for a private company. This lasted him a year or so, and he decided to move to the United Kingdom where he could got a job driving double- decker transit buses in London. His wife, Amarjeet moved in with us in New Delhi for a couple of months, as she was pregnant with their first child, before flying off to England to join my brother there, after he bought a house and settled there. Before Amarjeet left, I got a promise from her, to name their child "Dimple" if she was a girl. Later that year we received news that they had a girl whom they named "Dimple" according to my wishes. I was very happy about it and sorely missed them a lot.

The Sardar Patel road, on which all the foreign dignitaries passed by, from the Palam airport to the presidential palace, ran parallel to our house. So when Queen Elizabeth II and the Chinese leader Mao sing Tung came to visit India, their open motorcade passed by on Sardar Patel road which was lined by cheering crowds. I remember seeing them up very close. The Queen's dress and hat were a ruffled sky blue and she had short white gloves on, while she waved with a smile, as she passed by us. That was quite an event to remember. Years later Lali and I met Senator Ted Kennedy and Mrs. Indira Gandhi in an elevator at Hotel Ashok, on two separate occasions. When I was thirteen years old, I accompanied my father to a party at Maharaja Faridkot's house, where I met a gentleman who was director or producer of the movie "Lawrence of Arabia".

I remember when I reached my mid teens. My mother was very supportive of our love and talent in the theater industry. She encouraged us to put up a PLAY for her and the family at least once a week. We would use cots tilted sideways as the stage, and bed sheets as curtains and used the radio for music. Those were the beginning days of my acting debutante. In the meantime we had to keep our grades up. After school, we had a tutor come over to the house and help us in English, Math and science as I was in my high school years. My father and mother encouraged us to learn our own language, Punjabi. So, we had a tutor come in twice a week for that. So we would be able to learn how to read and write in Punjabi. This encouraged me to read our holy book and say my prayers, daily. If my sisters and I were not in school we had tutors for almost everything, even a music teacher, who was blind. My sister Lali and I hated the music sessions, so we would try to sneak out of it, thinking the music teacher would not know, as he was blind. That was wrong, he somehow knew, to our amazement. How come a blind person would know that we were sneaking out? That was a total mystery to me for a very long time. I remember that English language was my favorite subject and I graduated from High school with very high honors.

My maternal aunt introduced us to our first play "Prithviraj Chauhan", while I was still in school. My aunt who did soap operas on the radio had a friend, we called Sheila aunty, who was producing an Opera and thought my sister Goodi and I could try it out. Try we did, and were accepted in this play. Now here come the two months and more of rehearsals. My mother would chaperone us every day, after school for rehearsals. The opera finally came to town and here was our chance to shine. The opera was to run for two weeks, Monday through Saturday, daily. We had to get to the theater for makeup and dress fittings before the show. Finally the opera was on for about an hour or so daily. All of us got rave reviews in the newspaper and the show would end each night with a standing ovation. I felt like this was a dream, and I would soon wake up. The second week, we found out that our Prime Minister, Jawaharlal Nehru was going to make a showing at the theatre to see our play. That night the security people were everywhere and even in the 'Green rooms' where we were changing into our theatrical clothes and having our makeup done. Mr. Nehru was going to come in for 10 or 15 minutes only, but he stayed for the whole show. At the end of the show, the prime minister came on stage and presented the female cast a bouquet of roses. I had to pinch myself to see if this was real. This was the most exciting night for us all.

After this came two more plays for my sisters and I. These were again produced by the same lady who produced the first opera. The second one was an opera named "Heer Ranja" and a play named "Mada Cactus".   My sister Goodi and I also did a documentary on 'Punjab state' and Goodi played the leading lady role in the Shakespeare's play "Taming of the Shrew".   That night after the play, when the family got home we found our servant, another young boy who was dumped by his family at our house, lying dead.   The doctor said that he had a heart attack.   But he was only eleven or twelve years old.   We all suspected that our cook had scared him in the dark and his heart must have failed.

In the late sixties my sister Lali and I did a "Coca Cola" commercial, and played extras in a bollywood movie "Pyar ka Maussum".   I guess we were on to a life in the theatre.   Bollywood, here we come.

CHAPTER 3 – THE DATING YEARS

In the final year of my high school, I was introduced to my first love, Cucu, by my sisters at their friend's party. I was a slow starter. My sisters Goodi and Lali had already started seeing boys and I had no idea what they were up to. My mother had drilled it in my head that all the boys I see, are like my brothers. Only she and my dad would arrange a marriage for me and that good girls don't date. So, I believed her. My sisters were always sneaking out to meet guys and my mother would give me an extra allowance to snitch on them. Snitch I did. This would get them into trouble and they would be grounded.

One weekend, they said their friend was having a party at her house and I was invited too. When we went to the party, there were guys there too. This girl's parents were out of town. The music was blaring and there was drinking and cigarette smoking going on. Couples were necking. I decided that I was going to tell mom what was going on here. My sisters got scared and they fixed me good.

A cute guy, Cucu, came to me and asked me to dance and I glared at him and said no. Good girls don't do this kind of stuff, I thought. Someone gave me a glass of orange juice and unknown to me that there was booze in it, I drank it. The next thing I knew, Cucu and I were dancing pretty close and he kept nuzzling up my neck and his hands were all over me. Goodi came up to me and smiled and said that Cucu was our neighbor Jyoti's younger brother. Jyoti and her mom and my mom and I used to go for walks in the evening in our neighborhood, after dinner. I didn't know she had a brother, let alone three brothers. The oldest one was married, and then Jyoti, and then Cucu and Pappu.

That evening when we were ready to leave the party, I realized I had hickies on my neck. My sisters said to wrap my dupatta (Indian scarf) around my neck, so dad and mom would not see. I felt so ashamed that night for what I had some guy do to me. Yet deep down my heart, it all felt good. If this was love, I sure was in love. So I was fixed by my sisters pretty good. If I snitched on them, they said they would tell mom about me drinking and dancing with a guy, I hardly knew. I guess those days were over for me. Cucu would call me and pick me up after school and take me for a ride on his Harley motorcycle. We would make out in a park and then he would drive me back home. My parents were not to know anything about this. Cucu's younger brother Pappu was dating Lali and Goodi was dating Cucu and Pappu's good friend.

I started to see Cucu regularly. He would drive by my bedroom window and toot his horn, and I would run out to meet him outside, far away from our house, so no one would see him pick me up. One day he said we were going to see his best friend, Sammy, who lived at the Ambassdor hotel. I said okay and when we arrived there Cucu let himself in Sammy's room with his key. When we entered the room Sammy had left Cucu a note saying he would be back later that day, and for us to enjoy ourselves. That day I lost my virginity, a couple of months after meeting Cucu. I was so ashamed and it hurt me. Who said that sex was so good? I did not like it a bit. I don't know what the hype was all about sex. After that incident I tried not to be alone with him as I did not want deal with the sex part. He assured me that it would get better after a few more times. I was so scared that I would get pregnant. Cucu said from now on he would use protection and try to be gentler.

After months of dating and seeing Cucu on the sly, he said he wanted to marry me and gave me a ring. Since he was of the Sikh religion too, we did not think our parents would mind if they found out. He said first his older sister Jyoti had to get married first and then we would tell our parents about us. I loved him so much and since he was my very first love, I agreed to anything he would say.

In December of that year, I graduated high school with great honors. Now it was time to think about college. But instead we heard that the BEATLES pop group was coming to visit India. We also found out that they were booked at hotel Oberoi Intercontinental in New Delhi. It so happened that my dad was friends with the head of Security for the hotel, Mr. Singh. We pestered our dad to accompany us to the hotel and through Mr. Singh maybe meet the BEATLES. They were the next thing to ELVIS PRESLEY. I remember this was the most exciting thing that would ever happen to us. We had gone swimming at the Officers club, when we heard that the BEATLES had landed at the Palam airport in New Delhi. We rushed home. I had to drive my motor scooter and drop my sister Lali off at home and then go back to the club and pick up my sister Meera and bring her home. We all got dressed and my dad drove us to the hotel. We were met there by Mr. Singh who took us up the elevator to the sixth floor, where the BEATLES were staying in suites 601 and 602. Mr. Singh knocked on the door and the BEATLES' manager introduced himself to us as Brian Epstein. He said that we could not see the group as they were in India for a spiritual and learning tour only. They were not seeing anyone. We could hear the musical instruments being playing inside, including the Indian musical instrument 'Sitar'. Their manager said to give him our autograph books and he would have the Beatles sign it and give them to Mr. Singh and we could collect it from him later. We were so close and yet could not meet our Idol pop group. Well, unknown to us, that was the last we saw of our autograph books. The manager must have given them to a waiter who was to give it to Mr. Singh. Mr. Singh claims he never got the autograph books back. Someone must have stolen them. I had autographs from Mr. Nehru, Mrs. Indira Gandhi and a lot of Bollywood stars in it. I remember getting very mad about this.

One morning we awoke to a very sick dog Johnny. The night before the servant had given him a chicken bone and it got lodged in his throat. He could barely breathe and was choking to death. My mother hurried up to change her clothes and take him to the pet emergency hospital. In the meantime my father took him and had him put to sleep as he knew that Johnny was dying and suffering needlessly. After all he was fourteen human years old. When my mother found out she was livid with anger at my father and called him a murderer. The whole household was in tears. What would the household be like without Johnny sitting in the living room and greeting all that came in and out of the house. We cried a lot on his loss. He was not only a pet but part of our family. I remember my mother did not talk to my father for months after this incident.

My father was recalled to active duty just after his retirement. China had invaded India from the north. My father had to go to war with China with his regiment. The war ended almost as soon as it started. My father told us that India's weapons were outdated compared to that of China's. A truce was called between the two countries after China occupied some of India's land in the North. My father came home safe and sound.

That year I enrolled in college as a psychology major. Of course I was still seeing Cucu on the sly too. Lali and I and Pappu and Cucu participated in a dance contest at the Oberoi. TWIST by Chubby Checker was the craze then. We won the first and second prize in that contest among hundreds of contestants. That was such a big deal. We would all go out on dates and dance parties at hotels or our friend's houses. I remember my father was to drop us off at a girlfriend's party and he ended up not leaving and staying with us. My dad was drinking scotch and having a good time at the party among the teenagers. Someone yelled "Whose old man is he". We kept quiet, and stayed away from him, as we were so embarrassed.

There was the premiere of a big bollywood movie in New Delhi. The movie was "WAQT" meaning 'Time' in Hindi. We had just seen it and had a crush one of the big bollywood star, Raaj Kumar. We heard that the all the big stars were staying at hotel Ashok, which was pretty close to our house. My sisters and I started to walk to the hotel and told our mother where we were going – to meet Raaj Kumar, who was staying there. My father was mad when he found out that we had gone there alone. When we arrived at the hotel, we found out which room number he was staying in. We took the elevator and knocked on the door. Some guy answered the door and asked us if we were Kishan's daughters and we said yes and he let us in. Wow, we wondered who told him who we were. We sat down to chat with the movie star Raaj Kumar. He told us that our father called and told him that his daughters were coming to see him and that he better be nice to us. It so happened that Raaj had a friend named Kishan and when my dad called he thought it was his friend who was calling. My dad called while we were still in his room and invited Raaj to come over for dinner to our house. Raaj accepted the offer and his chauffer drove us back to our house. He had dinner with us at our house and my dad had drinks with Raaj. When it came time for Raaj to leave to catch his flight back to Bombay, he would not go. His producer had to come by and drag him to the airport. So after this incident, whenever Raaj was in town he would call my dad and come over to our house for a drink party with him. My friends would come over and get to meet him too; especially Cucu's sister Jyoti would come by all the time.

Over time my sisters started dating some other guys and this did not sit well with my boyfriend, Cucu. Here was the Indian male mentality talking again. He would urge me to talk to them about dating strange men. Personally I did not think it was my business as to who they dated as long as they were safe. I told Cucu this and he would argue with me that I was the oldest sister and should talk to my younger sisters and keep them in control. It seemed I was stuck in the middle of this dilemma between Cucu's beliefs and my younger sisters dating dramas. This made me hesitant about Cucu. We had been dating for almost seven to eight months now and instead of enjoying our time together, we ended up arguing about my sisters and what they did. When Cucu and I fought about this, he would take off to Missouri, a small town in the hills, with his friend Sammy, who was from the royal family of Nepal. Sammy had a family mansion there and they had billiards table in their house. Cucu loved to play billiards. Sammy also had a younger pretty sister living there too. I wondered what went on between Cucu and her. This meant I would not see him for weeks and this would break my heart, but I was so in love with him and waited for him to call when he got back in town. This went on for couple of more months or so. When we saw each other after a week or two things would be happy again and then they would go downhill from there.

In June that year, I had a terrible nightmare. In my dream I went to Cucu's house and his uncle came out and said that "Cucu was no more". I woke up crying and scared as the nightmare was so real. I called Cucu and when I saw him that day and told him about my dream he just started laughing and saying that it was only a dream. He was leaving for Missouri next month with his buddy Sammy and assured me that there was nothing going on between him and Sammy sister. He assured me that he loved me and no one else. In July he went out of town and came back safe and sound in a couple of weeks.

In the meantime my parents had been trying to arrange a marriage for me with some military guy, whose family was friends with mine. When Cucu was out of town, my parents invited this family over and have Ninni meet me, and most probably check me out. They were coming for dinner to our house. I told my parents that I did not want to get married yet and did not want to meet this person. There was a big commotion with my father yelling that I better say yes to this guy or some heads would roll. My mother was begging me to please say yes to keep the peace in the family. I could not tell her that I was in love with Cucu. My father would not take no for an answer from me, and asked me who gave me that ring on my finger. I told him that I bought it myself. My sister Goodi told our mother that she would get married to this guy, knowing my reasons for saying no. The family came over for dinner and I purposely dressed up in real ugly clothes and my sister Goodi was dressed to the nines. Later we found that the military guy Ninni liked Goodi instead and not me. I was really relieved. The next few days my sister had her engagement party. Everyone was happy and there was jubilation in both the households. Ninni was in town only for a week, before he left to rejoin his military unit in Jammu & Kashmir. That Friday Goodi invited Ninni over to one of her friend's house who was throwing a party for her she said. Cucu and I and my sisters Lali and Meera were invited too. We all piled up in two cars and went to this party. Goodi did tell us that this friend of hers was one of her old boyfriend. Without revealing this to Ninni and Cucu we told them that this guy's sister was Goodi's friend. I remember it was raining cats and dogs as the monsoon season was upon us. As we went to this house for the party, no one else was there, but us. We thought maybe more people would come by later, as the weather was rainy. Our host said that he would be back after picking up some booze and snacks for us. Cucu got very suspicious of this fella and told him that he didn't mind going to pick the stuff himself. As Cucu had already had a few beers, I told him I would go with him and he told me to stay with my sisters and that he would be alright and be back in a few. Ninni jumped in the car with Cucu and they both drove off. I asked Goodi as to what was really going on and she said that her old boyfriend wanted to give her a party on her engagement and no one else was invited but us. So, we waited for Cucu and Ninni to come back with the food and drinks. One hour passed by, then two hours but no word from them. We thought maybe his car broke down and maybe they would call us. After waiting for three hours we asked our host to drop us at our house, as there was no word from Cucu or Ninni. We thought as Cucu knew where we lived and would drop Ninni off later. I was very angry at Cucu that he did not call me if they had stopped off to get drinks at a bar.

When we got home past midnight my parents asked where Ninni was and why he did not accompany us home. We told them the truth that he and another person at the party had taken off to get food and drinks and never came back. This night was like a nightmare to us. Pretty soon we received a call from the police that there was a horrific accident and that Ninni was at the hospital in the intensive care, and may not be able to live. All this time I kept asking as to what happened to the person who was driving, Cucu. They told me that he was fine and had gone. How could he not call me, that's what kept running through my mind. I called the police station again for more information about Cucu and they put me on hold for a very long time. The daylight was now coming through the windows. My sister Goodi kept crying and I told her to stop crying and that Ninni would pull through and to be brave for him. Goodi's friend's mom came by and took the phone out of my hand and disconnected me from my call to the police. She said, "You need to put the phone down, as Cucu was killed last night in the car accident. They say that his chest hit the steering wheel and he died instantly." I remember screaming and hitting her with my fists and she just stood there and let me and then grabbed me in an embrace. I felt like my life had ended. I just kept getting hysterical and our neighbor the doctor had to come over and give me a shot to calm me down. After sleeping through the sedation, I woke up and said I wanted to kill myself. My mother had my aunt Darshan follow me and not leave me alone. I got dressed in a hurry and ran down to Cucu's house where his devastated parents were hesitant at welcoming me. I just forced myself in and hugged his mom and started crying. As we both cried Cucu's body was brought in to his house. He still had his red turban and cowboy boots on but his eyes were closed. I thought if I touched his face that he would wake up and my nightmare would end. But that would never happen and I would never see him again for the rest of my life. His funeral was set, which I attended by helping to carry his corpse to the cremation pit, along with his brothers and uncle. Only men are allowed this duty at the funeral, but I did not care. My Cucu was dead and I should be dead too. There were no other options for my life now. Darshan helped me emotionally, like a big sister would, as my world lay shattered in front of me.

CHAPTER 4 - LIFE AFTER THE TRAGEDY

Life went on whether I liked it or not. You know when someone close to you dies you think that it was only a dream. You would wake up and see that person again. But death is so final, and the person I loved was never coming back. I cried so much in the coming months after Cucu died, that I could not cry any more.

On the other hand, Ninni, my sister Goodi's fiancé was slowly recovering from his car accident injuries. He was in intensive care for three or four days, and the doctors at the army hospital would not guarantee that would live or not. My sister and my family would go visit him at the hospital. The hospital staff said that since he was in the military and was in good physical condition prior to the accident, that he would recover fast.

The accident occurred on August 9th and by October Ninni was recovering well. Since his jaw was severed he could not speak at all in the beginning. But slowly he could talk a little. The first thing he wanted was get married to my sister Goodi. Their marriage was set for December 25th of that year. My sister was still in High School and was to complete it by the end of December. While there was celebration for my sister's upcoming wedding, I could not get over my grief. In mourning I wore white for five months, until my sister's wedding, when I was required to wear bright colors.

The wedding was held in Jullundur, Punjab and not New Delhi, since my family did not want to upset Cucu's family who lived a couple of blocks away from our house in New Delhi. We all went to Punjab for the wedding ceremony. I hardly remember all the details of this celebration and my heart was not really into it. Even though I felt happiness for my sister, I was sad that I was not getting married to Cucu. We had great dreams for our future. Since his family was into building and selling houses, he wanted us to move to Beirut, Lebanon and form such a company for him.

I finished my first year of college and dropped out. A friend of mine took me to a party at the American Ambassador's house, around the corner from our house. She wanted me to cheer up. This was an afternoon brunch at the Roosevelt house, where Senator Chester Bowles, the Ambassador, and his wife were hosting it. For the very first time I drank the French champagne, Dom Perignon. My friend Maya and I mingled with other guests there. There were the usual Ambassadors and High commissioners from other countries among the guests. We got invited to several upcoming parties at this affair. Mr. and Mrs. Bowles were gracious hosts and loved the Indian culture. Mrs. Bowles was wearing a Sari, an Indian outfit and told us that she loved the Indian outfits as they were so colorful and bright. The official photographer took our picture with our hosts. Maya and I had a great time at the party and left with several more invitations to attend more parties at other such parties. We were invited to the British and Canadian High Commissioner's houses, the Argentine, Swedish, French, Chilean, and Italian Ambassadors houses.

I guess we got introduced to the Jet Set crowd. I asked for my sisters Lali and Meera to accompany me to these parties. The British High Commissioner and his wife sent their Rolls Royce car to pick us up for their party. The Congolese ambassador, Alphonse Lema had the greatest parties that one would hardly believe. He and his wife threw parties that lasted two days straight. Life did brighten up for me. My parents were also invited to his parties. Mrs. Lema was German and their only son, who was five years old, could speak five languages. He spoke French and Swahili, his father's languages and German and English, his mother's l languages and Hindi his nanny's language.

At one such party we got introduced to modeling. There was a model search for a fashion show by Pierre Cardin and Lali, Meera and I all applied for it. The designer was looking for tall and very thin girls to show off his collection of mini skirts and dresses. Unfortunately Lali and I did not get picked as we had curves and were not stick thin enough for his show. My sister Meera did get picked for it and did the fashion show at the convention center at the hotel Ashok. I did 'still' modeling for different products and my picture was on the last page of the Readers Digest publications. Lali and I did the Coca Cola commercial in New Delhi, Buddha Jyanti gardens. It took four days for them to shoot a two minute commercial, and was shown in the big screen movie theatre, before a Hindi movie.

Lali and I and some of our girlfriends were invited to fly to Sirinagar to act in a bollywood movie. Of course our mother accompanied us as our chaperone. The movie company paid for our flight and accommodation for a week in Sirinagar. This was a great experience plus vacation for us. Every evening after the days shooting, we would all get together and party with the movie crew at Oberoi Sirinagar, which included the actor, Shashi Kapoor, and actress, Asha Parakh, in the movie, "Pyar ka Maussum".

I also started dating again. My dates were usually Italian, French, etc. But, I met a guy named Chander, who was one of the Aid-de-camp to the President of India. My sister Lali and I dated Bunny and Chander for a few months. My sister, Lali and I would go meet these guys at the President's palace, where they lived, too. They would throw parties at the swimming pool at the palace, since the Indian President was too old and hardly ever used the pool. They let me throw a party of mine there too. The food was catered from an Italian chef and our friend Alphonse Lema, the Congolese Ambassdor, provided the music for my party there. One day while Lali and I went shopping at the Ashok hotel, we got in an elevator with Senator Ted Kennedy, who said hello to us. You know in such a situation, his face looked familiar, but we could not place his name. He got off at one of the floors with his secret service guys. As soon as the elevator door closed, Lali and I looked at each other and said "That was Ted Kennedy" simultaneously. We tried to go back to the floor he got off on, and ran up and down the corridors to see where he went, like idiots, but could not find him. Oh well, missed getting his autograph. We also met Mrs. Indira Gandhi, who at the time was the Minister of Broadcasting, in an elevator at the Ashok Hotel.

After a few months I started going steady with an Italian guy, named Alfio, who was twelve years older than I. He worked for the United Nations, peace keeping mission and was stationed in New Delhi. He would take me to various big parties around town and I would tag along with him as his girlfriend. When the Italians and South Americans would get together at these functions, they would talk in Italian or Spanish. I hated this, since I could not understand what they were talking about. I would ask Alfio, to please talk in English, in my presence since it was very rude otherwise. But he would slip and forget this and revert to his language again. All Italians and their better-halves, would meet at the coffee house in the Oberoi Intercontinental hotel, in New Delhi, at least once or twice a week. I met Rajeev Gandhi and his wife Sonya Gandhi, who is Italian, at one of these get-togethers. Rajeev was the son of Mrs. Indira Gandhi. Mrs. Gandhi, who was the daughter of Mr. Jawaharlal Nehru, later became the Prime Minister of India. Rajiv Gandhi took his mothers position as Prime Minister, after her assassination in the eighties.

I dated Alfio for about a year, and after a big fight, broke up with him. He had enrolled me in a class to learn his language, Italian, but when they all spoke the language too fast, I still would not understand them. This was the fight all about that and the fact that he was much older than I, and his views at life were much different than mine. He tried to makeup with me, but I had moved on to a much younger guy named Franco. I guess I was on a roll.

In the meantime, my sister Lali decided to get married, which was arranged by my parents. Her husband to be and his parents, who lived in Vancouver, Canada, had flown to New Delhi for this occasion. Lali got married to Amarjit Nagra within a month and flew off to Canada. We were all very sad to see her go so far away from home. Now it was Meera and I left at home. I had told my parents not to arrange a marriage for me, as I would pick the guy I wanted to marry. I started dating different guys, since Franco and I were not in an exclusive relationship.

Five months had passed, since Lali's wedding. One day we got a call from her that she was flying back home and leaving her husband, since he was still seeing his old Canadian girlfriend and refused to stop seeing her. She was about five months pregnant with her first child. My parents were devastated at this situation. Lali came home and we were very happy to see her. Even though she was pregnant, she started coming to parties with Meera and I. My Canadian friend David, who was the first attaché at their High Commission, told us that their Prime Minister, Pierre Trudeau, was coming to India for a visit and he was the one who was making the guest list for the party, which would be thrown in his honor. Of course all the big wigs were going to be at this party. I was trying to convince him to invite my sisters and me, for this event. We were at his friend's party that evening. I heard that some American Marines were there also. At one occasion one of the Marine came up and asked me to dance and I rejected his offer, since

I was talking to my friend David. I saw this Marine guy go up to both my sisters and ask them for a dance, and he looked very drunk. Lali told him that she was pregnant and finally Meera agreed to dance with him, but kept him at an arm's length from her. His name was Edwin Budd Jr. and his best buddy was Mike English and both were at this party that evening. Ed would not give up on asking me to dance again and again. Finally I gave up and danced with him. Somehow we started dancing slow and at the end of the night he took down my phone number. He called me the next day and invited me out on a date. I told him I could not, as I had a previous invitation to another party that day. He would not take no for an answer and I finally agreed to meet him at a softball game that the marines played at their compound, that weekend. He invited my sisters to the game too.

It so happened, that Prime Minister Pierre Trudeau canceled his trip to India due to problems in his own country. This canceled the party that was to be thrown in his honor in New Delhi, India.

My sisters and I went to the ball game at the Marine house across the street from our house. We did not even know what the game was all about and how it was played. Ed bought us hot dogs and soda pop before he went out on the field to play the game on his team, "Pan Am". Pan Am was playing against the team "Good Year". After about an hour the teams were tied in score, and Ed hit a "home run" and all hell broke loose as his teammates, hoisted him in the air for the victory of their team. Everyone ran on to the playing field cheering for "Pan Am" and Ed was their hero. My sisters and I sat our seats, not knowing what was going on, as we had no idea about the game. Until someone told us to go to the field as Ed had saved the game by hitting a home run, but we stayed where we were. Finally Ed came up to me and said, I his girlfriend, should have come up to congratulate him first. I thought as this was our first date, what made him think that I was his girlfriend. I was an acquaintance maybe, but not a girlfriend'. That first date did not go very well for us. I told my sisters that I was not going to see Ed again.

Just when I thought that Ed was out of my life, he calls me again insisting that our second date would be better and he would not take no for an answer. So I agreed to go out to dinner and dance with him, in about a week's time. He took me out to the Taj, a fancy restaurant at the Oberoi Intercontinental hotel. We actually had a good night out that evening. After dinner, we went to dance at the Tabela, an underground disco, member only, club at the hotel. I was impressed but he sure was not the greatest dancer or dresser. My sisters and I thought we would take it upon ourselves to show him how to dance better and dress better. He would wear these ankle length slacks, with matching satin color shirt and socks, which looked ridiculous. It was at Tabela that we first heard of an up and coming artist named CARLO SANTANA. From what we heard he was one of the top artists in America, and we would request his songs from the DeeJay over and over again and they were "The Black Magic Women, and Omay Cuomo Wa".

Ed and I started seeing each other regularly. My dad would invite him in for a drink, when he came to pick me up. Since my dad spent over forty years in the Indian Army, Ed and he would swap war stories. Ed was in Vietnam for a year and a half, with the United States Marine Corp, before he was stationed in New Delhi. He had a Purple Heart medal for being shot in the war in Vietnam. They hit it off pretty good. My dad would keep piling on drinks on Ed, and he would be drunk by the time we left on our dinner dates. After a couple of months seeing Ed, he popped the question to me about getting married. We were both the same age, in our early twenties. He even officially asked my parents for my hand in marriage. He took me shopping for rings and we selected a beautiful diamond engagement ring and two wedding bands with diamonds in them. We had to wait till his term ended in New Delhi, in November, to set our wedding date then. There were about six to seven months before November and this period would be a good time to get to know each other well before we took the big step towards marriage on November 10th, which we set as our wedding day. We were to get married in the Catholic Church on the 10th, and the Sikh wedding on the 11th. My parents gave us a fancy Persian rug as one of the gift from them for our engagement, and Ed kept it with his luggage at the Marine house.

In early spring, my sister Lali gave birth to her first child and named her Dixie. Dixie was born in the New Delhi Army hospital, and there was reason for us all to rejoice at her birth. Ed and I went to the hospital to see the baby, with gifts for Lali and her new born daughter. Lali raised her daughter with the help of our family members. As Dixie grew she would recognize Uncle Eddie, and look for lifesavers candy in his hands, which he always brought for her. We would all go to the American compound and go swimming at the pool and eat at their cafeteria and watch softball games.

One late afternoon, I came home from the Marine house and asked the cook where he had put the plate of okra that he had promised to save for me. He told me that he had put it in the refrigerator, and when I looked there the plate was empty. The cook said that maybe my sister Lali had ate it. I was so mad, that I took the empty china plate and broke it on my sister's head. She was sitting and talking to my mother and father, when I did that. My dad and mom grabbed my hands and Lali sucker punched me right between my eyes and nose. I started screaming in pain and so did Lali. I left the house to go back to the Marine house with my sunglasses on. Ed had a softball game that afternoon. He gave me a drink of scotch on the rocks, which I asked him to. While Ed went to change into his team uniform, I kept drinking straight from the Johnny Walker Black bottle. By the time Ed came out, I was belligerent and drunk out of my skull. I remember telling him, "If you love me, go beat up my sister". Ed started laughing so loud, and that got me furious. He left me at the Marine house, to go play his game. I don't remember what happened after that. I think two or three hours had passed and I woke up with a great hangover. I had practically finished the bottle of scotch.

On another occasion, Ed and I had another stupid argument at my house, and I told him that I was breaking up with him. I asked him to return the Persian rug my parents had given us and he mocked me and said that he was keeping the rug. I grabbed a butter knife and chased him around the house, with my dad yelling for me to stop my stupid actions. I guess we made up again after that drama. Ed grabbed the knife out of my hand and took me in a bear hug, saying that it was a butter knife and totally blunt and useless as a weapon.

All was not well in my relationship with Ed. There was a lot of dissention there. He had a quick temper and a short fuse if things did not go his way. By this time we had moved in together in an apartment, close to our house and the Marine house. We would fight a lot, whenever he started drinking, and I had my reservations about marrying him and telling my parents about our relationship. In the first place was a mistake. One time while we fought at the Marine house, I told him to shove off, and that I had decided not to get married to him. He broke a bottle of coke and came after me threatening to kill me if I did not marry him. I screamed and ran to the bathroom and locked myself in. But Ed pushed the door so hard that he broke the lock and was upon me with the bottle. In the meantime I was screaming for his friend Mike English to help me. Mike saved my life that day. He yelled at Ed to come to his senses and stop acting like fool, before he got kicked off the Marine Corps and put in jail. I left there crying and wondering what I had got myself into. I certainly did not want to marry someone who was physically abusive. The next day after getting sober, Ed came by to see me with bunch of roses to apologize. I did not tell my parents about the incident at the Marine house the day before. We went out and I explained to him if he ever behaved like he did the day before, we would have to end our relationship. He promised me that he was very sorry and it would not happen again.

In the meantime we started double dating with Mike English and his girlfriend Charmaine. These two were another couple who would fight each other like cats and dogs. At one point Mike English was banned from the hotel Obreoi Intercontinental as he smashed their front door of two inch thick glass with his fists while he was fighting with Charmaine. Charmaine would flirt with other guys in front of Mike and he would be ready to take her down. In these cases, Ed and I would intervene and stop them from fighting and vice –versa. Charmaine was quite a character and is a friend I call and talk to even today: she was very funny in a fun way. She and Mike had set their wedding date in the month of November, too. Mike was to be Ed's Best Man and my sisters were my matrons-of- honor at our wedding.

My father was running around trying to get my passport ready for me, for my departure to the United States, after our wedding. Despite the celebration of our wedding, there was a deep sadness on leaving my parents and moving so far away. I had never been away from my family for too long. This seemed forever. Ed told me that we were to travel to see his family in Keene, New Hampshire. He told me that it would be slightly colder there and not to worry, I would get used to it.

Finally, the sun was shining on the day of our wedding, November 10th. The temperature was in the mid seventies and very pleasant. Ed was getting ready at the Marine House and he sent Mike and Charmaine out to our apartment to make sure I was dressed and ready to go to the Catholic Church, on time. My family and I arrived there in a limousine. Ed was already there with all his Marine buddies. I had also invited all my teachers and nuns from my convent school, from which I had graduated my High school. Every one said that I looked very beautiful, with a white wedding dress, which I had designed, and a short veil, and carrying a bouquet of Yellow and white roses. My dad walked me down the aisle to where Ed was standing with the priest. The wedding ceremony took about half an hour itself, and after signing papers for the American Embassy officials who were preparing my paperwork for my transition to the US, we walked out of the church, with family and friends pelting us with rice. From there we moved to the Marine house lawn for a short reception and prepare for the Sikh wedding the next day. That night, I could not still see Ed, since we had still one more ceremony to go through, before we could meet for our wedding night. I went to sleep at our apartment, as I was coming down with a fever, while Ed went on to party with his buddies at the Marine house. I took some aspirin and lied down and fell asleep. When I woke up, there was the bright image of Jesus Christ in front of me. I know I was not hallucinating due to my fever, but I was actually looking at HIS image for a few seconds, and HE seemed to imply that "All will be well". That really scared me. I was not a Christian, yet I saw HIM. This was the second time in my life I had an encounter with GOD. I don't know but it sure seemed like a blessing. I kept this to myself and did not share it with anyone ever.

The next day my temperature was still high, but I had to go through the Sikh wedding ceremony, which my parents had arranged and paid for. Our house was full of relatives and friends. I was dressed in a red, green and gold sari (Indian dress) and Ed was in his suit and a burgundy turban, which my dad had tied for him. He also had an Indian sword in a sheath around his neck and shoulder, given by my dad. The ceremony lasted for an hour or more. We were buried with flower garlands placed around our necks by all our relatives. After the wedding ceremony, there was a big luncheon with Indian curries and bread. By this time I was feeling a little better after taking more aspirin, and enjoyed our lunch a lot. The wedding party ended and at the end of that evening and Ed and I drove away to our apartment for our wedding night. As we were exhausted, all we could do was fall asleep. Well now my name was changed to Mrs. Ed Budd, and we were officially married. The thought that I would be leaving India in two more weeks and leaving my family behind for a new home in the United States, was really scary to me.

CHAPTER 5 – COMING TO AMERICA

On November 21st 1971, Ed and I flew off for the United States of America by the Pan American airlines. I could not get the tear filled faces of my parents and sisters, out of my mind. Who knows when I would see them? Yet again, there was excitement too, for flying off to a new world, so far away. I hoped that I would like it there. Our first stop was in Tel Aviv, Israel, and then in Frankfurt, Germany. Our flight seemed to go on forever, and we finally landed in London, U.K. After twenty one hours of just flying, we finally landed at JFK airport, in New York in the evening. Looking out of the window, I was totally overwhelmed at the million of cars on the freeways. That was my first impression of America, of all the cars moving uniformly on the freeways. Not like in India, where the traffic is so unpredicted and everyone moves forward at the lights, causing so much congestion.

We took a cab from the airport to our hotel in New York. After we checked into our room, Ed called his parents in Troy, New Hampshire and told them that we would take a bus to New Hampshire the next day. In the meantime, he had to take the subway to go report to his Marine Corp. command there. He left me in the hotel to shower and rest, while he was gone. I had a bag of salt & vinegar Potato chips; we had bought on our way to the hotel. That was my dinner that night. Ed came back after midnight to the room. He looked so tired, and said that he had a horrendous time navigating the subways in New York. He took a shower and we went to sleep, as we had a long journey by bus ahead of us.

The next morning, we had breakfast and boarded our bus for Troy, New Hampshire. I could not help thinking how cold it was here. We had left eighty degree weather in New Delhi, to twenty degrees in New York. There was snow and ice on the roads and much colder as we drove north on the bus. After a very long bus ride we finally arrived at our destination in Troy that evening. The bus dropped us off at this little town's center and Ed called home to have his brothers pick us up and take us to his parent's house. I realized that I was very hungry, and when we arrived at the house. I grabbed an apple and pear off a basket on their dining table, not realizing the fruit was not real, but made out of plastic.

I met Ed's three younger brothers and his parents. The house had three very small bedrooms and only one bathroom. I guess all seven of us would be sharing that one bathroom. In India I had my own room with a bathroom attached. That was really going to be difficult. Ed and his brothers took our luggage upstairs to one of the small bedroom. After changing our clothes and freshening up we all sat down to dinner of New England boiled dinner. It was really nasty tasting to me. I ate the vegetables and could not eat the beef. We were to stay with his parents for a month or so, before we took off to Camp LeJuene, the Marine Corp headquarters in North Carolina. The next day we got dressed and went shopping to Keene, the next bigger town there. Ed and I test drove cars and we finally decided to get a 67 Ford Mustang (with hardtop). Ed had been in India for a while now, so when he got in the car to test drive, he followed the rule of driving on the left, like in India, and we almost got in a wreck. Next we went clothes and shoes shopping. He bought me a pair of boots, which were suede with sheepskin lining which would keep my toes warm. I had all open toed shoes from India, before. Even though I was shown a welcome by Ed's family, there was a certain aloofness and coldness towards me. If these were my parents, who had a welcoming and warm heart, they would have thrown a party for us. But there were no hints of a party from the Budds. All they wanted was to see, what their son got for them from India. Also, my bathroom dilemma was hopeless. There was never enough hot water left to take a good shower, when I was finally allowed in the bathroom, somewhere in the late afternoon. Ed would be making the rounds with his buddies and I would be left behind. I became more and more depressed and wanted to return home to India. After meals, Ricky whose job was to wash the dishes would leave me this chore, as the first time I offered this service for him. I felt taken advantage of. It did not occur to me to be more aggressive with my new family. I was taught never to talk back or be pushy with my elders. They intimidated me all the time. If I was not ready, my mother-in-law would tell her son in front of me to take off without me. It was not my fault that she would not come out of bathroom almost all day, as the washing machine and the dryer were in their bathroom, too. She showed me no consideration or apathy. One day I lay in my bed, not wanting to get out of my night clothes. When Ed came home and found me looking at his handgun, he freaked out, thinking I was going to kill myself. I never had such intentions. Since I hated the food here, I started losing quite a lot of weight. He brought me to the doctor's office and I found out that I was pregnant. Ed and his family were very happy to hear this news. Now they tried to be a little nicer to me. All I wanted to do was get far away with Ed, and away from his family. I wanted our own place so we could build a better relationship, now that we were expecting our first child.

This was the week of Christmas. That night I saw snow falling for the first time in my life. I was glued to looking out of the windows as the snow was fascinating to me. This would be my first Christmas with my new 'Budd' family. Not being a Christian we did not celebrate this holiday in the traditional sense, in India. I did not know why I was receiving all these gifts (cheap) from my in laws. Of course, there was the traditional Christmas dinner. I acted all excited in opening all my gifts. I received a lot of American clothing and shoes from my husband, which I needed. The jackets and sweaters were for this cold weather here. We did not need these heavy jackets in New Delhi, where the temperature does not dip down to below freezing, like in New Hampshire.

Ed had shipped our luggage, including heavy items like furniture, through the Marine Corp. He gave the address of his parents since we did not have our new address in North Carolina yet. My father's rug was included in these items. My mother gave us hand embroidered sheets and pillow cases and brass statues etc.as part of my dowry. This would take at least a month or more to arrive, and we alerted my in-laws to this.

During the month I was in New Hampshire, I noticed that my mother-in-law Kay (Katherine) seemed to be a heavy drinker and smoker. She would pop open a can of beer first thing in the morning with her cigarette and spend an hour in the only bathroom in the house. This sure was a problem for me. What would the rest of us do? My father-in-law Ed (Edwin Budd Sr.) would already have left for work, before we woke up. He worked in a Nuts and Bolts factory in the vicinity. My brother-in-law Jimmy was in the Marine Corp too, and had done a tour of Vietnam. My other two younger brothers-in -law, Bobby and Ricky were still students.

After a little over a month, we prepared to drive down to North Carolina, about a thousand miles, in our new Mustang. We were going to make stops on our way and maybe spend a night or so in motels. By this time, I was told to eat for two, but since I had acute morning sickness, I could hardly keep anything down. I could not wait to get out of New Hampshire. North Carolina, I was told, was a little warmer.

Finally, we started on our road trip right after Christmas. This got me all excited; as I would be traveling through several states and able to marvel at the beauty of this large country. That day we drove almost all day making small pit stops to use the restroom and eat at truck stops. The further we got south the temperature became more bearable. That evening, we stopped at Howard Johnson's lodge to spend the night. After dinner at their dining room, we retired for the night. The next morning, after breakfast at the lodge and getting gas for the car, we got on the road again. This was more fun as I could bathe at the lodge before taking off, and not worry about when I could use the bathroom. We would have the car radio on loud, and sing on down the Freeways. That night we arrived in North Carolina and made one more stop at another Howard Johnson lodge, for the night, as it was late at night for Ed to check in at the base in Camp LeJune. We decided that the next day after bathing and eating we would head on down to the base. We arrived at the base the next morning, and Ed checked in to our new home here. We were given base housing, which had two bedrooms and a bathroom with a living room and kitchen, with dining area. I was very happy with it. Even though there was no carpet on the floor, Ed and I furnished it with new furniture.

The weather in North Carolina, in the winter, was more bearable. There was no snow on the ground, which was a relief. Ed started his job at the base and I was a stay at home wife. I was not much of a cook, but I would clean house. I would meet Ed on base for lunch in the afternoons and check out the PX and the commissary for things for us and our new baby growing in my tummy. We also connected with Mike English and Charmaine who lived at the same base. Charmaine was a friend of my sister Lali first, who married Mike English, who was like a brother to Ed in India. Another friend of ours Dolly and Steve were at the base too. Again Dolly was another friend of my sisters' who was married to Steve who was a Marine there too. They would come over in the evenings and we would all play cards and watch television. Our neighbors were all nice and helpful. For food they introduced me to TV-dinners. In the evening I would put two of them in the oven and Ed and I would eat. Some evening he would order Pizza for us. I knew I would have to learn how to cook. I could make eggs and sausages for breakfast but the other stuff was a bit complicated. Charmaine taught me some of the meals like spaghetti etcetera. This food was much more bearable to me than the New England dinners I had up North. There was a fast food place named Yogi Bear, which served English type fish and chips. This was one of my cravings. I loved the fish and chips with vinegar on it. There was also a 'hoagie' sandwich at Pizza Hut which I craved. There was also the matter of washing and drying clothes. We did not have any washing machines or dryers in India. The washing guy would come in twice a week and we would count and give him the dirty clothes and viola the clothes would come back washed and ironed back in two to three days. The first time I went to the laundromat at base, close to our house, I asked another marine there washing his clothes to help me. He said that I should first separate the colors from the white. Put the whites in one machine and colors in another machine and put a quarter in each machine and push the lever and once the water was filled, to add powder soap (Tide) to each machine. After the wash cycle the machine would fill up with water again for the rinse cycle then to that add fabric softener to it. When the machine stopped transfer wet clothes to the dryer and put in quarters in it for the drying cycle. And when the clothes were dry enough, to fold and place them in my basket. And that was fairly simple and nice of the Marine to explain this to me. He asked me where I was from and I told him that I was an Indian. He asked me "What tribe"? My reply was "Sikh" after some hesitation. A quizzical expression came over his face. I bet he had never heard of that tribe before.

Ed and I decided that if the baby was a boy, we would name him Edwin Victor Budd and if it was a girl, we would name her Amber or Loretta (my picks) Budd. Finally winter turned into spring and we started going to the beach on the weekends together with Mike and Charmaine. I was about five months pregnant and I would make my doctor's appointments for checkups. We would go to the drive-in movies with Mike and Charmaine too, which cost only a quarter per person. I did not drink any alcohol but did smoke cigarettes still.

Once a month at noon on a Friday we would drive down to New Hampshire, so Ed would see his parents and brothers there. We would leave there on a Sunday morning drive all the way back to North Carolina, non-stop, since I had a driver's license now and could help with the driving. On our first such trip north, his mother told us that our luggage had arrived from India. When we checked it, the locks were all opened and the contents all picked over. We could not find the rug and the embroidered sheets and pillow cases that my parents had given us. When Ed asked his mother, as to why they had opened all the stuff as our items were missing, she said that she didn't know what happened to them and she never took anything. Obviously someone did take it. I was so angry at these thieves (his family). We took some of our statues and a hand carved wooden screen inlayed with brass, down South with us. We took a little, every trip we made to New Hampshire. I did not trust his folks at all. They were so grabby all the time.

By this time Ed bought a second car, a 1969 Ford Mustang-Mach II, in New Hampshire as there was no sales tax in this state. This was a superfast car. In North Carolina, they had drag races and Ed wanted to compete in these races with his new Mustang. We would go to these races, with Mike and Charmaine. The weekend Ed was racing his mustang, Charmaine told the spectators to move so I could see my husband race. When we finally got in front of the other spectators and the race started. Ed pealed out but stopped after only a few yards, as he dropped his muffler to the car, and was disqualified from that race. That was embarrassing. He came back with a red face. Nevertheless, whenever we went somewhere in it, guys would ask him if he would sell the car to them. Of course, our answer would be NO. I could not drive his car as it was stick shift and I could drive my other Mustang which was an automatic.

In the summer, Ed had to go to Puerto Rico, for six weeks for Marine Corp drills and I was left behind. That was a long time to be by myself. Lali my sister came from India to visit me before Ed left. That was nice that I had news from home through her. Charmaine, Lali and I would go out shopping, to lunch and to the movies together. It would take me two dollars to fill up the gas tank of my V8 car. The year was 1972 in the summer. After about four and half weeks, my car broke down and I decided to use Ed's car for small errands around the base. I did not know how to get it out of first gear, but managed somehow. Lali was nice enough to teach me how to cook some of the dishes. The only problem was that she drank and smoked like a sailor. The cloud of cigarette smoke was always hanging over our heads like a nuclear threat. She would light up another before the first one was still lit. I had almost given up smoking, but when Lali came to visit me, I would automatically pick up a cigarette.

Finally, Ed came back and Lali would be leaving soon. I told him about my car and he got it fixed by a mechanic and could not believe that I was driving his car around in first gear. Oh well, what could I do. We decided we were going to take Lali to the club with us. Mike and Charmaine joined us too. Ed invited one of the Marine buddies that worked with him, as Lali's blind date. Lali got in the car with him, Ed and I took our car and asked Mike and Charmaine to ride with us. Everyone had been drinking, except me, as I was pregnant. We were all dressed up to party that night, and party we did. On our way back, Lali and Ed's friend's car left first and we followed them. All of a sudden their car was weaving back and forth on the road. Ed got mad at his friend, and drove in front to block them. When he went to the driver's side, he found Lali behind the wheels; and when Ed asked her what she was doing behind the wheel, being drunk, she told him to "Fuck Off". That was it and world war 3 started between them. Lali told her date that she had an international driver's license and had coerced him to let her drive. She never knew how to drive and I knew that. When we finally reached our house so did their fight. I was the only calm and rational one and reprimanded Lali for putting their life in danger. At this Lali started sobbing loudly saying that I was taking Ed's side and that I did not love her. On the other hand the drunken husband of mine was saying that I was taking Lali's side and that I did not love him. This went on and on. Lali went to throw up and then Ed went to throw up, as they drank too much, and I was in the middle started feeling queasy too. Finally, Charmaine and Mike decided to separate Lali and Ed by taking Lali with them to spend the night at their house. What had started out as great evening ended in disaster? The next day all was forgiven and there was peace once more. We drove to New Hampshire with Lali and finally drove her to the Logan Airport in Boston, Massachusetts to put her on her flight back to India. My mother-in-law really liked Lali, as she drank and smoked just as well as her.

The next morning, we got on the road again on our way to North Carolina. By this time I was seven and a half months pregnant and hungry all the time. Ed told me that once we got on the road that we would stop in an hour to eat. The hour went and he still kept going saying the next stop and then again the next stop. Finally I could not wait anymore and put my foot on the brakes. This made the car swerve, and he finally stopped on the side of the road and started yelling that I almost got them in an accident. I told him that it did not matter if we lived or died, but I had to eat, as the baby in my belly was gnawing at me. We finally stopped at a truck-stop to eat and then got back on the road. This was much better. We finally made it back very late at night in North Carolina.

The baby was due in the middle of September and I could not wait for that day. My stomach was so big that ordinary chores had become tedious. In August, we watched the Olympics on our little black and white television every evening for two weeks. I had never watched the Olympics before and it was so fascinating.

One night as we were watching the games in the nude as the weather was hot and muggy, Ed had fallen asleep. I got up to say my prayers before retiring myself. I felt that someone was watching me, and as I turned around, I saw someone peaking through the blinds of the window. I screamed and fell on top of Ed, and startled he woke up as he heard me scream and knocked me off him as I fell to the ground now in my ninth month. He put his shorts on and ran out with a large machete chasing the guy outside our house. In the meantime some of the neighbors had called the MPs on 911. As they saw Ed, barefoot and half naked waving his machette, they presumed that he was the peeping tom, while the real one escaped back into the woods behind our housing. The MPs finally caught him about a week later in another such incident. We could finally rest at night in peace after this.

Finally, in mid-September, I woke up and felt contractions. I called Ed at work and he rushed home to drive me to the hospital. By the time we reached the Navel hospital on base, my contractions suddenly went away. The doctor said these were false labor pains and to come back in a week or so. Ed and I were so embarrassed by this incident. Finally on September 28th around 3 am I woke up to real labor pains and I was driven back to the hospital. The hospital staff admitted me and proceeded to take me to the labor room, where I could hear other women screaming in pain. I was scared to death; I thought I would not scream like these other women. But let me tell you giving birth was no child's play. You have to lay your body and soul bare for others to see. They first shave you and give you enema. Ah the puppies from my childhood were getting back at me from what I had done to them a couple of decades ago. After the enema they gave me some sort of pain medicine and lay me on a bed, with the water from the enema running out all over the bed. After that you lose all sense of time. You scream "Oh Ma, Oh Ma" when the pain comes and the nurse yells back at you "why are you yelling for your Ma, YOU are going to be a Ma?" I yelled back obscenities at the nurse. Was that really me? I guess it was the pain that was doing this to me. Finally, what seemed like an eternity the doctor and nurse came by and told me to stop pushing now and gave me spinal block. They could see the baby's head appearing, and now they would make an incision to take it out. They wheeled me to the birthing room, where my legs were raised, spread and tied up in stirrups. There was a whole classroom of interns watching the procedure. I thought "why don't you invite the whole hospital to watch me in this shameful position." There was a large mirror in front so even I could watch my baby making its grand entrance in this world. I should have charged tickets to this show. I saw the doctor take my baby out and he cried after he gave a slap on its tiny butt and the doctor said to me "Congratulations, you have a boy". I took one look at Edwin Victor Budd and fell hopelessly in love with him. I thought "He is all mine" and thanked the Lord for this beautiful child. All thoughts of pain disappeared and were replaced by awe. He was born on September 28th, 1972 at 6.58 pm and seven pounds and two ounces and twenty inches long. So I was in labor for fourteen hours. They wheeled me down the corridor and left me there for a good six or seven hours or more, as my room was not ready. I was falling in and out of sleep and Ed came by the hospital to see me and his new born son and brought me a dozen red roses. He was proud as a peacock. Finally my room was ready and they wheeled me in, and nurse came by to get me up and go to the bathroom. I said no thank you I did not have to go. She said you **have** to go or I could hemorrhage internally. The two nurses got my arms and yanked me up and I fainted. I heard my other roommate, who was in for the birth of her fifth or sixth child yelling at the nurses to get me a bedpan instead. They did better and stuck a decatherator in me. That was so painful.

So, Ladies if you have a child by natural child birth, make sure you get up slowly and go to the bathroom, or this could happen to you and you do not want this pain.

They had kept Edwin in the nursery as I was not going to breastfeed him, and cleaned him and surgically removed the skin on his little wee wee. They told me that I could go visit him in the nursery, as he would be kept there for twenty four hours for observations on his little surgery. I slowly walked to the nursery, which was lit up brightly. There were a room full of babies, who were all sleeping, but one that was awake and looking at the lights with his thumb in his mouth, and that was my Edwin. He had clear white skin with charcoal big eyes. He had no wrinkly skin at all like the others there. I could not wait to take him in my arms and hug and kiss him. They finally brought him to me in my room with a bottle of milk and showed me how to feed him, burp him, and change his diapers and lay him down in his hospital crib. Let me tell you, **I WAS THE HAPPIEST WOMAN IN THIS WORLD.**

CHAPTER 6 – WELCOME HOME EDWIN

We finally checked out of the hospital the next day. The hospital gave us a package of baby stuff, which included diapers, baby formula, bottles for milk, shampoo and soaps etcetera. Ed and I took baby Edwin home. The next few weeks were a learning process for me. I had never tended to a baby before and I realized I had a lot to learn. On the other hand Ed knew a lot more than I did. When he would cry I would feed him and change his diaper. He would start up crying again. I would think now what? My neighbor said that I needed to burp him as the gas pain in his tummy was making him cry. I was learning fast and needless to say that I loved him to death. Ed and I would take turns getting up at night to feed him. He would be up every two to three hours for his feeding. One of my neighbors, who was a nurse, told me to buy a package of rice cereal and mix it in with his milk and make a bigger hole in the nipple so the feeding would stay in him a little longer than just plain milk, which would go in and out much quicker. This made sense and it worked. So in the second week of his life, he was on the cereal already. All in all, he was a very good baby. Slowly I learned to prop up his milk bottle on a pillow next to his head and he would actually grab the bottle in his hands. This would give me a chance to run to the bathroom. I had stitches and it would hurt to go.

Since Ed did not re-enlist in the Marine Corp, we would be leaving for New Hampshire soon. He said he could get a job when we got back North, and would stay with his parents temporarily while we looked for a place of our own. Just the thought of living with his parents was stressing me out. We finally had the Marine Corp pack all our stuff and sent to New Hampshire. We would drive back in his Mustang. So we said goodbye to all our friends in North Carolina and headed back North. Winter time again, and it would be cold as the dickens up there. We took our time going back as we had the baby with us. We stayed a couple of nights at the lodges on our way back. We finally arrived in Troy, N.H. the third afternoon. Everyone was delighted to see Edwin and thought that he was the cutest baby on earth. His grandparents and uncles bought him gifts and they took their turns picking him up. That night I bathed him in the kitchen sink and put him down to sleep.

My mother-in-law, Kay was a really pain in the rear to me. I was so sick of her that I wanted to run away from him and his family altogether. I went to the Laundromat with little Edwin to wash my clothes and dry them and Kay must have told Ed that I ran away with Edwin. My spirits were low as I was going through Post-partum depression, and the fact that I had no family here to defend me, they made life pure hell for me. Ed and his brother Jimmy came to the Laundromat and Jimmy tried to grab Edwin out of my arms. The baby started to cry as he was pulling on one of his leg and it became a tug of war with my baby in the middle. I was crying and finally let Edwin go as I did not want to hurt my child. Ed said that he was taking Edwin home and I could finish my laundry and come back home if I wanted to.

In a couple of weeks, Ed did get a job loading and unloading trucks all day for the State owned liquor stores where his brother Jimmy worked in sales. It did not pay much, and the job was very strenuous and he would come home very tired. He would clean up and play with Edwin and eat and go to sleep and start the cycle over the next day. I started staying up longer and longer at night, watching television shows with my mother-in-law, the hawk watching every move of mine. I was bored to death here in this hick town. There was nothing to do. I could not go shopping as we had no money and also it was very cold for Edwin, as he was not even a month old.

I asked Ed if he would send me to India for a couple of months, and my family could meet Edwin, and by the time I came back, it would be a little less cold, and finally after a long argument he agreed. I did not want to stay in his family's home one more day, as I would go mad. We finally agreed that he would save money while I was gone with Edwin. So in mid-December we drove down to JFK international in New York, to catch a flight back to New Delhi, India. Since it was just before Christmas, the Pan Am flight I was on was totally full. I could not get the seat I needed for the baby up front, so they could put Edwin in a make shift crib on the plane. I had to put his baby carrier on my lap in the middle of the aisle. It was five and a half hours to London. There was an Englishman right next to me in a suit, and he had this look, 'Oh great there will be a crying baby next to me'. I had taken a lot of diapers and milk bottles and change of clothes for Edwin; but it looked like these would not be enough. That boy was going through them faster than I wanted him to. The stewardess brought everyone's food and I could not eat due to the baby on my lap, and the suited gentleman saw that. He offered that after he finished his meal, he would hold Edwin for me while I went to the bathroom and ate. That was very nice of him, after all. After arriving in London, this was his stop. I thanked him profusely for his help and said goodbye to him. Luckily some seats did open up so I had a crib for Edwin, as we still had sixteen more flying hours. The stewardess gave me some extra diapers and milk formula for Edwin. I thought what I was thinking taking a three month old infant across the world to meet his other grandparents. That was the worst mistake of my life. Edwin cried a lot on the trip and my heart was breaking to see his agony.

By the time we landed in New Delhi, he had not one stitch of clothing on him, as he had soiled everything. I just had him wrapped in a blanket and I was on the verge of a breakdown. The visa entry people said I had not obtained a visa for Edwin, but waved him in and told me to get one before my flight back. After gathering my luggage, I hailed a cab for the drive home. When I arrived home and saw my mother at the front door, I broke down into loud cries. My mom said what is wrong with the baby; and I told her that I, her baby, was exhausted not Edwin. I thrust the baby in her arms and cried my eyes out. My arms hurt and I had not had a wink of sleep on the plane. Mom took Edwin and bathed and dressed him in clean clothes for me and after feeding him, I took to sleeping. At least I was home and the weather was warm and wonderful. All my sisters were here and everyone helped me out. On the other hand Lali's daughter Dixie was almost three years old and she would come running to my room every morning to see her cousin Edwin. The problem is that I would finally get him to sleep and Dixie would come wake him up again. When I yelled at her, she would run to my dad and say Nalini auntie is beating me up. My dad would take Edwin from me in the morning so I would sleep, and he would take Edwin for a walk in our neighborhood. It was nice to be home where I had help in taking care of Edwin and I was among my family. By now my aunt Darshan and uncle Rajinder (my mother's half brother) had another child and his name was Bablu. They were still living at our house, since my uncle took care of the maintenance of our house. My maid would come by and wash Edwin's cloth diapers; as in India there were no disposable diapers.

My sister Goodi and Ninni and her two children Dolly and Sonny came to New Delhi to visit us from Chandigarh, where they lived. We all went to the New Delhi Zoo and picnics in the gardens there. In the evening we would all go out to eat chaat, an Indian appetizer. We took a lot of pictures of the whole family. My aunt Harprastish and uncle Brar also came with my cousin Bubbles to see Edwin the newest member of our family. All in all, this visit was a relaxing one for me, as I had a lot of help with Edwin and I could get tips on child rearing from my mother and other members of my family. I had to get a visa for Edwin since he was a US citizen.

When Edwin's milk formula from the US finished I had to buy the substitute formula in our stores here. This change gave him the runs for a week or so, until he got used to it. I told my parents I did not want to go back to the US because of Ed's parents. Ed would call me twice a week to make sure I brought his son back to him. I told him that there was no way I wanted to live with his parents. He promised me that he would enlist in the Army as the private jobs were few and far in between, if I returned back to him. This way we would have our own place like in North Carolina. I agreed to that. So by the end of February, 1973 we returned to America and Ed came to New York Kennedy International to pick us up. Edwin's eyes lit up when his daddy picked him up and kissed and hugged him. I guess no matter how young he was he remembered his daddy. We stayed the night in a New York motel that night. I bathed Edwin and myself and we fed him 'Gerber Bananas' that he loved so much. He was a very good baby and would eat almost all the foods we fed him, and was not fussy at all.

By March, Ed enlisted in the Army and his first duty station was Fort Carson, Colorado. He would start getting a regular paycheck from the military on his first day at work in Colorado and things got to normal for us again. In May he drove our car to Colorado, which took him two or three days. By about three days later my father-in-law, Big Ed drove Edwin and I, to the airport in Keene and off we flew to Colorado. Everyone on the plane said how good and cute a child Edwin was all dressed up in a cowboy outfit. We landed in Colorado Springs airport that afternoon, and Ed picked us up there and drove us to the military motel where he had checked in till we got our own quarters. I liked Colorado. We arrived there on a Saturday and he still had not received his paycheck. We had about ten dollars on us borrowed from Ed's Catholic Church on that Sunday. We bought some baby food in jars and baby milk formula and disposable diapers at the Military Commissary for Edwin and we bought a loaf of bread for us. We wanted to make sure our son got his full meal and Ed and I ate raw onion and mustard and ketchup sandwiches. The onions and mustard and ketchup were free from the café there. I would not ever forget those days of our poverty. On Monday, Ed left Edwin and I at the motel and went to check on his paycheck. I took Edwin for a walk and we both ended up at the playground. I held Edwin and got on a swing singing him lullabies rocking back and forth. I felt at peace even though we had nothing to eat, but I was very far away from Ed's family. Finally we walked back to our room in the motel. When Ed came home, he had good news for us. He got paid and that evening we finally ate at a local restaurant.

That week we found a nice two bedroom apartment in Security, Colorado, just outside the base, where Ed was going to be working and put a deposit and first month's rent on it. It even had a swimming pool. We furnished the apartment with new just some basic furniture and a color television, and we moved in. Finally now we had a home now.

Since now we only had one car, which Ed would drive to work, I had no problem walking across the street to all the stores and taking Edwin in a stroller with me. All fast foods like McDonalds, A & W root beer, etcetera were all within walking distance. Albertsons, our grocery stores was also nearby. Ed had left his Mach II Mustang with his brother in New Hampshire. We made a lot of friends here and we would visit each other's houses all the time. On weekends Ed and I would take Edwin to the Colorado Springs Zoo including some local attractions like Seven Falls.

Here, Ed also took up Karate (Tae Kwon Do) on a regular basis and would go to classes twice a week after work. Sometimes Edwin and I would join him to watch. He dabbled in karate back in North Carolina, but not like here; he was serious here. He felt that Karate was a calming influence on him. He participated in a couple of tournaments in Denver and did very well. The tournaments in Denver were where participants came to compete from all over the USA. There were names like Bill (Super foot) Wallace and Chuck Norris here officiating these tournaments. The news cameras from all major networks were also recording these fights. We would stay overnight in Denver on a two day tournaments. Edwin and I were there cheering his daddy on. Some other friends of Ed's were also participating and we would sit with their families in the auditorium. Karate became the focus of Ed's life here.

Well summer turned into fall and we celebrated Edwin's first birthday party by inviting some of our new friends and their children to his party. Edwin was so happy tearing open all the birthday gifts he received and his eyes lit up when he got a football in one of the packages that we gave him. I took several pictures of Edwin and his little friends all playing with his gifts. The party was a success.

I received a telegram from India that my uncle Rajinder had passed away. He drank some home brewed alcohol at a party and that is what killed him. Now Darshan was a widow who was taking care of her three children, Pinky, Neelu and Bablu. I wanted to be there in India for her, as she was for me, when Cucu died years ago. She was like an older sister while I was growing up, and my mother considered her as her daughter and not a servant. But I was not able to travel back home to India.

For Christmas we bought him a lots and lots of gifts. And then again he was so happy tearing the paper off his presents. This was the first real Christmas for me. Since not being a Christian, Christmas did not mean anything except a big holiday for me. But when you have a little child, and to see the happiness and awe in your child's face, was enough to make me a believer in Christmas. Okay now this will be the beginning of my celebrating this holiday for years to come. The winters in Colorado were ever changing weather wise. One day it would be snowing and the next day it would be 50 or 60 degrees temperature and the sun would be out. I took Edwin to see Santa Claus at our local grocery store, which was within walking distance. When he saw Santa for the first time, he started screaming in fright. He was so scared of him. Ever since I met Ed, he always went to church on Sundays. He told me that he would never miss church, as he had promised God that if he ever came out of the Vietnam War alive, that he would do this every Sunday. Now sometimes I would accompany him along with Edwin. On one such occasion, when we were at church, everyone started singing hymns and Edwin started singing too, in his baby talk. When everyone stopped we could not quiet Edwin down. Everyone turned around to look at him singing his own tunes and thought that was so beautiful. When I had married Ed in India, I had to sign some papers at the Catholic Church there, that I would raise my offspring as Catholics. Since I was such a believer in my religion, it did not matter to me that he would be raised in his father's religion as long as he believed in the Lord. In my opinion, God is only one, and we pray to Him in our own religions. Edwin turned two on September 28, and again, we threw him a birthday party.

Late that fall my sisters Meera and Lali came to America. Lali was in Germany and Meera was in Austria, in Europe with Neil Wildman and Dan Kennedy, the marines they had met in New Delhi, after I left India. Lali flew to Oklahoma, where Neil's family lived and Meera came to Colorado to visit me, since she had a fight with her boyfriend Dan Kennedy, who was from Cincinnati, Ohio. Since I did not want to Meera to go back to India, I filed papers with US Immigration service to become a US citizen. This way I could petition for her if she did not marry her fiancé Dan. She was a great morale booster for me and helped me with Edwin.

It was so sad for my mother that all three of her daughters were now in the US. Only Goodi was in India with her husband Ninni, who was a real fiend. He beat my sister if she did not obey him and harassed my parents all the time. Even though they lived in another city, Chandigarh, he would drive down with Goodi and his kids, Dolly and Sonny once a month to demand this and that from my parents. If he did not get what he wanted like a new air-conditoner for his house he would take it from my parent's house. My parents were getting old now, and they did not need to be treated like this. My dad would write letters to us on their situation with Ninni. We also learned that Goodi was sick of her in-laws that she wanted to divorce Ninni. He told her that if she left him, he would kill my parents, so she would have to stick around. At one point Goodi tried to commit suicide by taking a whole bunch of pills, but luckily was saved.

Edwin was now almost a year and half years old and running all around the apartment showing Mina auntie his toys. He would say "Meererr, see truck, see tires". I used to keep his milk bottles all ready in the refrigerator and he would run there take one out himself and drink it. In the evening before going to bed, I would wash and refill all his bottles and put them in the refrigerator for the next day. One evening I could not find any of his empty bottles. Meera said to look in the garbage can since she saw Edwin there earlier. She was right, and there in the garbage can were all his bottles. He must have seen us throwing our soda pop cans in the garbage can and he was doing the same. I told Edwin "No, No" we don't throw our milk bottles there. I told him to put them in the kitchen as mommy had to wash them for him. So after that he would look at me and say "No, No" and place his bottle in the kitchen. Now also, I noticed that whenever the National Anthem came on, no matter where he was, he would run in front of the television place his right hand on his heart and stand at attention and tell me to do the same. I don't where he got this from but was absolutely patriotic.

One day my sister and I took Edwin to the bank first and then shopping. While we were waiting in outdoor teller line at the bank, Edwin started stepping on dry leaves and liked the sound of crushed leaves. He missed a leave and very loudly yelled "FUCK IT". To my horror everyone turned around and gave me a dirty look. They must have thought that I was teaching my child bad words and I never ever used this expression. It was his father Ed who would be using these words while watching his games on the television. When we left the bank, my sister and I burst out laughing and told Edwin "No, No" we don't say this at all. He was so funny and giggled back saying "No, No". Edwin was an angel child.

There was a little girl named Wendy in our apartment building, living next door to us. She would come over every morning to see Edwin. She would come over and hug and kiss Edwin all the time till he cried. We would tease Edwin saying, that his girlfriend was here to see him. He hated that, even though he was less than a year old and she was two. She would come over and hang with Edwin and would not go home even when her mom called her and told her to. Since I wanted Meera to stay in the United States, I had to become a U.S. citizen, in order to sponsor her. I filled my application and turned it in to U.S. Immigration office in Denver, Colorado.

One evening Ed did not come home from work, or call me to say he was going to be late. Meera and I were watching the news and there was a story of a car crash, and car looked like our car. I really got worried. My friend drove me down to the base while Meera stayed home to watch Edwin. We looked for Ed on base and all the soldiers had already left for their homes. One soldier told us to look in the bar maybe he had gone there. When my friend and I arrived he was not there either. Well, we finally left to get back home. When I got back to the apartment, Meera said that Ed was home and he was in the shower, and looked pretty drunk. I went in the bathroom and asked him where he had been all evening, as I was worried sick about him, he smacked me hard on the head. I did not see that coming. This got me so infuriated that I took the sword from the wall in its sheath and whacked him real hard once, twice and three times. Since he was drunk, he could not defend himself, and he fell on the floor in a heap; and I whacked him a couple of times more, leaving large red welts on his bare bottom and back. Mina came running along with Edwin and saw our fight and took the sword out of my hand. Edwin started crying for his daddy and told me to "don't hit my daddy." I felt so bad and hugged my child and told him it would be alright, and no, I won't hit his daddy again. This was the pattern of violence all through our married life. The problem with Ed was that, when he could not argue with me verbally, he would use his fists first. This was the only time I ever got him back. That night he crawled up on the bed and went to sleep and the next day we made up and I cooked everyone a nice breakfast. We promised that since we had a child now that we would not use our fists when we fought and never to do it in front of Edwin. He was a very sensitive child and would not like to see his father or mother beaten.

Meera's Marine boyfriend Dan Kennedy would call her on the phone, from North Carolina and they finally made up their differences and were set to get married in his hometown of Cincinnati, Ohio. On the other hand Lali's Marine boyfriend, Neil Wildman, and she were also getting married, in Selma, Oklahoma and we were to attend their wedding that winter. By this time I discovered that I was pregnant again with our second child. I had morning sickness from hell. Meera decided to stay till Lali's wedding since she and I were to be the bridesmaids at her wedding. Ed was to give Lali away, to replace our dad, who could not be with us in the United States. We drove down to Selma, Oklahoma, to join Lali's wedding party there. We got to meet her in-laws, who were very nice to us and put us up in the local motel at their expense. The night before the wedding, we all went to the rehearsal dinner that the in-laws were hosting. We all had wild turkey dinner at their house. The in-laws were all ranchers and were used to waking up at the break of dawn and rounding up their cattle, including, Lali's mother-in-law. The wedding went off real well. This was Lali's second marriage, and Neil's first. Neil was dressed in his Dress Blues and Lali had a beautiful white wedding gown. They were to go to Camp Lejuene in North Carolina, after the wedding and we took Meera with us and headed back to Colorado.

Since Ed's time had come to re-enlist in the Army, he picked to be a recruiter in his hometown of Keene, New Hampshire. He said that there would be more money for us and we could purchase our own house there. We were to leave Colorado by car and drive all down the Southern States to North Carolina in January, the dead of winter, to drop Meera off there so she could meet up with her fiancé, Dan Kennedy, who was also stationed in North Carolina. After a few days there at Neil and Lali's apartment, Ed and I, together with Edwin were to drive up all the way to New Hampshire, stopping a couple of nights at motels on the way. This was the hardest drive ever and we left in a blinding snowstorm. While travelling through in Tennessee, the roads were slick ice on the first part of our journey. We could not go above 20 to 30 mph. after a few miles of this hard drive; we decided to stop over at motel at 2 am. It was impossible to find a vacancy as a lot of travelers had thought the same. Finally we found a motel to rest there a few hours and start afresh later that morning. By this time the salt trucks had spread the salt on the freeways to make the ice melt, so that the driving would be less hazardous to the drivers. When Ed got tired, I would take over the driving, and vice versa. We went through some beautiful country sides and crossed the Mississippi Bridge in Memphis, the home town of Elvis Presley, the greatest rocker of his time. We crossed the Blue Ridge Mountains of North Carolina. I was amazed at how big this country was and I would have the pleasure of traveling through so many States (about 25) that were absolutely beautiful and I had started falling in love with this country finally. That I would actually live in nine states, eventually.

We finally reached Camp Lejuene, North Carolina at Lali and Neil's place. We cleaned up and went out to eat. I was always hungry as I was eating for two now. The problem at Lali's place was that the water had a foul odor; we had to drink bottled water. The problem was when it came time to rinse my mouth after brushing my teeth, the odor from the water made me throw up. That night, everyone decided to bring in a bottle of booze each (Ed, Neil and Dan) and drink it all, while playing cards. That sounded like a disaster, and it definitely was. These guys started drinking as the evening progressed and got drunk as the hours passed by. The only one who did not over drink was Meera's fiancé, Dan. He could handle his booze better than Ed and Neil. I was tired and I put Edwin to bed and tried to sleep, with all the noise these guys were making. When I woke up the next morning, the guys went to sleep at 2 am that morning after puking all night, which was what Meea told me.

Ed and I finally got ready to leave for New Hampshire a couple of days later. Meera told me that she would stay there with Dan and leave for Cincinnati, Ohio that summer for their wedding, and I said to send us an invitation and we would drive up there for her wedding. I did remind her that the new baby was due on June 10th. She said that they would wed either before or after my due date. With that, we finally left on our thousand mile drive back to New Hampshire. We finally arrived there in a couple of days, stopping for the night at motels. My mother-in-law told us that they had moved to a trailer park house in Keene, and were going to sell their house to us, with the stipulation that we let Ricky, Ed's youngest brother stay with us till he finished his High School in Troy, that he was still attending. That was okay with us, as there would only be four of us and the bathroom situation would not be that bad.

Our furniture had arrived in Troy from Colorado already. It was already moved into our house. The next week or two we arranged the furniture the way we wanted to and I fixed up the house real pretty, the way I liked. Ricky would sleep in the upstairs bedroom and our bedroom was downstairs next to the bathroom. Edwin's crib was next to our bed. Big Ed and Kay had taken their washer and dryer from the bathroom and we had to purchase new ones for ourselves. We said we would do that in a couple of months after we saved some money for them. We had to open all our kitchen utensils and arrange those in the kitchen, which I did during the coming weeks, while Ed went to work in Keene as the new recruiter there.

Now I thought, everything should run smoothly for us. But I was wrong about that. Ricky would come home from school and bring his dirty snow covered boots and drape them on Ed's leather recliner or our grey eight foot velvet new sofa, to watch TV, leaving them wet and dirty. I asked him to take his boots off, like he used to for his mother, at the door before he came in but he never ever paid much heed to that. Now, Ed had to tell him to do the same which he said he would, but ended up doing what he wanted. Ed had long hours at work and could reinforce it. That left me to tackle this situation myself. Slowly, he started coming in and gobble up our food and take off drinking with his buddies, returning at 2 am, drunk out of his mind and turn the music on loud, and wake us all up. He would leave the kitchen sink full of his dirty dishes for me. The situation got so bad that Ed told him that if he did that, he would be thrown out on his ass. Ed had to get up early in the morning to go to work and he would not put up this situation with Ricky. Ricky resented this and thought I was turning Ed against him, and that I was the bad person. Ed told his parents about Ricky's behavior, but he did have to finish his High School around the corner from our house. The whole family was against me and I really did not care a hoot. Ed was making payments on the house and Ricky would have to abide by our rules. Not only was he coming home drunk but I had a feeling that he was also doing drugs. I had to look at his face several times daily, while I was in the last semester of my pregnancy. Edwin and I would eat and leave the house to go shopping or to my doctor's appointment at local hospital in Keene, where I was to deliver the new baby. I would also go baby clothes shopping for Edwin and the new baby, as I wanted to be absolutely ready before the baby came in June. I had a secret hope that it would be girl this time around, so I looked at a lot of girl's clothing while shopping, but only bought neutral colors and clothing for Edwin's brother or sister. Unlike in my first pregnancy where I craved 'fish & chips', in this pregnancy I craved hot Mexican food only. Everyone asked me if I was having twins as my stomach was huge, and I told them that as far as I was told, that it was only one baby.

In the meantime, Meera sent us her wedding invitation, which I told her about our situation here; and that it was too close to my due date, and I did not want to leave town this late in my pregnancy. She understood, and said that she would send the pictures for me and she and her new husband, Dan would come up to see us and the new baby soon.

Well, a couple of days before my due date of June 10th, my husband Ed took Edwin and me to see the stock car races that were being held in Marlborough, New Hampshire. That night I knew the baby would be coming very soon. The next morning my pains started and I had a load full of laundry and ironing to do for Ed and Edwin. I took the laundry basket into my car, but Ricky's car was parked behind mine in the driveway and I could not go to the Laundromat; and Ricky was nowhere to be found. He was told by Ed and me not to park behind my car but the jerk never cared to listen anyway. I was so mad that I called Ed at work to come home get me going here. He came home and tracked Ricky down at his friend's house and got me out of the driveway. In between my pains I finished the laundry and got home and started ironing. Now the pains were getting pretty together. Ed was a nervous wreck and told me to stop working so he could drive me to only hospital in Keene. This time I was more experienced than the first time around and finished all my chores before I left for the hospital. Both Ed and Edwin drove me to the emergency, where they admitted me and wheeled me to the delivery room. I hated leaving my Edwin at the mercy of his daddy for a couple of days for the first time in his life.

Finally after fourteen and a half hours of labor the baby's head appeared and was told not to push anymore. I told them that I could not hold off for long, and 'where the FUCK was my doctor'. He was standing right next to me and must have heard me cussing him. He gave me a pain shot in my lower spine to ease the pain and eased the baby out. This was the first time I laid my eyes on my second baby, just as the doctor held and gently slapped his tiny butt and he let out a big cry. The doctor exclaimed "Congratulations, you have a boy, Mrs. Budd"; and I said "Oh shit, he was supposed to be a she". They cleaned him up and put him in my arms and I was absolutely in love with my baby, BILLY JAMES BUDD. From now on I would devote my love equally between my two boys and adored them both so much. Billy was twenty-one inches long and almost eight pounds, born on June 10th 1975.

CHAPTER 7 – WELCOME HOME BILLY

Oh my god, I had two beautiful sons now. How lucky I was to have them, and my heart was so overwhelmed with love overflowing for them. I gave birth to them and they were all mine. Giving birth was the most awesome experience of my life. I thanked the Lord every moment I could. We brought Billy home from the hospital and there was my son Edwin waiting to meet his little brother. He hovered around me and Billy, as I was changing his diaper. When you have a boy, you have to be quick on the draw while changing the diaper or you will get sprayed by pee. This time around poor Edwin was in the line of fire and got sprayed by his baby brother. He said he did not like his brother now, and if we could take him back to the hospital and buy him a new brother. We thought that was so cute.

Seriously, over the coming weeks Edwin just adored his little brother and kisses him every chance he gets. He even brought out all his toys to share with him. I had to explain to him that Billy was too small to play with the toys right now and when he got bigger he would definitely play with him. Ed and I agreed that since I would be getting up several times at night to feed Billy that it would be best that I would sleep on our eight foot couch, with the baby. Ed would keep Edwin in his crib with him in our bedroom. We were in the summer season now and it was cozy on the couch with Billy tucked in my left arm. The only problem was that Ed's brothers Ricky and Bobby were in and out of the house at all times of the day like our home was their hotel. Obviously, Ricky flunked his High School graduation and had to retake his classes for another year. Also, Bobby and his girlfriend Becky felt free to have sleepovers at our house, like our house was their hotel. They would make a mess in the kitchen and leave all the dirty dishes for me to do. I told Ed that I would not keep living like this, now that we had two children that needed set nap times and I was not his family's maid and that we were not running soup kitchen here. Ed tried to talk to his brothers first, which really did not change anything. They kept doing what they wanted to do and even brought in their dirty laundry to do for free at our house.

I told Ed that we had bought the house from his Parents and that his brothers could go live there, or we would move out of here. I found nice apartment housing close to the Keene airport between Troy and Keene, which had two bedroom apartments with a bath, and large living and kitchen area. I kept pestering Ed, until he finally agreed with me. I took Ed to see the apartment that was open and he liked it too. I just wanted to be able to lock my apartment whenever I was out with the children and come back home with everything intact as I had left it. Only Ed and I would have the keys and not his brothers. Ed talked to his third brother Bobby and his girlfriend Becky to buy the troy house from us. Of course, we had to take a loss on it as 'poor' Bobby did not have that much of a down payment, but they would pick up the payments from us. Also, Ed's second brother Jimmy had married a woman named Laurie and they would buy one house and fix it up and sell it for a profit and do it again and again. They must have made good money this way. Jimmy worked as an assistant manager at the state owned liquor store in Keene.

Laurie had a son from a previous marriage and Jimmy and Laurie had a daughter together, who was slightly older than Billy.

In the meantime my sister Meera and her new husband Dan came over to visit us and see our new baby, Billy and of course Edwin. They had driven from Cincinnati, Ohio to see us. Now the only problem was that Dan was black and I had not seen one black person in Keene. It did not matter to me or Ed that he was black. We took them out to eat and went to the movies and even went to the only nightclub, at the Keene airport, leaving the kids with a babysitter for that night. I would notice people looking at Dan kind of odd, but he was such a cut up that he cracks us up. They stayed with us for a week and when they were leaving to go back to Cincinnati, I decided to go with them, as I was not Seeing Eye to eye with Ed. He was not very clear about us moving to our own apartment soon and I could not live around his family anymore. I drove my Pontiac with the children in their car seats following Mina and Dan back to their home in Ohio. I stayed with them for a month, with Ed calling me by telephone almost every day to come back. When he finally gave me a date that we would be moving to our own place, I said okay. He flew out there and we drove back to New Hampshire together.

Billy was a very hyper child, whereas Edwin was calm compared to him. He would move around so much, right after drinking his milk that he would throw up. I always had to have a wad of paper towels under his chin when I burped him, as I knew what would happen if I didn't. I would leave Billy at home with a babysitter, while Edwin and I would go out to eat and do our grocery shopping. So Billy was only accustomed to a few faces. If he saw a new face, he would start screaming in fear and would not shut up. When his grandparents would come visit us, he would cry if he could not see the familiar faces of me, his dad, Edwin or his babysitter. That is the only reason I would not take him to restaurants or shopping. He was also a very fussy eater and if he did not like a certain food and I forcefully put it his mouth, he would spit it out spraying the walls around him. I remember my mother telling me when I was little, that wait until you have children someday, and they would do the same to you. I was a very fussy eater too, when I was little. With Billy, I had met my match. At three months, Billy was unusually strong. If I laid him on his stomach, he would lift himself, like a little lizard and look around to see where his mommy and brother were. At six months, he was kind of wobbly walking, grabbing onto the couch. He would not wait more than a couple of minutes, and if I did not change his diaper right away, he would rip it off him, leaving his poop all over. One day his dad came home for lunch, and he stepped in it, with his dress shoes; as our carpet was mustard color too, did not help him see it. Compared to Edwin, Billy was a little devil; and my little beautiful devil.

We finally made our move to our little apartment that summer. My in-laws volunteered to take care of our children while we were moving our stuff to our new home. The grandparents came to pick up the kids and Edwin went willingly while Billy was sleeping. After an hour we got a call from big Ed and Kay that Billy woke up and has not stopped crying since they left. Their father, Ed had to go pick them up. I guess I had the moving left up to Ed and his brothers. We finally got everything from the old house to our new apartment. Now came the organizing of all our stuff in the new place, which I did, while Ed was at work. I was so happy to have a place of my own not be constantly interrupted by Ed's family, that I did not mind taking care of organizing our place and taking care of the children. We settled there very well. On weekends I got to sleep in late, and Ed would feed the children and bring them in our bed to see me. That was the best time for me as I would tuck Edwin and Billy in bed with me, and I would play hide and seek with them under the sheets. Billy of course would always half pick himself up like a lizard.

A couple of months went by and one afternoon that winter, I started having bad pains in my stomach. They got worse and worse, and by that evening I could not get out of my chair. When Ed got home from work he took care of the children and put them to bed, as I could not move from the chair at all. He told me that he would take me to the hospital if I wanted to go. I told him that if I took a hot shower I might feel better and told him to go to sleep, as he had get up real early the next morning for work. I slowly slid out of the chair, and dragged myself to the shower. I let the warm water from the shower fall over me and bend down to pick up the soap. I felt something slide out from between my legs and fall in the tub and the water got all bloody. That 'something', was clogging the shower and the tub was filling up with bloody water. But to my amazement, my pain had disappeared completely. I jumped out of the tub and called the hospital emergency, asking for my doctor. The doctor told me that I had just had a miscarriage, and to pickup that 'something' and put it in a container and get to the hospital as soon as I could. There was no way I was going to touch that 'something' and woke Ed up at 2 am. He got up and picked it up and put it in a large bowl for me, as I explained to him what had happened. I told him to go back to sleep and stay with the kids, while I drove down to the emergency room at the hospital. They admitted me there for the night, while they worked on me to do 'the cleanup'. Ed came to visit me at the hospital and pick me up later that evening, after they discharged me. After Billy was born and I went to the doctor for a checkup, and I told him that it had been a month and my period had not stopped, and he gave me some pills, he said would stop it, without even checking to see if I was pregnant again. I had just lost a baby and that was so depressing, while on the other hand Ed was laying this guilt complex on me, like it was my fault. Technically, it was the doctor's fault for not checking me thoroughly before he gave me those pills. I would always wonder if I had not miscarried, whether it was little baby girl this time around.

My relationship with Ed was not the best as he would be gone long hours for work, recruiting High School students in the Army. He would have to go to meet the parents of the Kids he was recruiting to answers their questions. Very often he would not be home for dinner on time. By the time he came home, we had already eaten and he would have to get his own food. While he was out doing his work, I was stuck with being the primary caregiver for our children. Not that I minded taking care of Edwin and Billy as they were the most beautiful children a mother could ever have. They were my life.

That fall and winter there was the campaign for a new President of the United States and all the big names and news media were converging upon our state of New Hampshire. Our current President Johnson and Senator Jimmy Carter and Senator Ted Kennedy were all coming to Keene to campaign for the Presidency. They would all fly to Keene airport and the road behind our apartments was the main route for them. There would be Secret Service men all around our apartments hiding. I remember taking my children to see Senator Kennedy to downtown Keene, where he was appearing. As I made my way up towards the podium where he was speaking, I was pushed and shoved by the news media people and the Secret Service people and they almost knocked Billy out of my arms and Edwin stomped on. Of course I could not get anywhere near the Senator? I was yelling his name hoping he would remember me that I had met him in the elevator in Ashok Hotel in India years ago. He just hurried and got in his chauffer driven Limousine and drove away. Ed's recruiting office was just across the street and we walked down there to see him instead.

Life went on for us and our children were growing up fast. The next year we celebrated Billy's first birthday on June 10th with cake and ice cream. I kept in touch with my sisters Lali and Meera by telephone and communicated with my parents in India via letters and pictures of the children. Lali's husband Neil had joined the Army also and they were being shipped off to Germany. Meera and Dan were still in Cincinnati, Ohio. Dan had got a job at his local post office and they lived in their apartment, there. In the meantime, Ed and I were looking for own house now instead of renting. The children soon would want to play in their own yard, and these apartments did not have anything like that around us. Bid Ed and Kay were living in their own trailer house and tried to talk us into buying a trailer home too. The school was very good in that neighborhood and close by. The hospital was across the street and Ed's office was not even a mile away. We looked at a few of the double wide trailer homes there. The one we picked out had three bedrooms and two baths and came with stove/oven, refrigerator and washer and dryer included. We also had wall to wall carpeting throughout the house except in the kitchen, dining area and bathrooms. It also had a space for parking two cars and a nice big yard. The only problem was it was too close to my in-laws place. Oh well, we moved into our trailer home after Billy's first birthday and Edwin's third birthday. We also bought Edwin his new full size bed with safety railings on the side. Edwin and Billy had one bedroom, with Billy still in his crib. Ed and I had the master bedroom and the third bedroom was a guest room or our working room. It was fun furnishing our house with all brand new furniture.

I got a letter from the Immigration office for my test date for becoming a U.S. Citizen. I had done this only to keep Meera in the U.S., but now since she was already married I did not have to do this. Ed told me to go ahead and take the test anyhow. We had to drive down to Boston, which Ed drove the kids and me there. I went in to take an interview with an Immigration office employee. I thought I did pretty badly in answering his questions, but they said I had passed. Oh well, next came the swearing in ceremony. There were hundreds of immigrants swearing in with me that afternoon. I had tears in my eyes when came the part that I had to forsake my old country INDIA, and take up arms for my new country UNITED STATES OF AMERICA, if need be. That day in March I was officially a U.S. citizen. There was happiness yet a lot of sadness too.

For Edwin's third birthday the four of us drove down to Disney World in Orlando, Florida. That was a great vacation and my first real vacation in the United States. When we left for Florida the weather in Keene was so hot. Billy slept in the heat, all the way down to Florida in the car, as we had no air-conditioning in the car. Of course we made a couple of stops for the night, on our way down. That trip was about a thousand and five hundred miles by car and we were all singing songs driving down the highway. I remember when we entered the state of Florida the sign said 'WELCOME TO THE SUNSHINE STATE'. We were all very excited. We checked into our motel close to Disney World late that afternoon and took the children to the swimming pool to cool off. Since we were going to be there for a full week, we decided we would visit Disney World the next day, after getting a good night's sleep. After swimming we went to eat dinner at the restaurant at the motel and settled in for the night after purchasing our tickets for Disney World. The next morning after eating a full breakfast at the motel's café, we drove to our fun day in Disney World. We parked at a massive parking lot and boarded the trolley bus that would take us to the Park itself. The park has their own strollers and we put both the kids in them and started walking towards the Park. The children met Mickey and Minnie Mouse and all the Disney characters. Once Billy got a hold of Mickey Mouse, he would not let go off him. It was a very hot day and we went on the rides but stayed away from the big roller coasters as I was too scared and the kids were too little to get on them. We spent the whole day there seeing all the attractions and parades. If you have little children DISNEY is a must. By the end of the day we were totally exhausted. As you cannot see everything there in one day, we returned there the next day. We shopped for the kids buying them Disney clothes and toys. The next two days we went to WATER WORLD. Before we knew the week was coming to an end. We also took a lot of pictures of the kids. Sadly, it was time to return home.

We had another thousand miles of drive back to New Hampshire. By the time we reached North Carolina the weather started cooling down and when we got home in a couple of days there was definitely a chill in the weather. The fall and winter were upon us. Ed had organized a Karate tournament in November and competitors from all over the US were coming to participate in it. We also invited the New England Patriots' cheerleaders for the half time show. Ed's family was all helping out. Ed's brother Bobby and his girlfriend Becky had a sandwich and hot dog stand there. His other brothers and I were selling tickets at the door. His parents were in charge of getting the trophies lined up. My sons Edwin and Billy had a mock fight match and the news media was there to cover this for the show "The Evening Magazine", which was to be aired the beginning of next year. Edwin being older knocked Billy down with one punch and Billy started to cry and their father Ed gave the point to Billy, saying Edwin had used excessive force. Boy that was it and Edwin also started to cry in front of the whole auditorium saying "that is not fair dad". Now here I had to care to crying children, and it was no win situation. Ed made about five grand for that one day, altogether. After the tournament Ed and I took his family and all who helped us to a, lobster dinner that night.

This tournament was shown on television the next January. Edwin's teacher sent out flyers to all the children in school that Edwin and his brother were going to be on television. My children, Ed and I were instant stars. As time went by I felt unsatisfied with my life and marriage, here in Keene. Ed's family was always disrupting our lives. Kay would come by unannounced every other day to our house. I would always have beer and an ashtray ready for her. She would smoke like a chimney her whole visit. Even though I smoked cigarettes, but not like her; she was a chain smoker. If I called Ed at the office asking him to pick up stuff at the grocery store, Kay would have a list ready for him too. If I was taking a shower, Ed's brothers would come by and shut the hot water heater off, thinking that was fun. I would end with freezing cold water in the shower. On the other had they would come by and shut our heater off in the house, until I would start getting cold, and find that the heater was off. With Ed gone long hours for this work, he had his family harassing me every moment they could. I was souring to my marriage to Ed. If I complained to Ed about his family, he never did anything to help me or our children. He said I was a complainer and imagining their abuse of me.

I was aware that my marriage to Ed was coming apart. There were times I hated him and these times were more often than any good times we had. I was spending more time with my precious sons than my husband, who was out of the house more often and would not come home very late almost every night. If I complained, he would say he had to work to put food in our mouths. I felt that there was more going on behind my back than his late nights at work. In the summer of 1977, he had to go to school through the Army to Indiana. I told him we could travel together and the kids and I could stay with my sister Meera and her husband Dan for the two months of his school, since his school was one State further from the State of Ohio, where my sister lived. My sister said it was okay for us to visit and stay with them for a couple of months. This way, I was away from his family in New Hampshire and Ed could drive down and visit us on the weekends. So that summer we all traveled to Ohio by our car and stayed with my sister.

CHAPTER 8 – THE END OF MY MARRIAGE

I was very unsatisfied with my life with Ed. In February of 1978 my sisters Meera and Lali were planning a trip back home to India and asked if I wanted to go also. My sons Edwin and Billy were five and two at the time. My husband Ed said that it was okay if I wanted to visit my parents in India and he would take care of our sons, while I was gone. This was something I could look forward to. We had a big snow storm in New Hampshire and the snow banks were twelve feet deep. I was definitely sick of this weather here. If someone has lived in cold places like New Hampshire would absolutely understand my feelings. The temperatures here dip several degrees below zero, and your water pipes freeze overnight with no water the next day and the electricity is suspended due to these big storms here, which they call NORTHEASTERS. I did not want to live the rest of life like this. I wanted to live in a warmer climate, where I could take my children to playgrounds and the swimming pools. Thoughts of Disneyworld and living in Florida kept coming to mind. We all had a great time in Florida, when we went to Disneyworld a couple years earlier.

My sister Meera, who lived in Cincinnati, Ohio, was going to fly into Boston Logan Airport and meet me there. From there we were to board our flight to New Delhi, India, together. My sister Lali's husband Neil was stationed in Germany in the U.S.Army, so she was going to fly in to New Delhi from there. This was going to be a surprise visit for our parents from us, who hadn't seen us for a while. I was going to miss my children terribly. I said a tearful goodbye to Edwin and Billy, telling them that mommy would be back soon. At the end of February, Ed and the kids dropped me off at the Keene airport to fly to Logan airport in Boston. I waited at the airport to meet up with my sister Meera, whose flight was supposed to come in later that afternoon. When her flight arrived we met up and proceeded to board our flight to New Delhi.

After a very long flight through Europe (London, Frankfurt, Tel-Aviv, New Delhi) we arrived in India in the morning. We took a cab from the airport to go home. My dad was emerging from the house when we arrived there and when he saw us he hugged us and was pleasantly surprised. He told us that mom was sleeping and to go and kiss her and wake her up. Our servant took our luggage upstairs to my old room and when we gently woke our mom up, she saw us and thought she was dreaming. She kept saying "Oh my god, oh my god" and started to cry. We hugged her and told her that we were here to be with her for a month or two. She was so happy that she kept hugging and kissing us. After eating something we went to sleep, after our long flight and the jetlag. Lali was arriving the next day and we were going to pick her up at the airport. Lali flew in the next day with her son Ryan who was just over a year old, and now my mom had all her girls with her. Of course, Lali's daughter Dixie who was now seven had lived with my parents since she was a baby. Lali had left her with our parents when she came to the United States to marry Neil, her husband. She grew up thinking that our parents were her parents too. Our father had enrolled her in our old school, Carmel Convent, in New Delhi. Dixie had a chance to see her new brother, Ryan and her mom Lali, whom she had not seen since she was a baby. Ryan was quite a spirited child and was everywhere and into everything, if not watched constantly. He would come into my room and pick up all our shoes and throw them out of the window into the street and then jump on my suitcases. Lali had never put any restrictions on him and he was totally a wild child. One day he threw a whole box of soap in the bathtub filled with water for the afternoon. The water company shuts the water down for four hours every afternoon, so all the tubs in the house are filled with water for use in the afternoon. On top of all this Lali would sleep till noon and Ryan ran around un-supervised all morning. One morning my mother tied him up to the foot of the couch in the living room. After a while when he realized he could not move about he started to cry out loud.

My aunt Darshan told us that there was an African guy named Charles living as a boarder at our house. When my dad took my brother and his family on their way home to England, to the airport about six months ago, a guy came up to my dad saying that someone had stole his wallet and he had nowhere to go without any money. Of course my dad bought his story, hook, line and sinker. He brought him to our house temporarily, but he was still mooching off my parents and making long distance calls to Germany on our phone. He was out of town, the first week we were home and finally we got to meet him when he came back. He was an American and not from Africa, like my aunt told us. Just because he was black, she presumed he was from Africa. I found out that he was quite a manipulator. He put his moves on my sister Meera, even though he knew that she was married. Meera told us later that her marriage to Dan was not on solid ground and that she was falling in love with Charles. This would be the worst mistake she was making, as she was looking at him with rose colored glasses and not for the shyster he was. But of course she was not going to listen to anyone but what she perceived of him. Every time I would go to the PX to buy myself some of the necessities, Charles would give me a list for himself. When I asked for his money in advance, he said that he would give to me later. I told him no, that I wanted his money up front. Of course, I knew that he had no money. Then he would ask Meera, and she would give me money for him. This aggravated me to the extent that, my sister was getting taken in by this thief. It was bad enough that he was staying at my parents' house and eating three good meals a day for free, and now he was hooking my sister in too. My mom asked me to ask Charles for the money he owed her for the telephone bill. If anyone wants their dirty work done, I was usually picked for it. I knew mom was not going to get anything from him and she was still in the dark as to what was going on between Meera and Charles. I was going to let Meera tell her that and keep myself out of her business.

Aside from that, the three of us (four including Charles) would go to the Marine house to party with the Marines there. Some of the servants who worked at the Marine house, when I met my husband back in 1970, still worked there, and knew us sisters. I met a Marine, John Smith, who was only 19 years old but was always hitting on me. I told him he was too young for me, but he wore me down to the point that I started going out with him. He wanted me to divorce my husband and marry him. I told him even though I was eventually going to divorce my husband, as I did not love him anymore; I was not going marry him or anyone else for that matter. We became sexually involved, and that is all it was for me. On the other hand Lali was also going out with another marine there. It looked like all three of us sisters' marriages were ending eventually.

When I left for my trip to India, my husband Ed told me that he knew that I would not stay without sex for two months and it was okay if I went out with someone, but when I got home to tell him. I told him that he could do that too, but tell me who he went out with. So this was our agreement and it was okay with both of us.

In the beginning of April, I got home sick for my children and wanted to return home to the US in the third week of April, as the weather in India was really getting too hot. On April 17 it was already a 117.00 degrees Fahrenheit and you could practically fry an egg on the sidewalk. I told my mom that I was going home to my children, and she said but I was already home. But she said she understood how I missed my children. In the meantime, I heard that Meera had a miscarriage. I did not know if the father was Dan her husband or Charles and she did not tell me either.

I booked my return flight back to the United States and left India to come back home. My flight was from New Delhi to Beirut, Lebanon, then to Frankfurt, Germany and then London, England and finally on to Boston's Logan Airport. Lali and Meera did not return with me as they were going to stay on a little longer in India. Lali was going to return to Germany with her daughter Dixie, who was now eight along with her son Ryan. She had to get a passport for Dixie, and that was going to take her some time and Meera decided to prolong her trip too, as she was now seeing Charles there. My parents were totally devastated on losing Dixie, whom they had brought up since she was born. This was going to kill them emotionally, but Lali being her mother, had her rights too. I felt sorry for everyone in this situation.

My flight from New Delhi was diverted from Beirut to Rome, due to the war in Beirut. After a layover in Rome we took off for London, where a lot of the passengers got off and new passengers boarded our flight on to Boston and then on to New York, which was the end of destination for this flight. A German passenger named Hanz had his seat next to mine. During the five hour flight to Boston we engaged in conversation in his broken English. One thing led to another and Hanz kept buying me champagne to drink. Before I knew it, we were in back of the plane lying down and I joined the mile high club with Hanz. He said he was married too and his wife did not mind him going out with other women. He was going to New York, and told me that he going to visit the Playboy club there and invited me to come with him and not get off the plane in Boston. He said that he would pay for my expenses back to Boston. I told him that he was crazy, as I was going to be re-united with my sons, whom I had not seen for two months now; also my husband was picking me up at Boston. I said goodbye to him and got off the plane at Boston, where I boarded my flight on to Keene, New Hampshire.

Ed came to pick me up at the airport. I asked him why he did not bring the kids with him, as I had specifically asked him to bring the boys to the airport. He told me that his mother was babysitting the kids and I could see them when I got home. After getting my bags from baggage claim, we started walking out towards our car. Ed, very casually, asked if I went out with a guy while I was in India and I told him that we would talk about it when we got home and I could see our kids. He insisted, just to answer yes or no. So told him yes and then he asked me if he was white or black and I told him black. That was it, all hell broke loose with him. He called me every bad name he could think of and threw my suitcases in the parking lot. We eventually got in the car and headed home. By the time we got home, Ed had calmed down a bit, when I reminded him of our agreement before I left for India. The first thing he tried to do when we got home was try to have sex with me. I told him I had to go to the bathroom and maybe bathe and rest after my long flight first. So he could not have his way with me. His mother brought the kids over from her house. I was so very happy to see them. Edwin came running to me, but Billy wasn't sure who I was, but when he saw me hugging and kissing Edwin, he also ran up to me. I could not let go of my children and was kissing them and crying at the same time. They were the cutest kids in the world to me. Billy was potty trained by now. My reunion with the children was the greatest feeling. I told them I would not leave them for such a long time, again.

In the meantime, I don't know with whom Ed had sex with, while I was gone, because he had a doctor's appointment to treat his sexually transmitted disease. He told me to call the doctor, also. I didn't see why I had to call the doctor, but I did, and he told me if I did not sex with Ed on my return, I did not have to go. So, that is why he was trying to get me in bed so he could blame this whole thing on me. I told him to stay away from me till he got better. I guess things were getting from bad to worse with our marriage. But now the spring was here and I would take my boys out to play and we would go shopping and go out to eat. Sometimes Ed would join us and mostly he would be on his recruiting for the US Army.

My brother-in-law Jimmy and his wife Laurie, who had a daughter Jennie and Laurie's son Mickey, were also having problems in their marriage. Laurie told me that things were not working out between her and Jimmy and that she was leaving him and moving to Florida. Our mother-in-law was our biggest problem. That drunken woman always got into her son's family life. She also told me that I could come to Florida and she would help me find an apartment for the boys and me. She had some friends in Winter Haven, Florida, who could help us look for jobs too.

Spring turned into summer and summer turned into fall. Ed was organizing another Karate tournament in November. In the meantime, he was invited to officiate at his friend's karate tournament in Springfield in Connecticut. So we travelled to Springfield on a Saturday morning, which was only a couple of hours drive from Keene, N.H. We took our boys with us and Ed's brothers Bobby and Ricky also went, to set up a hot dog stand there for their refreshment center. The boys were having a lot of fun, running around there. "Super foot Wallace" (Bill Wallace) who was a heavyweight in Karate world was also officiating and Ed introduced him to me. He played in a movie "Force One" with Chuck Norris. I thought that Bill Wallace was so cute and I had a celebrity crush on him and kept following him around the floor. And when he said he was hungry, I told him there was a hotdog stand there and if he wanted that, I would go get it for him. Ed heard me say this and pulled me aside and said I better stay put, and if he wanted to eat he could get his own food. I did not see anything wrong with this. It was not like I was asking him to go to bed with me. The ugly head of jealousy was rearing its presence in Ed.

Ever since I told him about my affair with John in India, Ed does not stay far from me, even when I went to the bathroom; he was lurking around outside waiting for me. This was really bugging me a lot. One day when I was coming out of the shower, he scared the heck out of me, as he was sitting on the toilet seat. When I asked him what he was doing sitting there. He said he likes to see his beautiful wife taking a shower. Well this was creepy on his part. He never did this before I went to India, so why now. When I asked him, who he slept with while I was in India, he said nobody. Then how the hell did he get his sexually transmitted disease, I asked him and he said maybe he got it from me. Heck no, I did not even sleep with him for two months. I wish I had not told him anything either.

That evening when we returned from the Karate tournament from Springfield, we stopped at Burger King to pick up food for us and the kids as it was late and we were tired. When we were eating our food, I don't remember what I said to bring out the violence in Ed. He jumped up and smashed the lights with his karate kick. The glass fell all around the area where we were eating. The boys got so scared and started to cry. I yelled at him as this ruined our meals as there was glass all over the food. He called me a bitch and some other names too sick to be mentioned in front of the boys. He showed me the note that I had started to write to John in India, saying I missed him and never intending to send it to him. Ed found it and that is why he was acting so strange with me at the tournament. I quickly calmed the kids down and got them ready for bed, as they were tired from the long day. When I went to our bedroom, Ed was sitting on the bed and crying and had his shotgun pointed to his head. When he saw me I told him to put the gun down and we would talk. He now pointed the gun to my head and said that I did not love him. I had to pick and choose my words very carefully. I told him that of course I loved him and in any case the gun is not his answer. I told him that if he killed himself I would have to explain this to his family and vice versa. Our families would be devastated if either one of us was killed.

Slowly I persuaded him to put the gun away and when he did that, we hugged and cried together. I told him that I loved him and we had two beautiful boys who would be devastated if anything happened to either one of us. We made a promise to each other that we would try to make concessions to make our marriage work. I told him that he would have to spend more time with me and the children and put that same dedication he put in his work. If we don't see him for long periods of time that puts a gap in our relationship. We promised to be faithful and truthful to each other. I had not kept anything from him, but he was not very honest with me always. Also, we made plans to go out on real dates with each other at least once a month if not twice. I missed the good times we used to have before we got married, in India.

The next day he took the kids and me out to eat at a restaurant. That weekend we got a babysitter for the boys and got dressed up and went dancing at the Keene airport lounge, where they had a DJ spinning tunes, so we could dance. When we arrived there, the lounge was pretty packed. As we moved to a table, a girl came up to Ed and said "Hi, I know you were my first" not knowing that I was with him and was his wife. Ed quickly steered us away from her. I was shocked as the girl was not that old, maybe high school age. When I asked Ed what she meant by that, he said she meant "my first recruiter". This was all BULL. The clouds of doubt came back in my mind again. Will I ever trust this man, again? We went out dancing a couple of times more and one time with another couple who were friends of Ed.

In mid November 1978, Ed held another Karate tournament and made out like a bandit, raking in over $5000.00 in ticket sales. I never saw him claim that on his taxes. He had our boys Edwin (6 yrs) and Billy (3 yrs) put in an exhibition fight, where Edwin knocked Billy out in one punch and Billy started to cry. His dad gave the point to Billy as Edwin had used excessive force. Now Edwin started to cry, saying it was not fair. The tournament was covered by a television show called "Evening Magazine". They did interviews with Ed and me and incorporated this in their show too. This event was to be televised on January 15, 1979. Edwin's teacher sent out flyers to all the students in his class to watch him do karate on the show. Edwin was an instant hero in his class.

The year of 1979 just flew by. Ed started staying out late almost every night again in the name of recruiting. I don't think he wanted to save our marriage. I would make his dinner every night and he was never there to eat it with us. I started getting a babysitter for the boys and began going to clubs with Laurie (my brother-in-law's wife) and her girlfriends. I would dance with guys at these clubs, and soon they would ask me out. I had one-night stands with some of them. I was not getting sex at home, so I thought that what was good for the 'goose, was good for the gander". If Ed was so busy working, which I did not believe entirely, I am sure he was getting this elsewhere too. Now I was sure that I did not want to be with him anymore. All I felt was anger at him, and not love. I decided that I was going leave him, but did not know how or when. Laurie told me in the beginning of 1980 that she was leaving Jimmy too and moving to Florida, where she had friends who could help her and me too, if I decided to move there. I called my sister Meera, who had left her husband Dan, and moved to northern California the previous year. She was working in Oakland, California now. I told her about my situation with Ed and told her that I would be moving to Florida maybe later in the summer. I told her if any job opened in the car brokerage she was working with to let me know.

Laurie told me that she was leaving for Florida in March or April. I asked her what she was going to use for money and she told me that she had got a lump sum price of $5000.00 from a used furniture company to take everything from her house in one morning and give her the money. She told me not to tell anyone about this, especially Ed. I thought that was cold, but I promised her that I would not utter a word to anyone. She said when she got to Florida, she would call me.

One evening Ed came home all shaken up. The first question he asked me was that if I was going to do the same thing that Laurie had done to Jimmy, his brother. I guess Laurie had left. I pretended I did not know what he was talking about. He told me that his brother called him at his work saying Laurie had not come to pick him up at work and if he could give him a ride home. When he dropped Jim at his home, they found the house was totally cleaned out. No glass even to get a cold drink of water, as the refrigerator and stove were also gone. I guess if the carpet was not wall to wall, that would have gone too. I told Ed that I did not know anything about this. I told him that I would not do this, as I wanted an amicable divorce from him, where he would pay me child support and spousal support. He sat me down and we talked about our marriage, and he told me that he did not want to lose me, so he would put in a transfer for us to move to Florida, with the army. He said that if I wanted to move to Florida sooner, he would drive us there and set the kids and I at a nice apartment and when his transfer comes through, he would move in with us. He did not want to lose his family. I told him fine. In the latter part of 1979, when the price of gold had gone up to nine hundred an ounce, I sold my gold jewelry and got cash for it for such an emergency.

Laurie called me from Florida, saying she was staying with a friend of hers till she starts working and then she found a nice apartment housing, which had a swimming pool for the kids too. I told her everything about her husband Jimmy that Ed told me about, the day she left. She said the weather was hot and beautiful there. Two weeks later, she called me again and gave me her new telephone number at the new apartment she moved into. She said that her kids Mickey and Jennie were having a great time at the swimming pool. She also enrolled them in school, there.

At the end of April and beginning of May I packed up my Ford Granada with all of mine and the children's belongings. I was going to drive my car and Ed was going to take his car too. It was a long drive of one thousand and five hundred miles to Winter Haven, Florida from New Hampshire. This place was between Orlando and Tampa Bay on highway four. I called Laurie and told her that we were on our way there and I would call her when we arrived there. Here we come FLORIDA…………….

CHAPTER 9 – I HAVE MY FREEDOM

We had a long trip ahead of us. I was going to follow Ed's car and make several stops on the way to Florida. After three days on the road we finally reached Florida. I called Laurie from the motel we were staying in and she gave us the directions to her apartment in Winter Haven. We stayed the night at her apartment. Our boys were happy to see their cousins Jennie and Mickey. Edwin was seven and Billy was one month away from being five. The next day we went to see the apartment manager, who showed us a two bedroom apartment with two bathrooms, which was very big and roomy inside. It was on the first floor. He wanted the first and last month's rent, which was only $290.00 a month. It also had rear balcony outside the kitchen and dining rooms, and orange trees growing outside our apartment. We moved in, that particular apartment that day. Ed rented some basic furniture for us from a rent to own company. The kids and I were set. I called the phone company and they installed a telephone for us in a few days. After we were set up and the kids were enrolled in school there, Ed took off back to New Hampshire. He said that he would call me when he got home, up North. He said that he was going to put in a transfer with the army to move to Florida immediately as he did not want to lose his family, like his brother Jimmy.

The week after Ed left, I would drop the children off at school, and started my job search. After getting turned down at several positions, I signed up at a temporary agency. This way the agency would send me to different positions. They sent me to a position for an office clerk. I got all dressed up very professionally, with the hose and all, in the extreme heat there. The Office Manager, who was an old white man, said that I should have applied for a job at the "Cypress Gardens" one of the local attractions. I told him that I was applying for a job as an office clerk at his office, as I considered myself qualified for this position. I thought in my mind as to why he was asking me this stupid question. I could type, file and answer telephone calls and perform all general clerical duties. After the interview, I knew I would not hear from him. He sounded like a racist. Since my skin was darker than his, I was not going to qualify for this position. Going to job interviews and not hearing from them, was getting me down. I knew I would not give up, as I had to feed my children and myself. On a Friday afternoon of the next week, the agency sent me for a job interview at a consignment store for sales clerk help. I went and talked with the store owner Dolores with whom I had my interview. I told her that I was a very fast learner and would be a good worker for her. She told me that she would call me with her decision by Monday morning. By this time I was pretty frustrated by being rejected again and again. I told Dolores that I could start working on Monday and if she could give me a week to prove myself. If she still did not want me after the first week's work she could let me go. She kept saying no I will call you on Monday, and I kept insisting, no that I would start work on Monday. She finally relented to my deal and told me to come in on Monday at 9am. I went home happy with the thought that I have a job now, which only paid $3.10 an hour. Now I could provide for my little family. I called the temporary agency letting them know that I had the job. I must have sounded excited about the job, as the lady could not understand why, as the job only paid $3.10 an hour. This was my first job that I got on my own.

After dropping the boys at their school, I went to work on my first day there. Dolores gave me a tour of her store. She had two other stores, one in Lakeland and one in Auburn. I was to work at her main store at Winter Haven. My job was to ring all sales and on down times tidy up the racks and put out new merchandise on the racks. When people brought in their used clothes Dolores was in charge of accepting or denying the clothes she wanted in her store. At my lunch hour I would pick up the kids at school and drop them off at the child care center close to our apartment and bring them home after work. I guess I was doing a good job, as at the end of week, Dolores was happy with my friendly manner with her customers. She decided to keep me on longer. Dolores had two daughters who also helped their mom with the other stores she had, and slowly she started trusting me more and more. After a month there, I was taking her deposits at the end of the day to her bank. One day while I was eating my lunch she told me that she was very happy with my job performance. She also told me that on the day of my interview she was not going to call me back for the job, as she was prejudiced, but she was glad to have me as her sales clerk now.

On Saturdays I would do laundry and clean up the place in the Mornings and in the afternoons I would take the kids swimming at the pool. Laurie and her kids would join us there. On some Sundays we would go to Disneyworld, which was only forty six miles away from our place. Ed would call now and then from New Hampshire. He would send some money to help me out financially. Laurie told me that she had been talking on the phone to her husband Jimmy too. She said that he was begging her to come back to him. I could not believe after all that Laurie had done to Jimmy, that he was willing to take her back. One day, Laurie asked me to lend her a hundred dollars, as she had lost her job and needed the money to buy food and clothes for her kids. I lent her the money, on the promise that she would pay it back to me. That was the last I heard from her. Ed told me that Laurie was back with Jimmy in New Hampshire. I also found out that Ed did not get his transfer to Florida, but they had given him the new duty station in the state of Maine, which was even worse than New Hampshire. I told Ed that was it, I would never go there. Well it was time to say goodbye to our marriage. I also found out that Ed was seeing another woman, whose name was Robin all the time he was professing his love for me. What a hypocrite he was telling me that.

I started dating other guys that I met in Florida, who would turn out to be losers and moochers also. There was one guy named T.J., who had no job, and while I was at work he would crash on the couch at my apartment and eat my food. I told him that he could not come by my apartment, while I was at work and harass my kids and their babysitter. One Saturday night he called me after midnight saying that he was in jail and to come bail him out. I asked him why was he in jail. He said that he was caught trying to sneak out a pair of boots from the store and was arrested. I told him I was not going to bail his sorry ass out. He might as well do the time in jail and not to call me anymore. Then I met another guy who was an ex-cop and can't even remember his name. He used to keep a snake in his car. That freaked me out totally. He would be looking for mice to feed his pet snake. I quit seeing him too. I started going to country western bars with my two friends who worked at the store too.

By now I had worked with Dolores for three months and she started giving me more responsibilities with her three stores. Sometimes I had to work at her other two stores and close the store at the end of the day after balancing my cash register and taking the deposit to the bank. The children were doing well in school. Edwin was in second grade and Billy was in Kindergarten. I gave them lunch money for school and always asked them what they ate that day. One week, Edwin said that they got nasty mashed potatoes at school. When I called their teacher she told me the kids did not have mashed potatoes that day but GRITS. I had never heard of this before. I did not even know what grits were. I guess it was some sort of food from the South. We celebrated Billy's fifth birthday on June 10th with a cake and ice cream and invited some of his and Edwin's friends. One day Billy came home and said that he met the love of his life. Edwin explained that there was a mini concert at the school, staged by teenagers, and the girl he was referring to was fourteen years old. I thought that was so cute. Also one week Billy's teacher wanted to talk to me. She said that Billy had taken a little girl from his class behind the door and was kissing her. When I asked Billy why he did this, he said "Mom next week was Valentine's Day and he was starting early". I told him that he could not do this and he was too young for this and his teacher would punish him for that. Boy, these kids were really working it with this kind of stuff.

Ed called me in early fall, that him and his new girlfriend Robin, wanted to come down to Florida and take the kids to Disneyworld and other attractions like Busch Gardens in Tampa for a week, before school started up again. I told him it was okay with me as long as he brought them back to me. So for a week the kids went with their dad and even went to Daytona Beach, where Edwin got stung by a jelly fish in the water there. Ed dropped them off at my work after a week around 2pm, after saying goodbye to them. Edwin was pouting and looked very sad and so did Billy. Dolores said it was okay for them to stay at the store with me for the rest of the day. Since it was Friday I was going to take the kids for pizza for dinner. My co-worker Sandi said she would meet us at the pizza place and she would bring her teenage boys with her too. I thought this would cheer the kids up, as they were missing their dad. They got to eat and play video games there too. When we got home Edwin broke down in tears and Billy saw his brother crying and he started crying too. Needless to say, I started crying too. Edwin kept saying I want my daddy too. I asked Sandi's son, Billy to talk to Edwin and my Billy, that it was okay to miss their dad but they should be with their mom as I need and love them the most. This whole situation was so traumatic for my eight year old and my five year old. I just hugged my boys and told them that they will be able to see their dad too, and I needed them too, and loved them very much. Somehow this seemed to console them and the next day they were my happy little boys.

Ed and I were trying to going through our divorce paperwork. I told him that I wanted the primary custody of our children and he could have visitation rights. I wanted child support of two hundred for each child and altogether four hundred dollars per month, from him. I did not want any part of our mobile home but just my belongings and my car. Since I could not afford a lawyer, Ed's lawyer was drawing up the divorce paperwork. We went back and forth over the custody of our children and he would call me in Florida and threaten to kidnap the kids, while I was at work. I would end up crying after these calls from Ed. I had no one to help me in my situation. This would upset my children too. One day when their dad called me and was threatening to take the kids away from me, Edwin took the phone from me and yelled at his dad telling him to leave his mom alone and he would have to deal with him from now on, as he was the man of house now. After hearing these words from his eight year old son, Ed finally realized what he was putting his children through. The only reason he was fighting over the kids was that he did not want to pay me child support for them. He finally relented on the calls after this incident.

I must be doing a good job for my boss, Dolores, at work, that she started sending me to manage her other two stores at Lakeside and Auburn too. But my salary still remained the same as I had a yearly review with her. It was hard bringing up two growing boys with my salary. I needed the child support check from Ed, to help with my budget. He would never send them to me in a timely manner and sometimes he would forget them, until I would call him and remind him. All in all, I was happy to be free of him. I did not realize how much control he had over me and my life and what total freedom felt like, until I moved away from him. This was my life and I could live it like I wanted to. There were times I was scared over our future; but whatever the future had to throw my way, I could handle it if my children were with me. They are my life and soul.

I tried to give my children all I could afford. I gave them an allowance of five dollars each a week, so they could save it and buy a toy or anything they wanted. One Mother's day they spent all their allowance on me. Edwin bought me a necklace with a cross, black on silver tone. When I asked why a cross, since I was not a Christian, his reply was "Mom this will protect you". Billy got me a gold tone necklace with a heart and arrow with a rhinestone in it. He said mama see I got you a diamond necklace. To this day, after twenty nine years, I still have their beautiful necklaces with me. I would not part with them for anything in the world.

In December of 1980 Ed called me to say that he wanted to pick up the kids for Christmas for about two weeks and take them to New Hampshire. I told him that it was okay as long as he brought them back to me right after Christmas. So this was our deal. He came by to pick up Edwin and Billy about a week before Christmas and took the kids on the long road trip up North. As soon as the kids left, I cried and cried when I went to their empty bedroom that evening, after work. I could not fathom the pain in my heart, as it was so acute. I tried to immerse myself in my work. Dolores, my boss and my friend Sandi both invited me to their houses for Christmas dinner, but I could not think of Christmas without my kids so I declined their offers. On Christmas day I went to the movies and sat way in the back and cried my heart out. I don't remember what movie I went to see. After the movie I rushed home to see if Ed would have the kids call me, but no such luck. So that evening I took the liberty and called them to see how they were doing. They were excited at all the toys they received from Santa. They said they would show me when they come back. I was glad that they were happy. I asked Ed if he could bring the kids back before the year ended. He started laughing saying what makes me think that he was going to bring them back. I was shocked at his answer as we had an agreement that he would bring them back right after Christmas. I could not go on another day without them. Ed would not give me a straight answer. I really got scared, thinking that he would not return them to me and he knew that financially I could not do anything to get them back.

That night I made a decision that I was going to drive back to New Hampshire to get them if I had to. I told my boss what my plans were and she said that I would have to quit my job, as I did not know how long this would take me. She said that if I come back and she still had not hired anyone yet, she would give me my job back. On 12/27/80, I put all my belonging in my car and took off on the one thousand five hundred mile drive up North. When I reached South Carolina, I got a flat tire on the freeway. I was so lost about what to do, as I did not even know how to open the hood of my car. I just stood on the side of the road with my flashers on. Finally a trucker stopped to help me, and replaced my flat tire for me with the spare I had. He also told me to go buy a new tire as I could not take a chance on my long trip up North. There are still some nice people like him left in this world. I took the next exit into a small town and stopped at the Goodyear store. Luckily, I still had an open credit with them. They replaced my tire with a new one and I was on my way. I only stopped at rest stops to fill up gas for my car, eat and use the restroom and kept driving, even though I was very tired. I felt if I did not see my kids before the year ended, I would not see them again. At 2 am the next day I was very low on gas outside Washington DC. I stopped at a gas station, which was closed for the night and would not open till 6 am. I decided to sleep in the car for four hours, even though it was freezing cold there. I covered myself with a couple of comforters and locked my car and fell asleep. In the morning I used their restroom to brush my teeth and wash my face and gas up my car. I was making good time. Hopefully I would be in New Hampshire by nightfall. I made it up there at about 10.00 pm. I parked at our mobile home and I still had the keys to it. I knocked and let myself in to my house. My brother-in-law Bobby and Ricky were watching television with their girlfriends. I asked them where Ed was with the kids. They had a shocked look on their faces, like what was I doing there. They told me that Ed was out of town for his recruiting and the kids were with their grandparents' house around the corner. I told Bobby and Ricky to take their sorry butts out of my house and take their girlfriends out with them, as I was back wanted to go to sleep after I picked up the kids. They were grumbling about how late it was. I told them I wanted them gone when I came back with the kids, and I did not care how late it was.

Next, I drove to big Ed and Kay's house and knocked on the door. Big Ed opened the door. Of course he had shock written on his face when he saw me, as he let me in. I told them that the kids were coming back home with me. Kay said, "I hope you have not come to steal the kids from Ed". I told her that for her information that the kids were under my custody not her son's. Edwin came running to me and Billy hesitated. But when he saw me hugging and kissing Edwin, Billy came running to me, too. I told Ed and Kay that I was taking the kids home as I had to go to bed after my long trip. They told me that Ed would be home the next day. I put the kids to bed and went to sleep myself. For the first time, since the kids left, I slept soundly that night.

Ed came home the next day and was shocked to see me too. I told him that since he did not have the time to bring the kids back to me, I was here to pick them up. He said that he planned to bring them back, but that is not what he told me over the phone. I told him that I would be leaving with the kids in a couple of days, after I had my rest back. He tried to seduce me into having sex with him and won. I had not been intimate with anyone for four or five months now, so that was alright with me. This time I packed some of my things that I had forgotten the first time. I had an Indian brass statue, which I put in my car. One by one, I started loading up my car with all my forgotten things. When Ed saw my brass statue in my car, he pulled it out and brought it back in the house and asked me if he could have it as a parting gift from me to him. I told him "Heck No" these were things that I had purchased with my own money and he could not have it. Here was a man who was having problems paying me child support for his children. What a dirt bag he was.

I wanted to hurry up and leave New Hampshire, before there were any snowstorms coming. My children and I hit the road in a couple of days. We took our time going back to Florida this time. I had my kids back and our drive back was an adventure. We finally got back to warmer weather and reached our apartment in a few days. I called my boss as soon as we got back. She had already hired someone to replace me. So that was bad news. Dolores told me that the new girl had just started and had been there for two days now. I was devastated at this news. I told her if she needed me in the future to call me. I had not only had to search for a new job but since I did not have enough money to buy food the next week, I had to register for food stamps and file for unemployment. Unluckily, I was not qualified for unemployment, as I had quit the job and not laid off. A friend of mine told me to go and sign up for 'Food Stamps' at least, so the kids and I would not starve. I did not even know what that was. I called up the social services and they gave me the address and to be there very early in the morning and get in line. The next day I went to that address and saw hundreds of people standing in line outside the office. They all looked like scum bags, I said no I could not do this. I still had a few cans of food left, and maybe I would get a job by then. So we would be eating things like beans and rice etc, even though the kids did not like it. The child support check that Ed gave me, before we left, went to our rent, utilities and the children's day care.

Two days later, I still did not have a job and my food had run out. This time I went to the food stamp office and stood in line at about 6.00 am and office did not open till 8.00 am. When I finally saw someone there and explained to them my situation, they qualified me for food stamps. I told them that this would be temporary and as soon as I got a job I would not need these. The lady had to explain to me how to use them. After I collected my allotment of food stamps, I picked my kids from school and we went grocery shopping. Edwin asked me if I would buy steak for them and I told them they could have whatever they wanted, including cake and other desserts. We bought all the food we wanted and headed home and cooked them a fabulous meal of steak, potatoes and vegetables. Even though the kids were eight and five year olds they could clear out a grown up's steak in no time. Edwin would eat the potatoes and vegetables too, but Billy was strictly a meat and potatoes guy.

The next day Dolores called me saying that she had let go of the girl who had replaced me. She said that she was lazy, and if I wanted the job back, I could come back to work the next day. At last the year 1981 was turning out to be good year. I had my job back and we all had our bellies full with good food. I went back to work the next day after dropping the kids off at school. It was just like old times. Dolores and her daughters were all happy to see me back and so was my friend Sandi who worked there. Dolores bought us all lunch in my honor. She said "Nalina, I am so happy to see you back again. That other girl did not work as hard as you did". They must have missed me. I was now fixing her store window mannequins with great displays, and when the time came for the ads of stores in the local paper, she had me model her clothing and those pictures appearing in the back to school magazine.

Life was good again, except I would never receive child support from Ed on time and some missed checks too. One time I had to call my brother Harbhajan, who lived in Derby (north of London), England to loan me some money. He wired me four hundred pounds (equivalent to seven hundred dollars) into my bank account in Winter Haven. This enabled me to pay two months' rent and some utilities. Also, now my sister had moved to Oakland, California after she got divorced from her husband Dan in Cincinnati, Ohio. She had been working with a car brokerage company, with the help of her friend Sumita, who referred her to the job where she worked, for over a year now. I told her that I was going to sell my wedding ring and engagement ring, which was appraised for a thousand dollars. Meera said that she would like to buy it and pay me five hundred dollars for it. I told her I would sell it to her. I mailed the ring set to her and she sent me a check for it, which I put it in my savings. She also told me if Ed gives me anymore trouble, I could move to California, and she would help me get a job at her company.

Of course Ed never quit playing games with me and still threatening to take away from me. Over the next few months I thought real hard to resolve my dilemma with Ed. He was now engaged to Robin whom he had been seeing since I left last summer. He basically wanted the kids so he would not have to pay child support to me. Even though I did not take any alimony or our any part of our mobile home together there, how greedy could he be? I finally decided to move all the way across the country to California. By spring of 1981, I had saved about a couple of grand and also after selling my car and television and electric sewing machine to my friend Sandi, I could easily have a total of about four grand to begin a new life in California.

Look out CALIFORNIA, here we come. I quit my job with Dolores and after attending a surprise party she threw for me, we started packing all our stuff. I sold the three big items to Sandi. Sandi was to drive me and the kids to the airport and take possession of my car there. I also called Meera in California and told her the day and time we would be arriving there. I also had to suspend my phone and electric services. And we finally got on our flight to San Francisco, California with a stop in Atlanta, Georgia.

CHAPTER 10 - WELCOME TO CALIFORNIA

Our first stop was in Atlanta, Georgia. We had to change our flights there and had about fifty minutes to an hour to board our flight to San Francisco. I had dressed Edwin and Billy in cowboy outfits, complete with Stetson hats on their heads. When we disembarked the plane there, we made a pit stop at the restrooms. I told the boys to come to the ladies bathroom with me. Of course, they would not hear of this and said they were going to the men's bathroom, since they were boys. I just did not want to lose them at this big airport. I went to the bathroom and when I came out Edwin was standing outside the men's bathroom. I asked him where was Billy, and he said "I don't know mom". I got real mad at him, as he was to keep an eye on his little brother. I told him to go back in the bathroom and look for him and I would look outside the bathroom. I frantically looked for him and just as Edwin was walking out empty handed, I heard an announcement on the airport loudspeaker that Billy Budd was lost, and for his mother and brother to come claim him at a certain gate. When we reached there, there was my little cowboy with big old tears in his big dark eyes. When he saw Edwin, he first kicked him saying 'you tricked me', and ran to me for a hug. We all got a bite to eat at a restaurant by the gate of our next flight out. As soon as we got done eating there was the announcement to board our flight to San Francisco. After boarding the flight, we settled down in our seats and waited for the flight to take off.

When the stewardess saw Edwin and Billy looking so cute in their cowboy outfits, she asked them if they wanted to go in the cockpit to talk to the captain who was flying their plane. I said we would love to. She said to me "not you ma'am, just the boys" and I told her okay you can take them. She took my kids up to meet with the captain of our flight. They came back real excited on seeing all the stuff they saw in the cockpit. Now we settled down for our long flight to San Francisco. We slept after we ate our meal on the plane. We arrived there in the afternoon of a Sunday. We looked for my sister, Meera, who was supposed to meet us there and take us to her home in Oakland. She spotted us first; as she said later 'I saw this family of cowboy hats and knew from afar that it must be us.' She came and hugged us all, and after collecting our baggage she drove us over the Bay Bridge. It was foggy and raining lightly. I asked her "where is sunny California?" To which she replied "we better get used to the bay area weather, which was unpredictable." It was cold and foggy one day and sunny warm the next. We drove down to her studio apartment in Oakland, which was in a secure building on the third floor, overlooking the Grand Lake. Her friend Sumita and her daughter Shalini came to visit us. We all went to the same school in New Delhi. It was nice catching up on old times. Both Meera and Sumita worked at the same car brokerage company in Emeryville, California. Meera took us to this Indian restaurant to eat and I felt like I died and went to heaven. I had not eaten Indian food for almost nine years since I left India.

The Bay area consists of various cities like Berkeley, San Francisco, San Jose, etc. I got a part-time job at Meera's work, as a receptionist after a couple of weeks being here. Meera was dating the Manager John, at this car brokerage company. He was a very nice guy and would put my kids to work washing and wiping down the new cars for sale, which made them feel important. And then he would pay them five dollars each. The next day they told John that they wanted a raise. John told them they don't get a raise after just one day of work. We were all laughing at that. One time John lifted Billy and put him on top of one new car, and did not know that he had iron brush in his hand and just when he was going to scrub the brand new car and scratch it with that brush, John yelled "Billy NO".

My problem was that I had no transportation. I attempted to buy a used truck at my brokerage company, but I was denied, as I had no credit history under my name. I had to take buses to work. Sometimes Meera would lend me her car to go grocery shopping, as it rained a lot here that year. My boys and I would get drenched while we stepped out to go shopping. One day we were walking down the street and a guy yelled to me "Hey Mama" and Edwin looked at him and then me and said "Mom that guy thinks that you are his mom too". I thought that was so funny and assured him that I was only his and Billy's mom. We stayed with Meera for a few weeks and then found our own apartment, also in Oakland. This was actually someone's condo, which they were renting out. After paying one month's rent, I realized it was too expensive for me. Another friend of Meera's named Maria, was going to vacate her very small two bedroom apartment with one bath in El Cerrito. She was going to move to a bigger one in El Sobrante and told me if I liked it (the rent was only two hundred and fifty dollars a month) she would ask her landlord to lease it to me. This apartment was okay as the rent was closer to my budget. With my savings I got some basic furniture like three beds, a couch, dining table and chairs from a rent to own company and we moved in July or August. The children's school was within walking distance. The grocery stores were also pretty close by. I enrolled the kids in school and they could walk to school, while I had to take a bus to Emeryville to go to work. We could walk to anywhere we needed to. On weekends Meera would either drive us to Sumita's house in Albany for small tea parties or my apartment for dinner. This way my kids could interact with Sumita's daughter. As a matter of fact, Sumita gave my son Billy a surprise sixth birthday party on June 10th. She invited a whole bunch of kids and their parents and Billy got a lot of presents. Both Edwin and Billy had a great time. As we were pretty new here in California, and did not know a lot of people, this was great gesture on Sumita's part.

In mid September the car company I was working for, filed for bankruptcy. The owner had squandered the customers' deposits that they had put down on the purchase of their cars. The rumor was that he was heavily into drugs and the FBI was investigating him. I did not know what was going on until the place was going to be shutdown in a week. While my sister and Sumita knew this all along; they said that they did not want to alarm me that was why they did not tell me. This was total bullshit. If I knew about this, I would have been looking for another job. I had to feed my children and only one or two weeks to find a job was not enough. I had to deal with customers coming in and screaming about their deposits and trying to drag the copy machine out of there, if they could not get their money. In other words I was there till the morning the office was literally closed. On the other hand Meera announced that she was going to take a long trip to India, and then would come back and file for unemployment. When I tried to file for unemployment, they told me that I would have to file this with the state of Florida, as I had not been in California for a year yet. I did not know how to do this plus look for a job and take care of my kids too. Again some friend of mine told me to apply for food stamps, until I found a job. Diana, one of Meera's friends, who was temporary job recruiter for her business, also started sending me for interviews for various jobs in San Francisco, where she and her husband, Sonny, worked. I went to several job interviews with no results. I finally applied for a sales clerk for a family owned stationery store in Berkeley, on San Pablo Avenue, which ran all the way to El Cerrito too, where I lived. All I had to do was, to catch a bus in the morning on this street and be at my job in about half an hour. It did not pay much, but a minimum wage in California. But that was better than not having anything. I really worked hard there for eight hours every day and took the bus home to arrive around 5.30 pm or 6.00 pm each evening. Then I had to cook a meal for all three of us and check the kids' homework and put them to bed after a little television. It would be 10.00 pm or 11.00 pm before I went to bed. I had a second set of keys made for the kids, which I placed around their neck, every day before they left for school. They were supposed to walk home after school, and eat some snacks and do their homework. At the store I had to put all the stationery on shelves and place the price tags on them. The store was in total disarray when I started working there. The store owner, Dan said to me that the job was a permanent one at my interview. I also had to ring in the sales, when customers walked into the store and answer the telephone.

In one month I had arranged the whole store and had everything in its place. A little after a month the store owner called me into his office on a Friday, after paying me for that week's salary, told me that my job had ended. This is what I got after working so hard for him. I asked him that he had told me it was a permanent position, to that he replied that they could not afford to have my position open anymore. I was totally pissed off. He let me off at around 3.00 pm. As I was getting on the bus home, tears from my eyes started to flow. I had done nothing wrong and I was back to square one. Now I did not have a job again, and had to look for one again, just before Thanksgiving holiday. Why was life so hard? From having everything with my family in India, I had nothing here in this country. When I got off the bus and started to walk to my apartment and saw Edwin in the distance. When he saw me I heard him say "Oh no" and started to run towards the apartment ahead of me. I knew something was going on and since they did not expect me home early, they must have done something wrong. When I got in the apartment it looked like a hurricane had hit it, even though the boys were attempting to clean up. There was peanut butter on the walls and food and toys all over the floor. As it is I had lost my job and now I come home to this. I just could not help but started to sob. The boys saw me and they started to cry too. Edwin kept saying "Oh no, mom now that you don't have a job how are we going to eat?" They both got away from being punished for all the mess they created. I found that they had put birthday candles on a paper plate on the dining table and lit the candles and were blowing them towards the kitchen curtain. What if the curtains had caught fire?

Meera had come back from India by now. She was getting her unemployment check every week, which would carry her financially well, each month. I did not have anything. She talked to another friend of hers who worked as a secretary to the Indian Council general for the Indian Consulate, on Geary Street in San Francisco. They were looking for a clerk at the Consulate temporarily and Meera's friend got me that job. I was to start working there after the Thanksgiving holidays. Meera came over for the holidays, and since I was broke, we had tacos for dinner and watched television, which was a small black and white and only got two or three channels. I had paid fifty dollars for it. Meera explained to me that the Consulate was far into the city. I would have to take a bus to the San Francisco bus terminal from my home. Then take another bus from there to Geary Street. This would take about an hour and a half each way. This meant that the kids, who were nine and six years old, would be left home alone longer than I wanted to. But I had to do what I had to keep working.

So on a rainy Monday morning in the beginning of December, 1981, I boarded my bus to work, after sending the kids off to school. I finally arrived at work around 9.30 am. They were going to pay me weekly, without taking any taxes out from my paycheck. I met another girl named Lena who worked there. We got along very well and she showed me the ropes at work. I had to process VISAS for people who were going to visit India, check their passports and collect all fees from them. Since we had an hour for lunch, Lena and I would go to the Indian restaurant around the corner for lunch. She lived in Burlingame with her daughter and her 'on again and off again' boyfriend. The days were long as my commute was longer. It was dark when I got home and I would worry about my kids all the time. They were all alone at home. Some days Meera would drive down to my apartment on her way back or to her new work in Richmond at a Mazada dealer, to check on them. It was harder on my children, as at such a young age, they had the burden of responsibility on their little shoulders. But somehow we were surviving. My boys had made friends with a boy named Roggie, who lived two doors down from our apartment with his parents and a teenage sister. He told me that Edwin got hit by a car as he ran on the street in between parked cars, one day. When I asked Edwin, he said the slow moving car had just nicked him lightly before it stopped and the lady in it asked him if he was okay. I told him and Billy that they would have to stay on the sidewalk and look both ways at crossings before they crossed streets from now on. I would die if something happened to them. Also, we had another neighbor who was a single mother like me, who had a daughter. All these kids were my boys' age and they all played together after school. The parents in the apartment building looked after each others' kids.

At Christmas time I had nothing to give them and not even a Christmas tree to decorate. The little I made went towards our food and other household expenses. I asked Meera to come by for tacos again for Christmas dinner, which she did. I thought if we had no money, at least, we have a family. While the kids played, Meera and I were talking about her trip to India and how our parents were doing. After a while the boys started arguing and fighting with each other. I told them to settle down and start behaving themselves. I said "Edwin and Billy, since you are being bad, maybe that is why Santa did not bring them anything". I did not realize how cruel a statement this was. At this Edwin started to cry, saying "No mom, Santa did not come to our house because we do not have a Christmas tree". Meera and I hugged the kids to comfort them. That day I promised myself that next Christmas would be different for my children. Since Meera and I thought of Christmas as only a holiday, but to the kids this was a big thing; The Christmas tree, Santa and presents from him. If I knew what I know today, back then, I could have gone to charities that collect toys for needy families and received toys for my children and wrapped them from Santa. I guess we live and learn.

I worked for the Indian Consulate for the month of December 1981 and since this was a temporary position only, I accepted another position as a collector for a collection agency on Market Street in downtown San Francisco. I was one of the three interviewees they picked from a large group of people that had applied for the job. The first two weeks of January 1982 I was in training. They showed us how to call people who were behind in paying their various bills and get an agreement from them to a payment arrangement with us. We handled Macys and some other business' delinquent accounts. After the two weeks they put us on the telephone with a list of people to call. Of course this process was supervised, until we got fully trained. I was good at tracing people down and calling them on their unpaid accounts. We would never give them our real name. I chose the name of Nancy for myself. Some of these folks would spew verbal abuse, one after the other, but most of them would agree to payment arrangement. Of course it was another thing for them to follow through on their promises. I did not know if this was going to be the job for me, as I was tired of the verbal abuse I was put through daily. One day I called a lady who was delinquent on her encyclopedia payment. She started screaming hysterically at me saying "I just lost a child, and you are calling me about a #@%$&*& bill" and hung up. She was crying and it brought tears to my eyes too. I know if something bad happened to my kids I would do the same too. I remember this incident to this day and knew I could not do this job too much longer. In the meantime I kept looking for job openings in the paper. I called on this one job and got an interview and when I asked for their address, it was about a block away from my apartment, in El Cerrito. I talked to a lady named Sally, and the company's name was Charge Card USA. There was no prior experience required but a willingness to work hard and learn quickly. I ended up getting the job, after my interview with the president of the company, Javier. He told me that there were only ten employees, including him and his assistant, Sally. I told him I could start in one week, after giving a week's notice at my job in San Francisco. That was okay with him and told me that my salary would be $8.00 an hour, slightly less than at my present job. But I did not have to spend any money on my commute now.

On March 2, 1982 I started working for Charge Card USA. This was the break I was looking for. My work and the kid's school were both close to our apartment. I could walk to the apartment at lunch time and check up on the kids after they came back from school. That was a total relief to me. My boss was a great guy and understood that I was a single parent and set up a late lunch for me. I would eat my lunch while working and spend my lunch hour on checking up on my children. Of course I still did not have a car. The employees were all very nice to me and trained me on my job. The company was a subsidiary of United Bank of San Francisco, the largest Southeast Asian Bank in the Bay Area. We processed all credit card transactions for smaller Savings & Loans, Credit Unions. We had about ten accounts, whose transactions we processed. That included customer service; payment and cash advance processing, disputes, regulated by VISA and MASTERCARD. I loved my job as it was a on-the job training. My immediate supervisor was Daniel. On the second week of my job I went to use the restroom just before closing time and by the time I came out a couple of minutes later, the lights were turned out and the office was locked and the alarm set. I could not believe this. Why didn't someone check the restroom before doing this? I started panicking but calmed down enough to call the bank downstairs from us to see if they had the alarm code for us to get me out. The manager said they did not, but they did have Sally's home number and for me to call her, as she would have the alarm code and the keys to the office. I called Sally and her husband told me he would relay this information to Sally when she got home. I guess she had a long commute to Fairfield from El Cerrito. I told him to have Sally call me at work when she got home. Next I called my kids at home and told them that mommy was locked in the office and I would be home as soon I get out of there. Edwin said, "Oh no mom, who is going to feed us now?" I told him to calm down and look after Bill till I got home. After about half an hour later Sally called and said she would drive all the way back to let me out and did not sound happy to do this. Well, if she had only checked before she took off in a hurry, we both would not have to go through this fiasco. It is me and my kids who had to suffer through this experience. I finally got home around 6.30 pm that evening and I had to cook and feed my children.

On days we were very busy; Javier did not hesitate in pitching in, and processed payments or answer customer service calls. He was from Panama and his wife Maria was from El Salvador. I could not have asked for a better boss. One day when my phone rang and I was processing payments, he picked up the phone, and said "this is Nalini, how can I help you. No I mean this is Javier". We all heard it and burst into laughter along with him, after the call. My other co-workers were Ione, Linda, Anthony, Cindy, William, and Danny. It did not take very long for me to learn things fast here. There were some things that had to be processed daily, like payments and cash advances. We also had a fraud department and I learned how to place certain bad accounts in the 'warning bulletin'. Before I knew, we had added more accounts and Javier and Sally hired more employees later that year; we got Gayle, Sandi, Debbie, Kathy, Mary, Annie, Lena, Helen, Harry and his wife, Cathy. If we worked on a Saturday, we could bring our kids in to work with us. Of course we would be paid overtime. Now my co-workers were like my new family. We would celebrate everybody's birthdays by getting a cake for them, by collecting money from everyone. We played softball on the weekends against our clients' teams from work. Our children were also included in these games.

About a couple of years ago, while I was still in Florida, I had put in a petition with Immigration office to have my brother, Harbhajan and his family to move to the United States. Since he had helped me financially I was repaying his favor. It took about two years for him to finally move here in California. They stayed at Meera's apartment till they purchased a small two bedroom home in San Jose, California. Meera co-signed their mortgage loan, since my brother did not have any credit here. He had lived in United Kingdom for about over twenty years, where both his children Dimple and Bobby were born, and had a house a little north of London, in Derby. My brother used to drive the double-decker buses in England for a living. He got a similar job here, driving buses for the San Jose Transit. My sister-in-law Amarjeet also got a job in a factory there. Dimple and Bobby finished their school and enrolled in the university. On weekends, we would drive down to San Jose, and spend a night there with my brother and his family. This was great way for my kids to bond with their uncle and aunt and cousins. We would all camp out on their carpeted living room floor for the Saturday nights. And leave on Sunday afternoons to go back home. It was great having family close to us. To think I spent the first eight years all alone back on the East Coast. Billy and Edwin turned seven and ten that year and we celebrated their birthdays with a party each. All their friends came to celebrate with presents for them. I was happy to see my children happy and all my friends loved them as they were very polite and had good manners too. That summer Ed, their dad sent two return airline tickets for them to visit him. I was scared to let them go alone on such a long flight, but the airline assured me that they would get back to the East Coast safely, under their supervision.

The Christmas of 1982 was much better for us. I had the kids make a list of things they wanted from Santa, and I tried to get all the toys on their list. Billy even had a hand grenade on his list, and wrote "Santa, don't forget the batteries for my toys". Now where was I going to get a hand grenade? I did find one made out of plastic at a department store. Now it was going to be hard getting all the gifts wrapped and hidden from the kids till Christmas Eve. I had purchased a 1978 Oldsmobile Royale for four hundred dollars in the summer of 1982, and hid the toys in its trunk. The car was pretty beat up but ran okay, but needed a lot of things to be replaced, like tires and a new radiator. I was talking to a customer at work. She was telling me that she was taking this car away from her teenage son, who had accrued a whole lot of tickets on it. She needed to pay these tickets by selling the car. I told her I would like to buy it from her, which, I did. She transferred the pink slip under my name at D.M.V., after I paid her by check. At least I had a set of wheels now. I could replace the needed parts slowly. The car was like a big old tank, and needed a lot of gas to fill her up.

Our Christmas holiday went pretty well and the kids were so excited on Christmas Eve that they would not go to sleep. I was waiting for them to go to sleep so I would bring the toys from the trunk of my car and start wrapping them. We had a Christmas tree that kids helped me decorate, and Santa was going to bring gifts for them; what more could a mother ask for. I just did not want my kids to be disappointed again. Meera was also working for another car brokerage company in El Cerrito now. She was close to my work and apartment. This allowed her to check up on Edwin and Billy too, at her lunch hour. One day she called me at work and told me that when she went to our house, the boys were playing with the candles, lighting them and had wax all over the floor. I don't know where they got matches from, as I would never keep them in the house. Maybe they got them from Rogee's house. Meera helped them clean it before she left, so they would not get into trouble with me. For Edwin's birthday he wanted a toy safe, which I got for him. When the boys went to sleep, I would occasionally clean out his safe, as he had a whole lot of junk in it. One day I found nude pictures torn out of a Playboy magazine in his safe. My first reaction was shock; where did they get that picture from. We did not have that magazine in our house. I asked my co-workers to help me deal with this situation. One of my friends advised me to not make a big deal, when I asked them about it. I found out that their friend Rogee tore it out of someone else's magazine in the mail slot at the apartments, and gave it to them and some other kids in the neighborhood. This whole situation created chaos with some of the other tenants' mailed magazines disappearing. I know my kids would not do this, as they told me that Rogee gave it to them and I believed them.

In February of 1982, I was surprised to see my maternal aunt and my uncle came to visit us. They stayed one night with me and the boys after being with Meera for a day. My uncle had family near Fresno, in southern California and they went to visit them after they left my house. They had a large house down there with a full size swimming pool and had business of growing grapes and making raisins. Their oldest daughter Meeta was married to a surgeon and also had a large house in Bakersfield, adjacent to the country club. Meeta had organized a fundraiser for Jerry Brown, who was running for the Governor of California. We were all invited to go down to it. Financially I was unable to go, but my sister Meera and her friend Sumita and her daughter Shalini all went down for this and had a great time hobnobbing with the bigwigs in their political circle.

The year 1982 rolled into 1983 and I was still working for my company. We also went for the company Christmas dinner in San Francisco through the United Bank. I took my sister Meera with me to the party. We had a great party and ate great Cantonese food. Meera's friend Diana and her husband Sonny loved my boys a lot and would invite us to their house in Arlington for dinner on weekends. Diana would treat my kids like they were grownups and served them soft drinks in a wine glass. If all of us would discuss politics and current news affairs, Edwin would join in with one hand holding his wine glass and the other on his hip, acting so grown up. They loved going to Sonny and Diana's house. The fact that Sonny did not want to have children before he met Edwin and Billy, their behavior changed all that. He was so used to seeing unruly children of his brother, that he thought all children were like that. I told him that is not the children but, it is the way they are brought up is what makes a difference.

That summer I knew we had to move to another apartment, as the roof in our living area leaked real bad, which I had to place a bucket on the floor. When I asked the handyman to fix it he told me that the building was sold to someone else and the new owners were going to tear down the whole place and renovate. We were given three months notice to move out. I finally found a two bedroom apartment in San Pablo, called the Montoya Garden apartments, which had two swimming pools. The rent was a little over half the amount I was paying before, but it was real nice. We were going to move in after the school was out, which meant I would have to re-enroll the children in another school in September.

The children were going back to see their dad in New Hampshire after the school closed for the summer. Ed and his new wife Robin had a daughter named Carla, who was two now. Ed sent me the airline tickets for the boys and I was going to put them on their flight in June. I somehow mistook the days of the flight. The flight was for a Friday morning and I thought it was Saturday morning. If I worked on Fridays why would he send me airline tickets for that day? Well, to make a long story short, we came back from one of our softball game, and Ed telephoned me and asked why the kids were not on the plane and I told him I was going to take them to airport today. He said did I look at the date on the tickets as they were for the day before. At that point when I realized I had made a mistake, he started yelling obscenities at me. I told him I would call the airlines to see if they could honor the tickets from the previous day as I had made a mistake on the dates. The lady at the airlines was very nice and when I told her my situation and the fact that my ex-husband was going to kill me for this, told me that if I could bring the kids to the San Francisco airport in forty five minutes, she would put them on the next flight out to Boston. I was so relieved and called Ed back and gave him the arrival date and the flight number. He told me to throw the kids' dirty clothes in the suitcase, as they would wash them there. I told the kids to jump in the shower for five minutes and pack their toys in their carryon. Luckily Meera came by the house, and Edwin asked her to drive us to the airport as my mom is a nervous wreck, which she did. We finally made it to the airport on time and when the kids went through the security screening at the airport, there were toy guns on their carryon and were told that these were not allowed aboard the flight and that they would have to package them as checked luggage. More delays and the kids knew that I was mad at them for this. Why couldn't they have brought their books? I finally got them on the flight.

Every time they left, there was sadness in my heart, for the couple of months they were gone to see their dad. Meera drove us back to my apartment and stayed for dinner, so I would not get too lonely. The next weekend she and my friend Maria were going to help me move to our new apartment in San Pablo. It took us several trips moving boxes and my furniture. The new twenty five inch swivel television console that I bought from Macys a few months ago was the hardest thing for us to move. It took all three of us carry that into Maria's truck and then unload and carry it up the stairs to my new apartment. We started moving at 8 am on Saturday and finally got done by late that afternoon. Maria had to go and since it was very hot, Meera and I decided to hang by the swimming pool. There were two pools on the premises. In the coming weeks I started unpacking my stuff putting it away. I would go out partying with my niece Dimple, my brother's daughter in San Jose. One night Sumita came by and asked me if I wanted to go to this club in Emeryville and I said yes. That night I met a cute guy named Doug, who took my phone number and called me the next day for a date. We went out for drinks and had a great time together. We started seeing each other quite often and he would end up staying the weekend at my apartment. Finally my children returned from their trip to New Hampshire to see their dad. Doug insisted that he would take all three of us to dinner. He even ordered Shirley temple drinks for the boys. After dinner we all came back to my apartment. After a while I told the kids to get ready for bed. Edwin being protective of me said, "So, when is he going home?" right in front of him. I was so embarrassed. So when the kids went to bed, I told Doug that it would not be right for him to stay over as my kids were home now. It was okay, while they were out of town. He agreed and left, and told me he would call me. We still saw each other at different events. Sumita used to have a lot of parties at her home in Albany and she would invite Doug also. Also at a party in Meera's house I met Aruni, another friend of Meera. She was from Fiji Islands and her husband was from a country in Africa. Aruni worked for Hyatt hotels and her husband was an airline pilot. She told me that one weekend they flew to London free, on a dinner and dance. Since Meera lived in a secure building on the third floor and her door buzzer did not work, Edwin and Billy were assigned to run down and open her door when she had a party at her apartment. They would say "Mom we love being the servants". That was so cute, I think they loved running up and down the stairs. All of Meera's friends including Sonny and Diana and John and Janet would be at these parties. Meera and John had stopped seeing each other and now John was married to Janet and they had a little boy. Once John and Janet took my boys to an amusement park with rides, for the whole day and they had a great time and came home tired. John had commented that how well behaved my kids were. Everyone that I would meet would come to love my kids. I could take them to fancy hotels for meals with Meera and I knew they would act like little gentlemen. At this restaurant the kids wanted to order steak dinner for grownups and the waitress said that the steak would be too much for them, but they insisted that's what they wanted to eat. They actually polished the dinner off their plates to the amazement of the waitress and other patrons at the restaurant, which brought out applause from them.

Slowly I started to see less of Doug as my schedule with the boys was pretty full. I had to take them to Boy Scout meetings twice a week in the evenings and of course I had to make sure their homework was completed daily and cook their meals. Edwin would make a drawing of a house with a mother and child looking out of the window in the house and one child standing outside in the front lawn. Meera and I asked him to explain the picture to us. He said that in the window there was Billy and I waving and the kid outside was him, protecting us by standing guard. His thinking was way beyond his years.

Meera was now seeing another person named Jean Paul, who was from Haiti; and our friend Sumita, was working with Meera and was dating a guy named David. Lali and Neil and their kids were stationed in Germany again. Lali had another girl named Annisa. Now they had three kids, Dimpy, Ryan and Annisa.

Later that December, I had a party at my apartment and invited all my family and friends including my co-workers at Charge Card USA. We filled up the bathtub with ice and put all the drinks in it. The kids would run down and get the drinks for our guests. I even invited some of my neighbors and the couple who managed the apartment building, as we had the music blaring. This is the year that Michael Jackson came out with the his best selling records with songs like "Beat it" and "Billie Jean" and we played it over and over again. Earlier that year I did not even know who Michael Jackson was, until Edwin and Billy introduced him to me. They said mom come and look at the Grammy Award show on television and pointed him to me. Edwin said "Mom don't freak out when you hear him speak". Then I heard his girlie squeaky voice saying "Thank you, thank you very much". As he was wearing dark glasses, I said 'maybe he was on drugs". To this Billy replied, "Oh yes, what if Kenny Roger's beard catches fire". They were insulting the artist I used to hear on the country western radio station. Everyone was dancing and having a ball. The boys were my servers and the deejays. Everyone was drunk including me and the party finally ended at 2.00 am the next morning and finally the last guests left. My apartment was totally trashed. We went to sleep and when I woke up it was time to clean up the place. I also realized that the emerald from my ring was missing. I combed the carpet looking for the emerald but could not find it. Finally when I was vacuuming the carpet, I heard a 'clunk' like a rock was sucked in. I tore the vacuum apart and found my emerald. I was relieved at that. Luckily I was off from work that Monday, so I could recover from my hangover. Even though I had invited Doug and his mom, Jane to my party, but they did not show up. He lived with his mom and sister in Berkeley. All my friends Gayle, Debbie, Curt, Jeannie, Ione, Linda, Cindy and Anthony were at my party and they told me that they all had a great time.

Now 1983 rolled into 1984 and in January my boss Javier had a meeting, when he announced that he had liver cancer and planned to fight it. That was devastating news to all of us. He said he was going to have intensive chemotherapy to fight this disease and on days he is unable to come to work, he left Curt in charge of our operations. That night when I was saying my prayers, I said a special one for him and his family. When I told this news to Edwin and Billy, Edwin told me "Mom, people who have liver cancer, usually never make it". I asked him how did he know this, and he said he read that at school's library. I just felt so bad for Javier and his wife Maria and their kids. I wondered why something like this would happen to such a nice person like him.

Well, this was in January and by that summer we got the news that he passed away. One day in April he came into the office on crutches, with the help of his wife. He had lost so much weight and when Maria was holding his arm to guide him to the bathroom, the bone in his arm snapped. She got hysterical and rushed him to the hospital emergency. One weekend some of us went to visit him in the Kaiser hospital in Fremont when he was at the last stretch of his life. He was in a lot of pain but asked me if I could give him a cigarette, which he was allowed to smoke in his bed. I remember that he smoked the same brand as mine, Marlboro. That was the last we saw him and joked with him to keep his spirits up. He died a few weeks later. Life is fragile and is a gift from the Lord, and we need to enjoy it to its fullest, as we don't know how much time we have left on this earth. Curt had moved into Javier's position as the president of our company and made Gayle his vice president, even before he died.

The summer of 1984 Meera was again in touch with Charles who was in Germany with his new German girlfriend. He told Meera to come down to Germany as Lali had been drinking booze for a week and was not eating and also her daughter Dixie had ran away from home and living with a foster family there. She would be put up for adoption by the authorities. Meera flew to Germany to talk some sense into Lali and rescue Dixie, whom Meera adopted and brought her back to the U.S. and was now under Meera's care. Since Meera never had any children of her own, she adopted Dixie as her daughter, legally.

I bought a brand new Ford Tempo at the Albany Ford dealership, through John who was a manager there now. My loan was approved as I had been working at Charge Card USA for two years now. I took possession of the car in mid January and had my monthly payments explained to me and provide my car insurance to the financial department of the dealership. I guess money was going to be tight with my car payments now, but on the bright side I had a brand new car now. The children were doing well in school. They still had a window of two hours after school when they were alone at home. After calling me at work, they were supposed to finish their homework after eating a snack, I left for them. Lately I noticed the milk and drinks and ice cream would be gone in a day. First week I thought maybe they were hungrier but slowly I realized they were eating a lot, which made me suspicious. I asked them if any of their friends were eating at our house. They said no. One day I found my cash missing out of my closet. Now I knew something else was going on, as my kids never ever touched my money. I finally got out the truth out of Edwin and Billy. They told me that there were these two older boys who would push their way into our apartment and knowing that I was not home, would drink and eat food from the refrigerator and took my cash. The next day I asked my boss Curt if I could stay home the next day; after I explained my situation, he said it was okay for me to take the day off. I asked Edwin what time the boys did come every day and they said about three to three thirty. I hid in the bathroom and told Edwin to tell them that they could not come in our house, but they pushed their way in and went straight for the refrigerator and one of them grabbed the milk carton and started drinking straight from the container and the other started eating an ice cream bar. This is the time I decided to come out of hiding. Their faces fell when they saw me and they started to dart out. I grabbed them by their collars and dragged them back in and asked them what were they doing in my house, as I was going to call the police if they did not give their parents phone number. One of the boys said his mother was at work and could not be called at work. I told him he had a choice he could either give me his mother's telephone number or I would call the police and have them hauled off for trespassing. To this, he quickly gave me his mother's telephone number. I called and talked to his mother and told her what was happening at my house by her son and his cousin. I told her if this does not stop I would have to fill out a police report. She assured me that the boys would be punished and it would not happen again. She even talked to her son over the phone and told him to get home immediately, and she would deal with him when she got home. Turned out, she was a single mother like me. That evening she returned my eighty dollars cash her kids had stolen from my closet and apologized profusely to me. That was the end of terror my kids had to endure. One day I encountered the boys on the street, when they saw me they ran the other way.

That summer the kids were getting ready to go back to see their dad again for the summer vacation. I had a birthday party for Billy when he turned nine. Not too many of their friends came. Billy had a friend named Dong Ding, and when I made a mistake and called him Ding Dong, Billy got mad at me. "Mom his name is not Ding Dong". I said "so what is the difference", and that got him even more mad. The party went okay and he did get a lot of presents from me and his friends. After all the kids left, the three of us went out to eat dinner. A few days later they were on their way to fly back East to see their dad. I did not know that I would not see them for a year. After they left I was in a financial mess; too many debts and not enough income. I had several credit cards which I had maxed out and the banks required their money as I was late making payments. And I found out I was pregnant with Doug's baby and he wanted me to have an abortion as he said he was not ready for a baby. On top of all my troubles, Meera was also insisting that I have an abortion, as due to my financial situation I could not afford a child now. I wish I would not have listened to anyone and had my child instead of having an abortion. Meera took me to the family planning center where I had the abortion. She brought me home after that and I could not stop crying and felt so sad and down. Meera left after I went to sleep. Doug came by that evening to check on me and I started to cry again. He made me a drink to calm my nerves. He stayed that night with me and we fell asleep in each other's arms. When we woke up Doug took his shower and I started making our breakfast. He asked me if I saw other guys since I was a pretty girl. I told him no, and I asked him the same question if he saw other girls. He said yes. That was it. I told him to get out of my house. He had the gall to ask me "but what about breakfast?" I told him no breakfast and to get out. He left in such a hurry that he left his watch on my night stand. I was so mad at him. Here I went through aborting my baby and here was this jerk telling me he was seeing other girls too. He had the gall didn't he?

I would talk to the boys over the telephone while they were with their dad. I called them and cried too. They did not know what I was crying about. Ed told me if I was financially strapped that he could keep the kids with him for a year and they could go school there, and next summer he could send them back to me. I agreed to it, and I know I should not have ever done that. People around me were taking advantage of my vulnerable state. This was the worse time in my life. My kids were gone and I was in debt and no one to turn to. At least I had my job to keep me occupied and on the weekends I started to make oil paintings. Also, I had some good friends at work, like Mary, Lena, Annie, Helen and Kathy who would keep my spirits up. Mary ended up being my best friend. She and I would go party together on weekends. Doug and I were still having an on and off relationship till the rest of the year. More "off" than "on". On the weekends I would still go see my brother and his family in San Jose and my niece Dimple and I would go out with Amarjit to the San Jose flea market. Dimple was now engaged to be married. Both my brother Harbhajan and Amarjit were arranging a marriage for her. She was getting married in 1985. I also became good friends with Aruni who lived in Fremont with her husband and stepson. She would call and tell me that she was going to leave her husband as things between her and stepson were bad as he tried to hit on her. She was much younger than her husband and closer in age to her stepson.

In 1985 I met another person named Nalini through my work. She worked for Berkeley City and County credit union, and we handled the credit card processing for their customers. She and I became good friends too since our first names were similar. She was from Fiji Islands and lived in Berkeley. She lived with her on and off boyfriend Tom. Since we both had an hour for lunch, we would meet for lunch somewhere in between Berkeley and El Cerrito. I missed my children very much and would talk to them at least once a week via telephone. They would mail me letters too. Before the Christmas of 1984, Billy wrote me this cute letter. "Mom can't wait for Christmas. Ten more days to Christmas. Dad took us to see grandma and grandpa. Nine more days to Christmas". Every other sentence was a countdown to Christmas. I kept that letter to show him when he grew up and I did that.

On mother's day in May of 1985 we went to see a baseball game between the Oakland A's and the Boston Red Sox through the church group of Sumita's daughter Shalini. After the game we were to meet the players through the church group. I called my kids in New Hampshire to see if they wanted the autographs of any player. They said they would like Jim Rice's autograph, who was a left outfielder for the Boston Red Sox. I went to the game with Meera and Dixie, and Sumita and Shalini, and David and his two twin sons. Sumita told us that the church group's meeting with the players was canceled. We all enjoyed the game but the visiting team the Boston Red Sox beat the Oakland A's. In the last inning after consuming two beers, I was brave enough to run down the field and quickly get Jim Rice's autograph. One of the security guard lady stopped me saying if I went on the field I would be arrested. She told me instead why not go where the Locker room was and wait outside and when the players come out I could get his autograph. So we all went down to the locker room after the game but they would allow only one of us, so I told them I would stay and I would meet the rest of our group outside a little later. As I was standing there with a bunch of children, an A's player came by and all the children asked him for his autograph so I figured I would also get his autograph too. He signed his name as Jose Canseco; I later found out that this was his rookie year with the A's. I asked him if knew if Jim Rice was still in the locker room and he said yes; I asked him if he could take it in and have it signed for me. He said "No lady, he will be out." I was afraid I would miss him. I only knew that he wore a number fourteen jersey, but he would have his street clothes on when he comes out. I voiced my concern to the security guard outside. He told me not to worry; he would point him out to me. When he finally came out, I walked up to him and asked him for his autograph signed to Edwin and Billy Budd and he complied with my request. I started walking out with him to the parking lot, where his bus was waiting to take him and other players to the airport. I realized that I had a camera and I asked him if I could take a picture with him he said okay. There was a little girl standing there and I had her take our picture. Jim put his arm around me and said 'Oh no bra?' and I told him it was Sunday. He boarded his bus and left. I had accomplished what I set out to do. My family and friends were impressed. They said if they wanted something done, they could not do, they were going to ask me.

My parents came to visit us for the first time in the summer of 1985. We all went down to the airport to pick them up. That was so very exciting for us. They stayed with Meera and Dixie in Oakland first and then at my brother, Harbhajan's house, in San Jose. It was so nice to see my parents, whom I had not seen since 1978, when I was in India. They wanted to see this and go there on their first visit to the United States. They also brought us all some gifts from India, like clothes and jewelry. They came by to see my apartment and my office, where they met my boss and co-workers. We would be invited to Sumita, Meera and my brother's houses for dinner parties. They even went to an amusement park where my mother actually got on a roller coaster ride, something even I could not do due to my fear of heights. But most of all they loved going shopping where they looked like little kids in a candy store. My mother helped me to clear my financial debts and told me to cut all my credit cards, which I did.

Edwin and Billy returned from New Hampshire and could meet their grandparents for the first time. It was so sweet the way my mother tried to communicate with them, as she did not speak English. A lot of hand communication. By now it was my turn to have mom and dad to stay with me. During the week when I was at work, I would stop by for lunch in the afternoon to make sure that my parents and children had lunch already, if not, I would fix them something quickly. The kids would tell me that mom and dad would be constantly talking over their television shows and they would miss out a lot. On the other hand my mom told me that the boys were hanging off our balcony on the second floor and she was scared that they would fall down and she could not tell them to stop in English. There was a communication problem between my parents and Edwin and Billy. My dad was hard of hearing and my mom could not speak English. On Fridays after work I would drive the kids and my parents to the Fisherman's Wharf, where we would get a bite to eat and the kids would play video games and my parents and I would window shop. It seems the kids were not very happy as they did not have any friends at our new apartment and I had to work and they were not connecting with their grandparents. My parents now wanted to go to my brother's house in San Jose. On the weekend we all drove down to their house and spent the day with them. The kids always got along with their uncle and cousin Dimple. They loved wrestling on the living room floor for entertainment, as they loved rough housing. The next day Edwin, Billy and I left to go back to our apartment and left my parents there. The next day my friend Nalini and Tom invited us to their house in San Francisco, for dinner, as they wanted to meet Edwin and Billy. We drove down there in my car and I had country and western music on the radio, and my kids did not like that so I changed the station on the radio, to what they wanted to hear. We had a nice visit and dinner at Nalini's house. She had cooked Indian food. On our return trip, the kids were not behaving themselves so I told them I was going to change the radio station to my kind of music. This irritated the heck out of them. They would not speak to me when we got home and that really got me mad at them. I yelled at them saying I was bending over backwards to keep them entertained and they did not appreciate what I had done for them. Edwin and Billy were very protective of each other and if I yelled at one the other would say "don't yell at my brother, mom".

Later that week, they both came to me and said they had decided to live with their dad. I felt like someone had stabbed me in the heart. I knew their dad had put them up to it. I was poor and could not afford to buy them all they wanted. Their dad had most probably told them that if they lived with him he would buy them this and that. I knew that he wanted to get out of paying child support which is something the kids would not understand. Also the fact, that the boys, did not want me dating other men. I should never have let them stay with their dad for a year. Edwin was twelve and Billy had turned ten. I was so hurt and told the boys if that is what they wanted they could go and live with their dad. I called Ed and told the kids decision to live with him and his wife Robin. He told me that he would send me a return airline ticket for me to come visit them every summer back in New Hampshire. I must have cried many a tear on this situation. I decided to honor my children's decision and told them that if for any reason they decided to come live with me again that they could tell me and I would bring them back.

At the end of summer, I packed all their belongings like books, toys and clothes, and put them on their flight back East to be with their dad. I have never felt such loneliness, like felt right then watching their flight take off. My parents also left back for India a couple of weeks later, promising to return the next year.

After my children left, and I started going out to party with my friends, almost, every weekend. Mary and I would go to Alameda and go to bars on the city's main drag or the Naval Enlisted men's club, when the naval ship came into town. I met a lot of guys that way, mostly one night stands and some lasted maybe a month or two. I cannot even remember their names now, as they were just insignificant to my life. Sometimes Lena would come too. I met this nice Arabic guy named Khamiz. He would pay for my drinks when we were out partying with the girls. He would also drive us in his Trans Am there. He told me that he loved me and that we should get married. I know that was because he wanted to live in this country legally. I told him that I was not into marriage at this point in my life. His English was not very good. Lena and Mary used to make fun of him, behind his back, when he danced with us. I thought that was a bit mean. Khamiz lived in Fremont and would drive down to my place almost each weekend. We would all leave to party on Friday nights at 9.00 pm and return at two or three the next morning. We would come home and sleep the whole next day away, nursing our hangovers. Lena became my roommate and was supposed to pay me half of the rent. She was the worst nightmare as a roommate. Her boyfriend would come by and stay with her all the time. They were loud and messy. There were always dirty dishes in the sink as Lena would always be cooking something or the other. I told Lena that her boyfriend could not come and stay with her during the week, as I needed my sleep before going to work. They would come in at 2.00 am in the middle of the week and make all kind of loud noises and even fight loudly, and how was I to get my rest. This was the worst decision I ever made to have her as my roommate. After a couple of months like this I gave Lena notice to move out at the end of that month.

In August Doug called me out of the blue and said that he had two tickets to the CARLO SANTANA'S concert at the Concord Pavilion that evening, and wanted to see if I wanted to go. Like a fool I said yes. He came to pick me up in his old beaten down Mercedes, which broke down a few yards from the apartment. I told him that we could take my new Ford Tempo. Of course, I let him drive it, to make him feel like a big man. I don't know what it was about him that he would have me eating out of his hand. I was so mesmerized by him that I could not see what he really was – a wolf in sheep's clothing. But I did have a great time at the concert. I had a following of the CARLO SANTANA band since I was in India. I still think that he is the greatest guitar player in the world. He could make his guitar strings scream. Of course we were drinking and he was smoking something else beside cigarettes. He dropped me off that night and his car towed back to his apartment. Meera had a party at her apartment and invited all her friends and included Doug. I arrived late to the party and Doug was already mingling with Meera's guests. He was paying special attention to Aruni, who was single now. I stayed at the party for a couple of hours only and left. The next morning Meera told me that Doug and Aruni left the party together. Aruni turned out to be such a bitch. She knew I still had feelings for Doug and how could she take him to her place and have a one night stand with him. I would never do this to her. That was it; I finally saw their true colors. I was never going to see either one of them again. Now my only real friends were Mary and Nalini. They would never do this to me.

We all attended Dimple's wedding in Fremont's civic hall, which was booked for eight hundred people but I am sure at least more than a thousand showed up. Before my kids left for New Hampshire and my parents left for India, in the summer of 1985, we all attended the wedding and had a great time. Champagne was flowing and there were all kinds of Indian food served. Indian weddings are long and drawn out. Late afternoon it was time for the bride (Dimple) to leave her parents' house and go to the groom's house. The bride gets in the car with the groom, and everyone in the bride's family is crying as they are losing their daughter to the groom's family. When my kids saw this they were bewildered as to what was going on. They looked at me and said, "Mom what is going on?" and I had to explain this to them. Earlier, we were in the big parking lot adjacent to the building, where the wedding was held, I was teaching my kids to drive my car. I sat on the passenger side and let Edwin drive first and then Billy. As a matter of fact they did pretty good. At this wedding I met Mickey, who was like a cousin to us. His dad and our dad were best friends while we were growing up in India. My mom told him that she would give him Indian money in India and if he could give me US dollars here and he did. This helped me to pay off most of my debts.

In December of 1985, about two weeks before Christmas, I flew in to surprise my kids in Massachusetts, where their dad was stationed on base. I had talked to Ed and his wife Robin that I would fly in for the weekend and not to tell the kids I was coming. I flew the redeye after work on Thursday night and Ed came to pick me up at the Logan airport, in Boston the next morning, and we drove to his and Robin's place. The kids were in school and I decided to sleep for a few hours before they came home, as I was very tired. It was Edwin who came in first and Robin told him to come in the living room, when he saw me his eyes almost popped out of his head. He was so happy to see his mom. I hugged him a lot. Then in walks Billy and it was snowing lightly outside. He said "Mom what are you doing here?" I was so happy to see them both. They were very happy to see me too. Ed's daughter Carla, who was only about three or so, was so jealous when I picked Billy up like a baby and took him to his bed upstairs. She wanted me to pick her up and take her upstairs too. She said "How come Edwin and Billy have two moms, and I only have one?" I told her that I could be her mom too then she would have two moms too. This made her happy. I was there Friday and Saturday and left on Sunday. Ed's parents Kay and big Ed also came to see me. Kay told me that I was the best daughter-in-law she ever had. So I thought why she didn't she treat me better when I was married to her son. I had a nice and short visit with them. Edwin had a part time job delivering newspapers and collecting money from his customers. On Saturday he had to get up like 5.00 am and go out in the snow storm to do this. I felt so sorry for him. My kids were so dedicated in performing their tasks. They took me to the airport for me to catch my flight back to San Francisco and I cried all the way back. They told me to come visit them next summer for maybe a week this time, and I said I would.

In March of 1986 my friend Nalini and I made plans to go to Monterey for the weekend. I told her I would drive and she could pay me half the cost of gas and hotel. It rained a lot that month and the Friday before our trip on Saturday I came home from work, and tried to call Nalini to confirm and found the phone dead. It was pouring cats and dogs outside and the wind was howling; but I knew I had to call her so I got in my car and went to a phone booth to call her. Every time I tried her number it was constantly busy. After fifteen minutes I gave up, as I was getting soaked and very tired at week's end. I went home and ate and went to sleep. At 2.00 am in the morning I heard loud banging on my front door. I went to the door and asked who was it and he answered "Ma'am this is the police". I would not open the door and asked him how would I know he was the police and what did he want. He said for me to open the door, as he wanted to know if I was okay. I told him I was okay and still did not want to open the door. He explained that my friend Nalini had been calling his department repeatedly to go check on me. Oh I could have killed her. Just because my phone was not working no one had kidnapped me.

Also in 1986 Mickey had left his family in England and was in the process of moving permanently to the United States, and he needed a temporary place to stay and I told him he could rent my kids' old room from me. He agreed and paid me the rent and moved into the old room that Lena was renting from me. He was a better roommate as he drove taxis and was hardly home. He would come in late and quietly go to bed without disturbing me and was not always cooking like Lena. His younger brother came from England and they wanted to go to Reno in Nevada, so they asked me if I would show them around there, if they flew me down there and we would be back in the afternoon. I told them I would go with them. We drove down to the airport in San Francisco and parked my car there and boarded the flight to Reno. We arrived there in about forty minutes and it was the shortest flight I had ever taken. At the airport there, we took a cab to downtown Reno and walked around the main drag. I even gambled a little and lost some and won some. We had lunch and took a cab to the car museum there. This was fun. Late afternoon we flew back to San Francisco and got home that evening.

My parents could not come back to the USA in the summer of 1986, as I heard that my aunt Darshan had passed away from cancer of the mouth. She used to smoke a lot. She had been pretty sick for some time. Two weeks after she passed away my maternal grandmother died too. Now Darshan's kids Pinky, Neelu and Bablu were orphans and of course my parents looked after them. My mother was totally devastated. She treated Darshan like her daughter and now she had lost her along with her mother. I also, lost an older sister. It was hard to believe that she died at such a young age. My dad would write us the news via letters. He wrote they would return in 1987 now. After spending tons of money at Dimple's wedding, my brother and sister-in-law, Amarjeet, told me that Dimple had separated from her husband and was back home with them, in San Jose. Her mother-in-law was the main problem. That was pretty sad for their family. Bobby was still in college.

My friend Kathy B. at work, was moving from one apartment to another in El Cerrito, and had a gap of a week when she did not have anywhere to live, as her new apartment would not be ready for her. I told her that she could stay with me for a week but would have to sleep on the couch. Kathy, who was diabetic, was a very nice person and all alone in the world. Her parents had passed away and her only relative, a sister who lived in another State, had not been in contact with her for years, mainly because they never got along. I always felt sorry for her. I had to take her to the hospital, when she had a bout with her diabetes. She passed out in the bathroom at work, and since she could not afford an ambulance and had no car either, I volunteered my services for her. She used to travel to Reno by bus at least once a month for weekends. When Curt told us in the fall of 1986 that our office would be moving to San Ramon in the Central Valley, in May of 1987, she was devastated saying there was no way she could go with company that far, with no direct public transportation. I told her that since we got about eight month notice, she should start looking work in the El Cerrito, elsewhere. After that she grew more withdrawn and her trips to Reno became more frequent. I felt terribly sorry for her. She did not come to work on Monday. Our boss left her a few messages on her phone, without any response from her. After further investigation by Curt, we found that she had committed suicide by overdosing on her medicine for diabetes. Later we found out that she had maxed out her credit cards and was deeply in debt, and left a suicide note. That was an absolute tragedy. Curt lived in San Ramon so he was going to move all of us, who lived in the vicinity of our current job location, all the way to where he lived. This was not fair to us, but we had no choice or say. If he had not done this maybe Kathy would still be alive.

I asked Ed to send the children to me for Christmas this year, since they were always away from me for the holidays. He said he would. I was so happy and arranged a Christmas party by inviting all my friends and family for dinner for Christmas Eve. Edwin and Billy were going to be with me for two weeks and that was absolutely great. When they came to California the first thing Edwin said was "Mom we have to have a Christmas tree". I reminded him that now they were older and knew that there was no Santa, and two days to the holidays, why did we have to get a tree. But the kids insisted on getting a tree. We went to K-Mart around the corner from our apartment to shop and we got a blue light special small fake Christmas tree for two dollars. Edwin had everyone cracking up at the store. He comes around the corner with a women's hat, scarf and a handbag on his shoulder and asks me "Mom, how to do I look?" Other shoppers looking at him were cracking up with laughter. On the day of the dinner, I cooked a turkey and side dishes for us and our guests. Meera, Dixie, Sumita, Shalini, David and his boys Omar and Andre, Sonny and Diana, my brother and his family, Amarjit, Dimple and Bobby from San Jose, and my cousin Mickey were all invited. We all had a wonderful dinner at my place.

Now that I knew the Kids were happy living with their dad back East, I was also looking for a smaller apartment as my two bedroom apartment was too big for me to afford and I did not want to have a roommate anymore. I was keeping the apartment thinking that the kids would change their mind and come back to live with me. I found a one studio apartment in Richmond, near the Hilltop mall. My co-worker Gayle also lived in that complex just down the corner. I went and paid my deposit on this studio apartment and as soon as my kids went back to their dad, I was going to move. Some of my co-workers were going to help me. I was babysitting for Anne's girls for free occasionally, and she said she would help. I was going to donate some of my furniture to needy families as all this would not fit in my compact apartment, which was in a secure building with an elevator and a swimming pool, too. I finally moved the first week of January, 1987. My commute to work in El Cerrito was slightly longer, but I loved my place a lot. I had been working two jobs for the past two years. My second job was through Quaker State Oil, they would place me at different car dealerships to call the customers who bought their cars there to see if their experience was a good or bad one. It was a kind of courtesy call. The past two years the dealership I was placed at was Tim Southwick's Toyota dealership on Ashby Avenue in Berkeley. I would work from 8.00 am to 5.00 pm at Charge Card USA in El Cerrito during the day, and 6.00 pm to 8.00 pm at the dealership. I would get home by 9.00 pm change my clothes and eat my dinner and go to sleep and start the next day the same way. Except on Friday nights I would go to party with my friends. I had decided not to date any one guy as I did not want to meet more scumbags and bring them to my new apartment. I broke off with Khamiz but we were still friends.

CHAPTER 11 – I MEET MY SOULMATE

A month before our office was going to move to San Ramon, Curt told us to drive down there and see for ourselves how long our commute was going to be. I asked my co-worker Helen who used to ride with me to work, to see if she still wanted to commute with me to San Ramon. This time we would share the cost of gasoline, since our office was much further away and would take about an hour to get there in the commute traffic. She agreed to that. One Saturday Thelma and I drove down to San Ramon to check out our new office and where the fast food places were for lunch. Curt also told us that there was a restaurant called Bobby Mcgees, which was bar/lounge at night and a block away from our work where we could go work and it had a "Happy Hour" from 4.30 pm to 7.00 pm daily. We all were going to check it out when our office moved out there. On the actual day of our move, we had to pack our personal belongings and everything else was going to be moved by a moving company. The movers were there at about 9.30 am and they spent most of the day moving. Curt gave us the rest of the day off on a Friday. The company had the whole weekend to arrange our office equipment at our new office. The following Monday we started our first day in San Ramon. I first drove down to Helen's house in San Pablo, and took the San Pablo Dam road to highway 24 and highway 680 south from there. The traffic was horrendous, but we got there somehow but a little late. Tomorrow we would have to leave a little early. After a week there, Mary, Lena, Annie and I decided to check out Bobby McGees lounge for happy hour. The beers were seventy five cents each and the food was free. Later the disc- jockey came in at around 8 pm and the party was on. Since we were in there since 6 pm we did not have to pay the ten dollar cover charge which people had to pay after 8 pm. Oh my god, we had so much fun that night. Guys were asking us to dance, and we were having a blast and did not leave till after midnight. The party crowd, were other people who also worked in the vicinity, like Chevron, PG&E and other company employees. We all decided that we were going to come back here every Friday night for happy-hour, which we did.

On June 24th which was a Friday, just Mary and I stopped by Bobby McGees after work. As usual we drank our Happy Hour drinks and were having a great old time and had a good seat in the little lounge. After 9.00 pm the place was totally packed. The guys were just standing around with their drinks with no seating available. One guy came up to Mary and me and asked if he could join us and have a seat with us. We told him, of course, he could join us. We all started talking and he told us that his name was Marc and lived in Richmond. I told him that I lived in Richmond too. We asked him for his birthday and he told us, it was May 15th, and I told him that my birthday was May 19th and Mary's was May 9th; we were all "Bulls". He asked us what we were doing all the way out in San Ramon; we told him we worked just around the corner. We asked him the same question, and he replied his buddies at work in Berkeley had told him that this place was a great place to meet girls. He asked me to dance and I said no and tried to push him towards Mary, and Mary was pushing him towards me. In the meantime a great dance song came on and I took him up on dancing to it. I don't remember much that night as we were pretty drunk by then. He told me later that we kept buying him drinks and he ended up drinking seven Long Islands. At the end of the night, after a lot of dancing and fun, he asked me for my telephone number and I wrote it down on a paper napkin and he gave me his number. He told me that he had moved back with his parents after breaking up with his ex and he would like to take me out on a date. I told him to call me.

We all left for the night and Marc says that he tried to follow me, but I lost him somewhere along the way.

A week passed and Marc never called me back. Well this was another jerk I thought. One evening I found his telephone number in my purse and decided to call him. He sounded very happy to hear from me, and said that he had lost my telephone number that night. He asked me out on a date that Friday and I told him that sounded alright. I told him that I would call him when I got home from work. He told me that he was going to take me out for dinner and dance place called 'Baxters' in Larkspur. On Friday I called him after work and he came by my apartment to pick me up in his truck. When I opened the door, he gave me a dozen roses and I was pretty impressed and touched. I had never received flowers on a first date ever before. Marc was not much taller than me but he seemed like a nice guy. We drove down to Baxter and talked a lot about ourselves on the way. I told him I had two kids, who lived with their dad back east. They were going to come visit me in a month or so. He told me that he had moved out from his parents' house to live with his girlfriend in Vallejo, when he was nineteen. He said that he broke up with her in the early part of the year, as she was heavily into drugs and would not quit. He quit, and moved back with his mom and stepfather. Once we reached Baxters he asked what I wanted to eat, and I told him I wanted a meatloaf and mashed potatoes with gravy. He was surprised, thinking I would be ordering the most expensive thing on the menu, and I told him that I was a cheap date. After dinner we moved to the lounge for drinking and dancing. We had a wonderful time together. He drove me home and I asked him if he wanted to come in and he did. Since we both had some drinks, one thing led to another and we were in bed making out. He stayed the night. This became quite a regular thing as he would come by on Friday night and usually stay the weekend and leave on Sunday night. We would go to the beach fishing or to a movie and go out to eat. We would have sex all the time, and sometimes six times a day, whether we were at the beach and walking through an isolated part of the park. I guess we were making up for lost time. Pretty soon I told Marc that my kids were coming to visit me and he could not stay with me when they were here. He said to call him when my kids left as he was not very good with kids. I thought what a jerk. He better know my kids come first to me before anyone else in the world.

Edwin and Billy flew in to be with me for three or four weeks. I had two weeks off and we made plans with Meera and Dixie to drive down to Los Angeles to visit Disneyland. Dixie's paternal aunt Sunita and her husband Ashok lived in Anaheim and told us to stay with them while we were there. We drove down there in my car. It took us a while of driving to get there and arrived at about 3 am in the morning. Sunita had two sons and other nieces and nephews there also. We slept a few hours and spent the rest of the day shooting the breeze and getting to know each other. That evening we all ordered several pizzas for dinner. The next day we drove down to Disneyland to drop the seven teenagers off there. After buying their tickets we left enough money so they could eat there. When asked when we should come back to pick them up and they all replied after midnight, as they wanted to see the fireworks at midnight. That was twelve hours there. Meera, Sunita and I drove off to go shopping and out to eat at a restaurant and came back to their place in the evening. Sunita made tea for all of us and we sat and talked and watched television. We had to stay awake so we could pick all the kids later. Their house was large and very fancy with central air-conditioning as it was pretty hot there. Ashok had his own business and Sunita worked for a company there. That night when we went to pick up the kids at Disneyland, they were totally exhausted. On our drive home they all fell asleep in the car. That was good as they got their fill of Disneyland.

The next day we the grownups wanted to go to the Universal Studios, but the kids all said they rather go to the beach. It was overcast at the beach and pretty cool that we had to wear our sweatshirts. Edwin and Billy were chasing me around with seaweed on the beach and I was screaming and running away from them. They would run into the water and get washed up by the waves; they were totally soaked with the water and sand. They were having a ball, which made me happy. I wanted them to have a lot of fun while they were with me. The following day we decided to return home to the Bay Area. We left early in the morning and reached home that evening and dropped Meera and Dixie off at their house in Oakland. Meera was now renting a house there. Two days later we decided to go to an amusement park near San Jose, called Great America run by Universal studios, one of the largest one in Northern California. My nieces Dimple and Dixie were going to meet us there. So there were five of us spending our day there. It was a nice and sunny day and I was not going to get on any scary rides except the water rides, as it was a hot day and didn't mind getting wet to cool off. We all ate snacks at the park and I could buy beer for myself, which made me feel goofy. I was cracking up the kids. We were all waiting in line to go on this one water ride where we all get in this barrel type ride, and water shoots at you at various spots. I had been drinking beer, which made me want to go to the bathroom. I told the kids that I was going to pee in the barrel. They started screaming "No Mom, No Auntie". I said too late. Their laughter still remains in my mind to this day. At the end of our day we started to leave for the parking lot and I was going to make one more pit stop at the restroom by the exit. When we got there the restroom was closed temporarily. By the time we reached my car, I really had to go, so I opened the passenger door and made the kids stand in a circle around me facing out, despite their objections, and I went to the bathroom in the parking lot. Well when you got to go you got to go. Luckily a police car went by as soon we were all in the car….PHEW……that was a close call. We all burst into laughter, due to the fact that I got away with it. After dropping Dimple and Dixie in San Jose at my brother's house, Edwin, Billy and I headed home after a great day.

It was getting close to the time when my kids would be leaving to go back East and I was feeling sad. We went to the grocery store and ran into Marc and his mother, Toni, also shopping there. I introduced Edwin and Billy to them and Marc said that he did not realize that my kids were teenagers. Marc told me he would call me when he got home that evening. When he called that night, he invited us to a lake in the hills of Berkeley that Saturday for a picnic. I asked the kids if they wanted to go, as they were leaving the next day and they said that they wanted to go. On Saturday Marc came to pick us up and we all went to the lake for an outing. The kids had a great time playing outdoors. We took a lot of pictures and instead of a picnic we all went out to eat. The next day on Sunday the kids were all packed for their flight back home to their dad's place and I drove them to the airport. When I returned to my apartment, I cried all the way home as usual. Marc called me and came over to keep me company. We talked on the subject of my kids and I told him that if he wasn't comfortable with my kids there was no reason for us to see each other anymore, as my kids came first in my life. He said that when I mentioned my kids to him, he thought I had very young children and he had no idea that they were teenagers and after he met them he thought they were cool boys. He said that it was an honest mis-understanding, and he wanted to be with me and see me again. I forgave him and we started dating again. On Friday evenings he would meet me at Bobby McGees after work. Usually I would ask Mary and some of my other friends to join us. We would party there and we would return to my apartment and Marc would stay the weekend with me. We would go to Point Reyes beaches, go fishing and go out to eat. On Saturday nights he would rent porn videos, which I did not like to view, really, and we would make love several times at night. One hot evening on a Friday, Marc had come over to my apartment to spend the weekend with me. I had left the left the sliding door to my balcony open, with the curtains drawn and Marc and I were making out on the carpeted floor and without realizing that my screams (of delight) were a bit too loud. We heard a guy downstairs yell "Hey you stop that and leave her alone" thinking that I was being beaten up. I burst out laughing at the incident and Marc got mad at me for spoiling his mood. I thought it was hilarious.

The kids called me to tell me that their grandmother, Kay died of emphysema finally. I thought good riddance to bad rubbish. She was always a bitch to me, while I was married to Ed. She was an alcoholic and smoked like a chimney. I even remember Ed telling me that his parents had told him that he should have married his own kind. I was actually glad to hear that she was gone forever, and may she rot in hell. I am not a mean person, but in her case, I don't mind saying the truth about her, as she had my life hell.

My parents came back and this time they stayed with Meera for some time and the other half with my brother and his family in San Jose. They could not stay with me as my apartment was too small for three grownups. But Meera brought them over to my apartment, along with Dixie and Lali and her baby son, Daniel. They all got to meet Marc for the first time. My parents liked him a lot. Unknown to me, Marc had consumed a whole lot of vodka and orange juice, before meeting my parents. He said he was nervous meeting them. They stayed at my place for over an hour and we all had a good visit and then Meera took them back to her place. Meera would invite us to her place in Oakland for dinner, while our parents were still staying with her. Sumita would also have dinner parties at her house in Albany and we would all meet there too.

Aside from our ups and downs, our relationship survived till the end of that year and he invited me to go to a new year's party in San Francisco, organized by KMEL radio station and one of their hosts, Renel, was present at that party. This was at the Galleria in the city and Marc had bought two tickets for us. That night turned out to be total chaos. It was totally packed in there and no place for us to sit down. We danced to the music played by the DeeJay. I was waiting in line to go to the restroom, just before midnight. I finally got out of line to go kiss Marco at midnight. I saw a girl fall off from the second floor, and luckily landed on the awning of a booth downstairs. I decided I did not want to be there anymore and wanted to go home and Marco agreed too. I still could not go to the bathroom and had to go outside in the dark street where we were parked.

The year 1988 began bad, due to the party, but got better when Marc started teaching me how to fish with him. He bought me a fishing pole and a nice reel and it turned out to be a nice hobby for me. We would take a picnic lunch and a lot of beer to drink and would sit by the water and fish and enjoy the nature. I would somehow hook the larger fish than Marc's and that made him jealous. In May just before my birthday he said that we were going on a trip for the weekend and to pack a few things and also a bathing suit. He would not tell me where, but his mother let the cat out of the bag and told me that we were going to Monterey, California, where we were booked at a hotel. After work on Friday we left on our road trip to Monterey in the most horrible traffic. We arrived at the hotel there late in the evening and checked in. The room had a huge fireplace. We changed and went out to dinner and came back and made out on the kitchenette counter and in front of the fireplace. The next day went down to the swimming pool to catch some rays and that night went to dinner and a discotheque afterwards. On Sunday we checked out and drove to the Monterey Bay Aquarium. I had a beautiful and fun filled birthday and returned home that evening.

That summer I went to see my kids in New Hampshire for two weeks. Both Edwin and Billy were growing up. Edwin was almost sixteen and Billy had turned thirteen. Edwin was a great clown and Billy very straightforward and to the point. While I was with them I noticed that their stepmother Robin would always make my kids do all the dirty work, like doing dishes and taking out the garbage while her daughter Carla did not have to do anything and was terribly spoiled. She would cry and get whatever she wanted. Edwin had an old car that he bought for about two hundred dollars from the money he saved while working as a manager at the local McDonalds. It was a piece of junk but still worked. The radiator would heat up all the time. I was very proud of him. They both had their bedroom in the basement of the house, where it was very cold in the winter. I was staying there during my visit and only one bathroom to the whole house and of course Robin and her daughter Carla were the first ones in it. I would also notice that Robin would always pick on my kids and complain to Ed about them all the time. I am sure they could not wait till they were eighteen and join the Army and get out of that house. In a way, they had learned to be self-sufficient and were good students in school. We all drove to a water park up north. Edwin drove his car with Billy and I, and their father took Robin, Carla and some other friends of the kids in his van. Poor Edwin's car was constantly heating up on our way there. We spent our day at this park. It had a very large wave pool, water slides and other water attractions. The kids and I had a great time there and the kids even stole an inflated rubber raft for me which had the name of the park on it. One day Edwin drove Billy and me to an amusement park in Springfield, Connecticut. I was so proud of my children that they were so grown up now that they drove me down about three hundred miles both ways to go to this park. Of course I drove on the way home and we took a lot of pictures there. Another day I took the kids fishing as there are several lakes close by. Marc had let me borrow his fishing pole and other fishing equipment to bring with me. I guess fishing was too slow a sport for the boys, as they kept playing pranks on me. Like putting grass and leaves in my open beer can. When I would go to throw my line out into the lake, it would get hung up in the tree branches. Edwin would tug at the branches to get my line off the tree. Edwin told me not to feel too bad as pointing in the trees up, there were several bobbers caught from previous fishermen. In the afternoon, there was a big thunderstorm and we had to scramble into the car and head home. Time was getting close for me to leave and head back to California, which was always one of the hardest things for me to do. With the promise that I would come down and see me next year, I left. Of course I cried all the way home. Mina came to pick me up at the airport as my car was parked at her home in Oakland; I drove back to my apartment in Richmond. I called Marc to let him know that I was back. He came by to see me later that evening.

Marc and I got pretty close the rest of the year and I went to his mother's house for Thanksgiving and Christmas Eve, where I met Marc's sister Sheila and his niece Marie and nephew David. Sheila was a single mom living in Richmond and worked in Oakland and had a boyfriend named Gary. Marc and Sheila's dad died when Marc was only a little over a year old. Marc had a stepfather, Jack. He also had a half brother George and a half sister Cheryl, who lived in Oregon and northern California. Their father was Marc's mother's first husband. Our relationship was blooming like the spring flower and I felt that he was my soul mate even though he was younger than me. I was only working for my second job, Quaker State four evenings a week. I asked them to move my second job closer to San Ramon, so they transferred me to Dublin Toyota, which was about ten to fifteen minutes from my main job at Charge Card USA. Our Christmas party from work was at the Concord Hilton, on Diamond Blvd. this year; just for Charge Card USA employees, instead of joining the United Bank's employees in San Francisco. Marc came with me for the party; which turned out to be very boring and he got into an argument with Harry's daughter who lived with her mom in Brazil and was here visiting with her dad.

In the summer of 1989, I finally got tired of commuting to San Ramon and having to work a second job, as I was not making enough at Charge Card USA. Also my car, Ford Tempo, was giving me a lot of trouble and I had to have a new transmission on it. I heard of another bank called Western States Bankcard Association (WSBA) which was within five minute drive from my apartment. My friends Helen, Mary, Debbie some others had already got a job there. Helen told me that I should give her my resume with a cover letter and she would give it to the Vice President, Tim. I did this and got a call for an interview at this bank and finally hired by WSBA. I gave my two week notice at Charge Card USA and Quaker State, my second job. My boss Curt was not very happy, as about four or five of his employees had already moved over to WSBA. This was time to celebrate as I was going to make more money at one job than I did at my two previous jobs and also, it would take me only five minutes to get to work. My last day at work on Friday, Marc met me and my girlfriends at Bobby McGees, and we all partied At my new job they also had free lunch meat and condiments too in the second refrigerator in their lunch room where the employees could make our own lunch free. I loved my new job. We did merchant chargebacks here, unlike the cardholder chargebacks at Charge Card USA. My first day here was June sixth. My life got a lot better. On Thursdays after work Marc and I would meet at my apartment and we would drive down to Point Pinole Park to go fishing; as Marc, who worked in Berkeley for Courtaulds (previously known as DeSoto) would get off at 3.30 pm and I would get off at 4.00 pm. I made a lot more friends at my new job. We had about seventeen employees in our merchant chargeback department, and our boss was Flo, and her assistant was Lee. My co-workers were Ruth, Kinney, Marylou, Josephine, Carolyn and William from Charge Card USA. We also had a fully equipped workout room with shower facility after a workout. My hours were from 8 am to 4 pm and our half an hour for lunch was paid by the company. I also heard they had great Christmas parties for the employees.

In April, Meera took Dixie to Hawaii for the very first time on a one week vacation. They went to Honolulu and stayed at hotel at Waikikki beach. When they came back I learned that Meera almost drowned in an undertow up in the North shore. She told me that she and Dixie rented a car one day and drove up to the North shore of that island, where there are several beaches. Being a good swimmer, she did not think twice about jumping into the ocean for a swim. She noticed a guy sitting on the beach, fully clothed in white pants and white shirt, who was dark complexioned and could be a Fijian Indian. She saw a red flag day posted and still went in for a swim. In a matter of seconds she lost control as she was in an undertow and started to panic and was being thrown in and out of the water by strong currents. She said that she finally stopped fighting, and started to go all the way down through a tunnel with a bright light at the end of it. All this while she kept thinking why didn't that guy sitting on beach come to save her. In the meantime when Dixie saw what was happening to her mom, she started to scream for help. Dixie said that the guy sitting at beach was the one who saved my sister. He pulled her out of the water and before she could come to consciousness, he was gone. He must have been her guardian angel. I don't think she ever went back in the water. Ever since that day my sister was never the same. She started thinking of that day as her new birthday. She joined a guru's ashram and started following her sayings. All they do is brainwash people to join their groups. When a person is drowning, I am sure; the oxygen to the brain is cut off temporarily.

Edwin and Billy came down to visit me in July and I had not been at my new job long enough to take a day off. On Friday my manger told me to call in sick, as I had to go pick up my kids at the airport; so that way I would have three days off to be with them. Marc and I took my kids out to eat and over the weekend took them fishing to Point Pinole Park and Point Reyes beach. The next Monday I had to go to work and told the kids I would be home for lunch and fix something for them too and if they wanted they could come back with me to work, where they could use the workout room for the afternoon. One day they walked down to the Hilltop Mall to hang out there. Edwin said he wanted to work part time at the pet store at the mall and Billy would go with him. Since he was not yet seventeen, he needed my permission. I told him he could have my permission but all this would be a long process and by then he would have to return to New Hampshire, as they would be with me for about a month. During the day they would either hang out at my work or the mall, and especially at the pet store. In the evenings we would do something with them. Pretty soon it came time for them to leave, which was always heartbreaking to me. But having Marc in life would lessen this pain in my heart.

At my new job everyone was into baseball and football pools, and there would always be football pools to bet on. I would call the boys, who were experts in predicting the wins, and I would ask them to pick the teams for me when I placed my money on a bet. I won almost all the time and I would send the kids half the money I won. The baseball season was coming to an end and bay area teams, Oakland A's and San Francisco Giants were the top teams in 1989 and had to play each other for the final winner. The first three games were played in Oakland and won by the A's and after the weekend the games were to move to San Francisco, home of the Giants. Our Vice president at WSBA, Tim kept saying that the Giants would win now. I told him that the A's would sweep the Giants. So we made a bet that if I was right then Tim would owe me lunch and if he was right, I would owe him lunch. The game in San Francisco was set for October 17 at 6.00 pm. That morning when I woke up to get ready for work, the weather started out to be pretty cold. I wore my warm dress with my pantyhose and a jacket to stay warm. After work I was going to stop over at the mall to buy a pair of jeans from Macys. At about lunch time the weather got warm and muggy and I took off my pantyhose and rolled over my long sleeve dress for the rest of the afternoon. At close of work, I drove down to the hilltop mall. Marc was going to take his mother grocery shopping after work and said he would call me that evening. I walked around the mall doing my shopping. At Macys I looked for these stretch jeans that they had come out with. These jeans had little bows at the ankle area and they fit pretty snug, so I took one to try them on. I noticed a very big woman go in the stall next to mine. I put one leg in the pair of jeans and was about to put the other one, when I heard a great rattle in the ground and my booth started shaking. I thought it was the woman in the next booth, and I yelled for her to stop shaking the booth. All of a sudden someone yelled EARTHQUAKE and soon the power went out in the mall; it was two minutes to 5.00 pm. I still tried on the pair of jeans and they fit perfectly, and went to pay for them. The cashier had just moved to California from Ohio, and she was freaking out because of the minor earthquake. When the power came back on I paid for my jeans and someone said that the Bay Bridge had fallen. I thought oh yes, that's how rumors get started. The mall that was crowded emptied real fast. I felt now I could shop for the rest of my stuff without the crowds. I left the mall around 7.00 pm to go home to my apartment. As soon as I got in, my telephone started ringing. It was Marc and he was yelling where had I been as he was trying to find me because of the major earthquake we just had. Marc had a one hundred and fifty gallon fish tank at his mom's and they had to hang on to it so it would not tilt and empty out on her carpet. He told me to turn on my television, which I did and saw the total chaos everywhere. The Bay Bridge had actually fallen and some cars had landed in the water as the road suddenly parted and the cars went flying into the water. But the worst disaster was at the Cypress structure, where people were still trapped and sandwiched in their cars. The top structure fell over the road below. There were fires in some places. Some of my pictures on the wall had fallen to the ground in my apartment and I straightened these out and tried to call my kids on the east coast but I could not get an outside line. I did not realize the havoc the earthquake had caused in the Bay Area. Some people did not have electricity for a day or so and the phone lines were down too. Travel between San Francisco and the East Bay was virtually shut down. The Bay Bridge was shut down for almost a month or more for repairs. You had to take the Golden Gate Bridge or the San Mateo or Dumbarton bridges to connect to the San Francisco Peninsula. There were also, the extensive searches for survivors at the Cypress structure collapse. Luckily, due to the baseball playoffs, the fans were already at the stadium for the game, or there would have been a lot more casualties on the bridge and people were just getting off work and had not got on the bridge yet. It was nightmare for people to get home that night as there were several aftershocks also. I got dressed and went to work the next day and some of the people who lived in San Francisco could not come in to work. Finally when things came to normalcy in the Bay Area, the Oakland A's beat the San Francisco Giants to take the baseball trophy for 1989. My boss Tim had to take me to lunch to settle our bet. That is how the year ended.

In 1990 Marc and I made plans to go on vacation to Hawaii, and picked the Island of Maui. I had a friend named Kathy, who was a travel agent, who booked our vacation for a week through Pleasant Hawaiian Holidays. Our package included air fare, hotel and a car rental for a week. We started practicing our snorkeling in the swimming pool at my apartment building, for weeks before our trip. We also bought our own snorkeling masks and fins and mine were shocking pink. We left for our vacation in the last week of April. We were nearing our three years together anniversary on June 24th. Marc's sister Sheila took us to Larkspur where we were going to catch a tour bus to the San Francisco Airport. We boarded our flight to Maui through a short stop in Honolulu and then on to Maui. When we landed in Maui we felt we were in the ultimate paradise. When we looked out through the plane window, there was green and blue water everywhere. The Pleasant Hawaiian Holiday people placed Leis around our necks. We picked up our luggage and loaded it in our rented car and after getting directions we drove to our hotel, The Royal Hawaiian on the Kanapaali beach. Our room was in a four-plex building next to the golf course of neighboring Westin hotel. In the parking lot there were mango trees growing and all through the gardens were full of tropical flowers. We were both very excited. Marc had only boarded a plane once before this, when he flew to Ohio with his ex. He had never even gone to Reno before he met me and I had never ever gone on a real vacation in this country, even though I traveled extensively in this country with my ex-husband. So this was a win-win situation for both of us.

The next morning we had a breakfast meeting with the Pleasant Hawaiian club, along with all the other guests at our hotel. At this meeting Marc and I purchased almost two events per day through them, for the duration of our stay and spent about nine hundred dollars. That afternoon we had nothing planned so Marc bought a map of the island and we took off to visit the IAO NEEDLE PARK. We parked our rental car and ventured into the park, where there was a huge waterfall. Of course we were drinking beer and were on our last beer can which I was sipping through. It was so hot so I took off my sneakers and started playing in the water. The sound of the waterfall was so loud that we had to talk real loud to hear each other. Marc was busy taking pictures. I was stepping over rocks with my bare feet, and heard Marc yell "Honey, don't step on any green moss stones". Just then my foot was poised to step on the green stone and it was too late. I slipped and fell, full force into a giant rock in front of me. I almost passed out and Marc's back was to me and he did not know what happened to me. I lay in the water motionless until the water hitting my face revived me and I could not get up. Marc turned around and said "Honey, what are you doing lying in the water and where is the beer?" On impact the can of beer floated downstream. I told him to come help me get up and in turn he started taking my picture. I knew something major had broken in my body, as my breathing became labored and my voice seemed to be coming out of voice box, I could have almost punctured my lung. Marc got real mad at me for hurting myself on the first day of our vacation, as if I had planned it. It happened and I could not reverse this. He asked if I wanted to go to the doctor who might wrap my body up. I had left my medical card at home in California, so I could not even go to a doctor. I took some painkillers to ease my pain. We went back to our room and realized I could not even lie down as my ribs hurt real bad. We take it for granted that the muscles we use on the upper part of our body, to sit down and get up and lie down, when nothing is broken in our chest. I could not do these without extreme difficulty. But I was a trooper and tried to enjoy my vacation as best as I could by washing down my painkiller pills with several Mai Tai drinks. We went to our dinner show at the Hyatt Hotel, called "The Drums of the South Pacific" that night and then the next day, a snorkeling trip on a boat ride to Lanai, a smaller island off the Maui coast. I just tagged along as I was just going to get bombed on drinks. On the boat trip to Lanai we were entertained by the crew to Hawaiian songs on their guitars. Once we got there, we were served lunch and a lots and lots of Mai Tais. I had my painkillers and drinks and I was just fine. This Hawaiian crew member tried to get me on a boogie board.

As soon I got in the salt water its buoyancy felt like a big rig was sitting on my chest. What was I thinking I could not do it? The rest of the group was all out snorkeling, and I sat and chatted with some of the crew members. There were other activities like canoeing, tug of war but I sat through it all. Soon it was time to return back to Maui on our boat. Now the crew sang all the hip hop songs and we were all dancing on the boat. Another activity was a dinner cruise on a ship and a discotheque on the top floor. After dinner we moved upstairs to have drinks and dance. We were there only half an hour when the ocean got real rough and they had to cut our event short and transfer back to shore. This trip was one of the best one so far. Even with my injuries I had a lot of fun.

On our last day we had hired a Hawaiian guide to show us around the island. His name was Randy and he drove us around the island taking us to hidden waterfalls up the mountain to a little community he lived in, showed us houses for sale and an idea on their prices. He even took us to sugarcane fields and cut down the tropical flowers to take back with us. It was too bad as we were leaving the next day, and should have done this in the beginning of our vacation. Marc kept saying that he wanted to take home a coconut and a gecko back with us. That night there was a rain storm and we heard a thump on the roof. It was a coconut and we packed that in our suitcase also. By the time we arrived at the airport and turned in our rental car, we did not know about the agriculture check at the airport. They took out all the stuff our guide gave us and even the coconut. We could not take that back with us, which was so disappointing.

We arrived back home to California with our beautiful Hawaiian tans. The first thing I did was go see my doctor, who after getting my x-rays found out that I had three cracked ribs. He said that there was nothing he could do, as the ribs would heal on their own in time, except prescribe stronger painkillers. If I had known this, I would have not done all that I did in Maui. I went back to work at WSBA and showed all our pictures to my co workers. But I found out the ribs were going to take a very long time to heal. We loved our vacation so much that we booked another one for fall to go to Cancun in Mexico. That was also a great vacation. We stayed in the Sheraton Towers there. Our room faced the Ocean on one side and the bay on the other. We visited all the local haunts and went on fishing trip. The weather was rough on the fishing trip and I was busy catching all kinds of big fish, while Marc was too busy throwing up that the crew hand asked me if he was pregnant. That was a great laugh for me, but Marc did not like that comment. We also went to a big discotheque named Gloria, there. It had large television screens, where we first saw the video of Mariah Carrey, and did not know who she was then. The waiters there were Hollywood wannabees and so funny. They were pouring tequila in people's mouths on the dance floor. The last day we went out to eat and Marc ordered mixed drinks and the ice in it which was not pure gave us the monazuma's revenge. We suffered all the way back home.

When I talked to Meera she told me that she was dating a new guy named Boyd for some time now and that she was going to move in with him in San Francisco, as Dixie was going to room with Shalini, Sumita's daughter. Dixie had already graduated from high school and had a part time job. Of course Meera was going to help her if she needed it. Boyd had a beautiful three story Victorian home in the heart of Haight Ashbury area. After Meera moved in there she invited us over for dinner and Marc and I loved the house. Meera was still working for the car brokerage company in El Cerrito but quit working there within six months after moving to San Francisco. She said she was going to start her own business doing flower arrangements for different companies in the city. She also made jewelry and sold it and did flower arrangements for weddings.

The beginning of 1991 my bank started getting too many merchant chargebacks. These were all fraud by one or two merchants that had accounts with a bank we handled. After their accounts were closed, they came and opened accounts under another name with another bank that we were handling at WSBA. These merchants would fraudulently charging cardholder accounts and the cardholder banks charged them back to us and we would debit our merchant bank which in turn would debit their merchant and settle the money back to us. I kept telling my superiors that what if the merchant bank did not pay us. They kept assuring us if they don't, VISA will make them pay us. Well, my suspicions were correct the merchant disappeared and their bank was not signed up with VISA, and our bank was out of over five million dollars. Our bank started layoff for several employees. We were all worried who would be next. So far everything was alright. Marc and I moved in together on March 31st in an apartment in El Sobrante. He was practically living at my old apartment and we had known each other for almost four years. It was time he paid half the rent. This was a two story duplex type apartment, with two bedrooms and a bath upstairs and the living, dining and kitchen downstairs. It also had a swimming pool and a small backyard for Marc's gardening. Instead of paying $525.00 a month at my old apartment I was only paying half of $700.00. I liked this arrangement. But all was not well in my relationship with Marc. We would argue a lot, especially about his friend Bob who was always popping in to have Marc go on Bike rides with him or they would go camping by themselves to Yosemite, and not inviting me, which was really weird.

After talking to my mom in India, she told me that Lali had returned from America and was now living with them. Neil gave her one way ticket back home. She left her kids Ryan, Annisa and Daniel with Neil and signed some paper saying that she would pay him child support, in her drunken haze. This was some kind of joke, as she had never worked a day in her life so how was she going to pay. I think Neil was looking for some sort of handout from my parents. That girl had lived in America for over twenty years and never ever became a citizen here and she was now home in India, making my parents' life hell. She said she would run away if my parents did not buy her booze and cigarettes. They did try to place her in rehab, but she would not go.

In May for our birthday week Marc and I went to the island of Kauai in Hawaii. It was a fun filled week. We stayed at the Astin hotel and there were peacocks roaming around the lobby and live fish in their fish pond. We went on a fishing trip on a boat, went on a snorkeling trip, discovered and went to a deserted nude beach, went on a zodiac boat to view the Napoli coast which is inaccessible by car. On Marc's birthday he wanted to spend the day at the nude beach fishing and running around in his birthday suit. The whole day we did not see anyone else there so that is why they called it the Secret beach. In the evening there was restaurant called BUBBA'S BURGERS AND PIZZA, where Marc wanted to eat. He ordered ribs and pizza and pigged out on that. Four days later, on my birthday, we went out to breakfast at a Sizzler there and then we went shopping to buy momentos for us and our family and friends. Marc bought some very large sea shells from an outside vendor. When we returned to our room, we changed into our bathing suits and went down to the swimming pool. For the evening Marc had booked a dinner and comedy show for us, which was great. I laughed a lot and afterwards there was dancing there. The day ended very nice. The next day we went on a riverboat to where Elvis Presley had filmed his movie "Blue Hawaii". There were waterfalls all around that area, and we were on a guided tour of that place. Soon it was time to leave Kauai and return home.

That summer my parents came back to visit us and stayed with Marc and I after staying with Meera and Boyd in San Francisco. They left Lali in India with their servant Nabu and his wife. My mother said that they liked living with us. Our apartment was more user friendly for them, than Meera and Boyd's place, which were three stories tall. In the

Summer my mother would walk down to the swimming pool with Marc and I and watch us have fun in the pool, splashing around. On Sundays Marc would take her to the produce store down the street in his truck and they would buy veggies and fruit for us. Since my mom could not speak English and Marc couldn't speak Punjabi, our language, it was almost comical to see them communicating. We took them fishing and shopping too. When we went to Costco, a wholesale store, my mother was looking at a knife set and fax and copy machines. I bought her the knife set at the store to take back home. We all had a lot of fun together. My parents were like little kids in a candy store. My dad was in his late eighties and was always dressed immaculately in a suit even when we went grocery shopping. They stayed with us for about a month. My dad would tell us about the time Meera and Boyd took them out for dinner over the Golden Gate Bridge, maybe to Marin County. He said they took us to this expensive restaurant and it took them about an hour, stuck in traffic, to get there and my dad said he was starving. When they finally got there they fed him leaves (must be a spinach salad as Meera is a vegetarian) and spent a lot of money. He said he got back from the restaurant still hungry, as he was a meat and potatoes man. When they stayed with us Marc would buy a whole cooked chicken from the grocery store and my dad would clean it off to the bones, himself. Sometimes I would cook for them frozen fish sticks, tater tots and canned corn and dad would love that. Of course he would always have a glass of wine before his dinner. After their stay with us, they went to stay with my brother and his family in San Jose. We drove them down there on the weekend.

I called my ex-husband to see if he would send Edwin and Billy to see me before Edwin had to leave for his duty station in Germany, as he was in the ARMY now. I knew I would get laid off from work and could only buy one airline ticket and if he could buy one and the boys could come to see me. Ed called me back and left me a message saying that he had good news and bad news. The good news was that yes the boys could come to see me but the bad news was that I would have to buy both the airline tickets. They were buying a dog for their daughter and could not afford to buy even one airline ticket. By now I was very mad and called Ed back and his wife Robin picked up the phone and she said that Ed was not home and what part of NO I did not understand. Boy that got me totally steamed. I told the bitch to butt out as this pertained to mine and Ed's children. She had no business butting in and I was practically screaming and crying by now. I told her to put Edwin on the telephone. When he got on the phone all I could do was cry. My children did not have to go through this trauma again in their young lives. After I hung up I kept bawling and was inconsolable. Marc told me to let him buy the other ticket which was so sweet of him but I could not take him up on that. They were not his kids. I just had a feeling that I would never see my children together again. Their damn dog was more important than our boys. What type of father was Ed? Edwin left for his duty station soon after that and he did not even call me back for a long time after that as he was stationed somewhere in Germany for four years.

I got my final paycheck at WSBA on September 12th and I did get laid off.   It was so sad to leave my coworkers who were like my family by now. They told me to stay in touch with them; which I did as I would go by there to meet Ruth, Josephine, Mary Lou and my manager Lee and of course Tim too. Marc had bought another vacation package for us to go to Puerto Vallarta in Mexico for the latter part of September. I was pretty depressed and did not want to go anywhere, but since Marc had already paid for it we did go. Leaving on September 21st and returning on September 28th, which was Edwin's nineteenth birthday and I could not even contact him to wish him a happy birthday. We stayed at the Sheraton bougainvillea.   Our trip to Mexico was intermingled with fights Marc and I would get into. The fact that I did not have a job had a lot to do with our arguments. He was acting all high and mighty with me, which I did not care much about. We went to a nightclub there and he started to flirt with other women at the club, which pissed me off. And of course we had a fight about that. I was glad when we returned home after that trip.

I came back and applied for unemployment at their office in Richmond. The lady told me that I should not have any problem finding a job in the banking industry. This was not true as I looked and applied but would not hear from anyone. Mom and Dad came back to stay with us for a couple of more weeks. Then they were going to stay with Mina for a few days and leave for home, back to India. I had to go to the unemployment office once a week to let them know where all I had looked for jobs so I would keep getting my unemployment check, which was barely enough to pay half my rent and some other small bills like car insurance, telephone bill. One week my mom asked me if she could come with me to the unemployment office, and she would stay in the car. I told her it was not a very nice neighborhood in that part of Richmond. I finally told her to hop in the car with me. Dad stayed in the apartment. I could see in her eyes that she just wanted to be with me, no matter where I was going. They had a very short time left with us before their return to India. I told her how I missed Edwin and she told me that is how she missed me too. I guess we both knew how each of us felt. On October 15th Meera and Boyd came to pick mom and dad to take them to their place in San Francisco. They were leaving for India October 18th. Marc and I drove down to the airport to meet them there. Mina had requested wheelchairs for both of them as it would be easy to navigate them in it. They were too old to walk the long distance to the airport terminal. The airline personnel told us that their suitcases were too heavy. All of us were reprimanding my mom for packing too much stuff in her suitcases and she started to cry. We kissed her and apologized and tried to shuffle some things from one suitcase to another lighter one and the guy passed his inspection for them. Finally it was time to take them to their flight terminal and say goodbye to them. Even though we knew that they would come back next year, there was sadness in our hearts.

The next day October 19 which was a Saturday, Marc and I decided to go to the nude beach in the Marin headlands. The traffic was pretty heavy on Interstate 101 south and just before the Sausalito exit we noticed that there was black smoke coming from the East. The smoke was so thick and the wind was blowing it west towards us. On the radio we heard that the Oakland hills were on fire but did not know then, how catastrophic it was. When we hiked down to our beach, the sky got dark and had an orange halo, due to the sun shining through the haze. This fire was the second disaster to hit the Bay Area in two years after the big earthquake. Hundreds of homes were burned down and there was loss and injury to humans and livestock. Of course I was still looking for work and even went to my old job Chargeback USA, where I worked over seven years, to see if they would hire me back. But no such luck. I am sure Curt was laughing behind our back for leaving his company and joining WSBA. Gayle was still working there and said they did not have anything available. I also heard through Debbie who was still at WSBA that Tim and Curt did not like each other and had animosity towards one another. Tim did give me a nice recommendation letter when I was laid off, saying if the company recovered from its losses they would hire the old employees back. The president of WSBA, Dwayne, was not an advocate to this idea. They were all under the suspicion that the building, we were located in, had a bad vodoo spell on it. Someone suggested to them to place mirrors at critical points inside, which they did. They acted as if that was going to help them.

In 1992 I was actively looking for a job. I even gave my counselor at the unemployment office several of my resumes. She said that she gave them out to prospective employers. Then in April Well Fargo Bank was hiring temporary employees for their twenty four hour customer service, through a temporary agency. Our training was for five weeks. And the job would end in July; but it was a part time job only, about twenty or thirty hours a week. I took this position. I went to my five week training in Concord. Our trainer's name was Mona. She actually left a good impression on me as she was very thorough in every aspect of the job we would be performing. They even had a chargeback department, and I would always bug her about a position in that department. I had to take a test for it, which I did not pass. Although the test had nothing to do with chargebacks, yet why would they administer such a test? I continued with my training in Mona's class. After practicing taking test calls in the last week of our training I was assigned a shift which was sometimes a graveyard shift or worse yet Swing shifts on the weekends. I would come home in the middle of the night and sleep all morning. They had a very busy customer service line, and soon as one call would end another one waiting to be answered and I would come home with my jaw aching from non-stop talking. I could not be with Marc on the weekends, or go fishing with him. I did not like my job at all.

I came home from work one morning at 3.00 am on a Monday morning and went to sleep. Marc woke up at 5.30 am to go to work. At about 9.00 am my phone rang and a lady named Helen from a credit union in San Francisco asked me if I was still looking for a job, and I told her yes I was. She made an appointment for me to come down to the city for an interview on Wednesday, which was my next day off. She gave me directions and address on Fremont Street in San Francisco, and the name of the credit union was Spectrum. My interview was at 11.00 am, so I took BART from El Cerrito station to Embarcadero but got lost looking for the address. The numbers on Fremont Street ended at a low number of 50 and I had to go to 150. I tried to stop and ask someone but everyone I passed seemed to be in a hurry. I finally had someone give me directions and arrived at the credit union a little late. I met Helen, who was the manager, and she introduced me to Cheryl and they said they were looking for someone who knew chargebacks on the FDR system. She said the position was for a VISA SPECIALIST for their credit union, which had members that worked for Bechtel and Charles Schwab. They could not get over the fact that I knew the system, as I mentioned on my resume. Helen said the manager of their other branch had given her my resume back in January and she forgot and put it away until now. They were very impressed by my knowledge in the credit card processing area. Helen told me that she would call me after she conducts two more interviews she had scheduled. I thanked her and left, knowing in my mind that I had the job. She called me the next day that I had the job and when I could start. I told her that I had given my resignation at Wells Fargo.

I started working for the credit union on June 6th 1992. I would ride the BART train to Embarcadero station and walk two and a half blocks to my office. The lady who worked this position before me left me with a real mess to clean up. She would be hiding the dispute letters from members in her desk drawer, as she did not know anything about the dispute system by VISA, and how to retrieve money back for the members. It took me a couple of months to clean up her mess, and had an excellent visa department in place. I even ordered the dispute manuals from Visa, to keep up with their regulations, in processing chargebacks. With the help of some of my friends at WSBA, I also created form letters to be sent out to members. One day during the week my sister Meera came to my work to take me out to lunch and had a surprise guest for me. She brought my friend Charmaine, with whom I had lost touch over the years. We had a nice reunion at lunch time going over old times. She was now married to Mike Green another Marine and had a daughter with him.

The Ceo of the credit union was Hope. Aside from my visa duties I had to be on the switchboard and help with servicing our ATM with another employee named Roy. The assistant to Hope was Michelle. Lynn was the head of their accounting department. Judith and Alex worked in accounting. Cheryl and Roy took care of the member's retail banking needs. Van Dyke was the marketing director there. Bill was in charge of the collections department. The last Thursday of the month our Ceo, Hope would conduct a meeting for all employees which included our one branch on Beale Street; John was the manager there and Andre, Sandra and Andrew all worked at this branch. The credit union also had two other branches, one in Houston, Texas and the other in Maryland. I liked all the people I worked with who became my friends too. I asked my boss, Helen if she would send me to a VISA seminar to San Mateo, as there were changes in the regulations which I need to catch up on. The seminar was booked for me for November. I was also learning a lot of other duties at work.

My friend Ruth from WSBA was also laid off and pregnant with her second child and she told me that she was going to take her time to have her kid before looking for work again. Since she lived in Vallejo, she would drive down to our place and then we would all drive down to Bobby McGees to party on Friday nights. We would meet Mary there. I did not mind going to party but since I was driving my car, Mary would not let us leave by midnight and it was always past midnight when we finally got to leave. On one such night we left and driving through Orinda to come home, there was a road block. The police was checking for drunk drivers. Marc was totally freaking out and saying "Oh no, you are going to jail" and I had to tell him to shut up. Marc was the one that was drunk, I had stopped drinking that night around 9.30 pm and Ruth would never drink, as she was five months pregnant. The officer came by my window and asked me if I had been drinking tonight, and I told him yes but I had stopped drinking around 9.30 pm. He told me to step out of the car and gave a whole bunch of tests, which I performed without any difficulty. The police officer told me even though I had passed, he would not let me drive my car. He looked in the car and asked if anyone in it had not been drinking at all. Ruth piped in "Me, I am five months pregnant" and he asked Ruth to drive us home. Phew, that was a close call. I told Marc that this was not going to happen to me again, and if we were going to Bobby McGees, we had to leave earlier or I would not subject myself to go through this dilemma again. But when Marc and Mary would start drinking there was no stopping them and on another night we did not leave there till after midnight again. When we came through Orinda and there was the road block up the road again, and we took the first right without hesitation and looking suspicious. All this time my hands were shaking but went around the block without any problem. That was my last drive down that road and I told myself I would never volunteer to drive like this late again and would take another route home.

One late morning in the middle of the week, as I was on the switchboard and super busy, and I got a call from Edwin from Germany, where he was stationed. I was so thrilled, but had to put him on hold, as there were other calls coming in. When I finally talked to him, I asked how he was doing and if he would call me at home. He said he was doing alright and got my telephone at work from Billy, who was still in New Hampshire and coming to visit me soon. I asked him if he would come home to see me, too. He said he could not come right now but he would soon and stay in touch with me. I was so thrilled that I heard from him after a little over a year. I was on cloud nine. At least, he was alright, and I need not worry so much about him. Billy did come to spend a week with Marc and me. I could tell he missed Edwin also and hated being alone in New Hampshire without him. Since I had a few days off to be with him, I even brought him in to my work to meet all my coworkers. They all thought he was a nice and good looking young man. I was so proud of him. That Friday Marc and I took him to Bobby McGee and met Mary there for happy hour. Bill was only sixteen but was very tall and he was dressed great. We all partied there till the wee hours. I would order a coke for Bill and a shot of tequila for myself and put that in his coke. After a couple of those he was totally buzzed and we could not tear him away from the blondes to go home. Of course I did not drink. He wanted to come back again on Saturday night too and we did. I was happy to see that he was enjoying his stay with his mom and Marco, his step-daddy. I also took Bill to different place in the city during the day and we got on the Bart train and the Ferry service from Larkspur to San Francisco. Visiting the city, we went to Planet Hollywood restaurant and Virgin Records store and had a lot of fun together, both of us wishing that Edwin was with us too. One day we drove down to San Jose to have Bill see his uncle Harbhajan and his cousins Dimple and Bobby. I also took him to see my sister Meera and my niece Dixie in San Francisco and Meera invited us to go see her Guru

Mai's ashram in Emeryville. I had not seen a spectacle of hundreds of her brainwashed followers in a large indoor auditorium, totally mesmerized by her presence, where she was sitting on a raised platform with a bright spotlight on her, like she was god. Billy and I looked at these people who were all chanting something and then we both looked at each other and decided to leave. By the way Meera and Sumita had been following this Guru Mai since 1989 or 1990 and tried their best to recruit everyone that they came in touch with. Marc and I also took Bill and Marc's niece Marie to Great America. Marie thought that Bill was cute and asked me why Bill would not talk much and I told that he was a person of few words and maybe too shy. We had a lot of fun while we were there and let the kids go on the rides. Bill returned back to New Hampshire, as he had to finish his last year in High School.

That summer I also learned that Tim at WSBA had hired my old friend Gayle from CHARGE CARD USA. I was pretty mad as he should have hired me according to the letter he gave me when they laid me off. I called him and he said their business still had not picked up, and I asked him about Gayle, and he made some excuse about that. Gayle told me that CHARGE CARD USA was getting ready to be shut down by its parent bank, United Bank. Curt fought the CEO of United bank from being shut down, and police was called to physically remove him and the rest of the employees there, in San Ramon. I guess what goes around, comes around. Now Curt was out of a job.

My nephew Bobby finally got married to Sukhwant, who was a childhood friend of his in UK. The marriage was held overseas and their reception was held here, at a Vietnamese restaurant in San Jose. We were all invited and Marc and I attended the celebration. There was a DJ and open bar and lots and lots of Indian food. All the women were dressed up in our fanciest Indian outfits and we danced the evening away.

I attended the Visa Chargeback seminar in San Mateo in November. It was a two day seminar, which was held at the Marriott Hotel; and they covered all the reason codes for chargebacks and one of our trainers was Steve M. Both, he and the other lady covered all the topics in the dispute rules and regulations. There was a lunch provided at noon for an hour, and it was for a full eight hour sessions from 8.00 am to 5.00 pm. This was my second Visa seminar. I also went to my first one from WSBA in 1990. But by the second one the Visa regulations had changed a lot and I learned a lot. My work load was increasing by the day and my pay raises were small, comparatively. I was learning lot about the daily functions of my credit union. Every Thursday night after work we had our department meetings, which lasted an hour long and I would not get home till after 7.00 pm. I hated these meetings, as my favorite show "In Living Color" would come on at 8.00 pm on Thursdays. I hardly had time to get home change and have dinner going and miss parts of it, but I was glad that I had a job now.

Marc's sister Sheila got married to Robert on Valentine's Day in 1993. She met him in October of 1991. They drove down to Reno and got married there. This was the second marriage for Sheila and the third one for Bob. Sheila had been a single mom to her son David and daughter Marie. They moved from Richmond and bought a five bedroom and three bathroom houses in Pinole a year later.

In March of 1993 Marc and I booked another vacation trip to Belize, which is small country between Mexico and Guatemala, and in the Caribbean. Now that I had a job we could afford to go on vacation. In 1992 we did not go anywhere. We paid our travel agent, Kathy for the vacation inclusive of all meals. We were to leave for our birthday week in May. Marc got a terrible cold and a fever from someone at his work and gave me his cold too. He started feeling better when I was going through the worst of it. This kept going on when I got better he got it and vice versa. This cold was still with us when we left for Belize. We were to fly through Houston and Marc's fever was so high that he was shivering all through our transition. He kept taking aspirin to keep his fever down. We finally arrived in Belize City and boarded a small plane to fly to Ambergris Caye our resort. It was very hot and the small plane had no air-conditioning and only a large fan blowing on us. When we landed we had to drag our suitcases to a small boat waiting to take us to our hotel called "Journey's End". I wish I had not put on my jeans and had shorts on instead. I guess we were on an adventure. I just wanted to dive in the water and get soaking wet. We figured once we checked in we would change and go soak in the swimming pool with the swim bar and have some drinks. After checking in, the attendant took us to our room, which was nice and spacious inside, but there was a very strong stench in the area of the room. The balcony opened to the swamp in the back and toilet was leaking. We asked him to assign us to another room preferably facing the water, where there was a constant breeze, which he did. The new room was like a small cottage with a bathroom with a small shower and there was no phone or television in any of their rooms. This was fine with us as we wanted to spend most of our time outdoors. The bad part was that the swimming pool was being worked on and would not be available for a couple of days. They told us to dip in the Caribbean water in front of the hotel which was not at all deep and we could stand in it. Marc and I changed into our swimsuits and went into the water right away and stayed in it, next to the dock for over an hour and swam and played in it. The waiter brought us our drinks there. Just when we were ready to get out of the water, Marc told me "Honey I don't want you to freak out, but look at the stairs leading out of the water are covered with millions of little fish". Just then I looked down into the water and there were millions of fish there by our legs and I totally freaked out and insisted that Marc pick me up and get me out of there.

At the hotel they told us that this was the largest living Reef here, second only to Australia. We also discovered that you could go out a mile past the shore and be able to stand up in the water in some areas of the water. Marc started to feel a little better and we went to our room to shower and get dressed for dinner, and shoes or sandals were optional. As a matter of fact when we arrived at our hotel to the time we finally left to go home we never wore our shoes once. There was nothing but sand everywhere and it was not hot to step on. We had brought a lot of mosquito repellent with us, as soon as we stepped out of our room at dusk, there were swarms of mosquitoes. I had not sprayed my hair and found out I had do that quickly as they were ready to attack any unprotected area. The dining room was outside and we had a nice meal of seafood and washed it down with beer. They had an outside bar where they had a piano player and our entertainment was talking and socializing with other guests at the hotel. We went on several snorkeling trips and two fishing trips on the boat. On one of the snorkeling trip traveling to the fish preserve in a four-seater boat, I got hit in the head with a flying squid. It must have been coming at me maybe twenty miles per hour and my first reaction was the guy sitting behind me hit me and the guy thought that I hit him, as he got hit too. But the boat driver pointed at the dead squid in the bottom of his boat. The chance of this happening was one in hundreds. Once we arrived at fish preserve, all the snorkelers jumped in the water, but I stayed in the boat as I was not a very good swimmer. Couple of big barracudas swam by the boat and I was glad that I was not in the water. I could see all kinds of colorful fish just by looking down into the water from the boat. On our first fishing trip we rented a boat for the day with a local of Belize named Ramon, and for only a hundred and twenty dollars he took us out on his boat and provided us lunch and drinks. He took us further into the deeper water and we kept catching barracudas one after the other. As soon as he pulled the fish in the boat, he would hit it hard in the head with a baseball bat. This was the part I did not like; why kill the poor fish? I like to catch and release the fish but on these boats the captain gets to keep all the fish caught for the day. He said he said he was going to feed his whole village. The barracudas have razor sharp teeth. In the afternoon since it was very hot we took a dip in the water. Marc just jumped in and I was holding on to the stairs on the boat. We had a beautiful day and returned to our hotel to bathe and eat a hearty meal. On our second fishing trip we went on a much larger boat, which also cost us three times the price of Ramon's boat and we shared it with several other guests. The owner of the boat was also an American from Houston, Texas. Marc caught the largest Wahoo on the boat and we brought it in to the cook at our hotel who served us our cooked fish for dinner and rest of the diners also ate the same fish.

Aside from fishing and snorkeling there, we also went sailing. They also had canoes that guests could use. Marc told me to get in one and he was going to take me for a ride. I did not know he had never done this before, since I was sitting in the front of the boat, he was rowing me straight into the pier. At that point I started yelling HELPPPPP. The hotel employee saw us and came running to help us. I put my oar out to stop the boat from colliding with the pier. Marc got mad at me for embarrassing him. I told him I was only concerned with my well being and was not going break anymore ribs on vacation and he should get over his embarrassment. One day one of the hotel employees was feeding an eel and told us to come and look. This BIG eel would peak its head out of a hole in the water and guy was feeding him. He said that it was the hotel's pet. It looked very fearsome to me. I bet he could rip his arm out if he wanted to. We were happy that the swimming pool was finally fixed and we could chill out there. We made a lot of friends while we were there and promised to write or call our new friends when we got back to the United States. Like all vacations they all end and it is finally time to go home and back to work.

We returned on a Sunday and were off from work on that following Monday too. We had to unpack and do all our dirty laundry and settle back at home before we had to go to work. I started getting sick with a cold. I went to work Tuesday and Wednesday but my cold turned into bronchitis and I knew I had to go to my doctor Wallach to get medicine for it. I had fever and a nasty cough. The doctor gave me a big lecture about my smoking and that I should quit. The reason I picked this doctor at his practice at El Cerrito Medical, was that they were open on weekends too. The doctor prescribed me a cough syrup with codeine and an antibiotic. I took this and after two days the antibiotic he prescribed was not working at all. I was in such bad shape that I could not lie down as the fluid in my lungs would make me cough so hard that I would pee my pants. I called the doctor's office again and complained that the medicine was not working, and the nurse kept saying that I had to give it some time to work. I could not take this anymore and called the emergency room for help as I could not breathe, the lady said that it sounded like I had pneumonia and to call my doctor and come in immediately. The doctor told me to come back to his office, which I did. He checked me again and gave me free samples of another medicine. I took it at the doctor's office, and within an hour the fluid in my chest started to dry off. I went home and was able to fall asleep. As a matter of fact, I slept the whole weekend into Monday and Tuesday too. The doctor gave me a note for my work that I should rest the remainder of that week. I slowly started getting my strength back and was able to return to work. I don't think Helen was not too happy while I was gone on vacation and then sick leave, as my work had piled up, as no one knew my work. I worked real hard to finally catch up. Billy called me that summer to let me know that he had also joined the US Army and was leaving for boot camp. I told him to call me to stay in touch with me and he promised he would.

Roy was our ATM specialist and since two people have to go in to our ATM, which was located in the Bechtel building on Fremont Street in San Francisco, I was pulled away from my work to go with him on Thursdays around 10.00 am, first to service the ATM and add money to it. After that we had to walk to our branch at Beale and pick up the deposit from them and take it to California Bank and deposit it there in our account. My left knee was giving me a lot of problems and my doctor had me going to therapy which never really helped it. I finally quit therapy. One morning we did this whole process and Roy used to roll up the deposit in a grocery bag to hide it, in case someone decided to rob us. We walked up past California Street chatting the whole time. Roy was deathly afraid of pigeons which are all around the streets here in the City. I asked him why he was so afraid of these dirty old birds, as they were totally harmless; and he told me that when he was a kid, a blue jay attacked him and pecked his head. We walked past this tall building at 101 California around 11.00 am and headed back to our office at 150 Fremont. I always had my radio tuned to my station at work. In the afternoon there was an announcement on the radio station that all businesses in the vicinity to close our doors, as there was a sniper loose and was shooting everyone around him. That is what we did, and closed our doors and locked them from the inside. All this was occurring between 2.30 pm and 3.30 pm. The radio station also announced the BART trains were not stopping at the Embarcadero station, where I had to leave from to go home at 5.00 pm. We learned that there was a lone guy who went to see his lawyers at 101 California building around 11.30 am that day and learned that he had lost all his money and was arguing with the people there who were handling his financial transactions and never got the right answers from them or even sympathy on his loss. He left and came back with an automatic weapon and shot all the people on that floor who had been giving him grief and as he descended the building on stairs, from floor to floor, shot all that came in his way and finally shot himself too. There were hundreds of innocent people that died and more injured by him. There was total mayhem in the vicinity of this building. Hundreds of police cars were swarming there too and all traffic also halted from entering the Embarcadero area. If we had to board BART we had to take the New Montgomery station, which was a long walk or we could choose to take a bus backwards. I called Marc and of course he heard of this on the television at home. The trains were jam packed and I finally got home late that night.

The reason that Marc would catch these colds at his work was because he needed to remove his tonsils, as suggested by his doctor. He finally took this step and was off from his work in August to have the surgery. He recuperated for a week. It was painful in the beginning as any surgery would be but I know he took the right step, as I was sick of catching his cold every other week and I could not take any more time off from work. That weekend it was our company picnic at the Candlestick Park, just before the Giants home game, which we were all attending. Marc and I got to know Sandra and Andre well at the picnic. We also made plans to go to Bobby McGees with them in the fall. After the game we dropped them off at the Bart station as they both lived in the City. We had a great time that afternoon. One Friday I gave directions to Michelle, Sandra, Cheryl, and Andre on how to drive down to Bobby McGees in San Ramon after work. Marc and I drove down from home to meet them there. Mary was there too. We all had a blast partying there. They all left a little earlier as they had to drive down to San Francisco in one car, but Marc and I stayed there with Mary longer.

My parents came back to visit us in November and this time my mom said that they wanted to stay with Marc and me only. This was fine with us as they felt more comfortable with us. Meera and Dixie came to visit them at our place in El Sobrante. Our apartment was falling apart as the roof under our bathroom leaked into our dining room downstairs and we had to keep a bucket on the dining table. We had notified the manager, and the handyman told us this was major repair job for him and he could patch it up and could not guarantee if that would work. Marc and I decided that we were going to look for a house to rent this time around. We looked and looked and always took mom and dad with us. We looked at this one house which had pine trees in the backyard and the ground was covered with pine needles one inch thick on the ground. It overlooked the bay from the backyard. We really did not care for it and mom agreed too, saying that we would always be cleaning the pine needles which also tracked into the house. Our agent showed several houses and we finally decided on one that was located in Hercules, California on Pepperwood Street. It had three bedrooms and two and a half bathrooms and even a separate laundry room, and pretty spacious both inside and outside. The backyard was very big and since Marc loved gardening there was plenty of dirt back there for him to play with. It was in a very nice neighborhood too. Mom and dad both loved it too, for when they returned next year we would have plenty of space for us and them. So in December we paid them our deposit and the rent would be $995.00 per month and could move in on the end of January, 1994. On a visit to San Jose with my parents to see my brother and his family, we found out that Bobby's wife, Sukhwant had returned to UK to her parents' house and was not returning.

Our Credit Union had moved to another location on December 2nd, 1993, which was also my boss Helen's birthday, as our lease was up at our present location. We moved to 2nd Street about two very large blocks away from our present location. I used to eat Mexican food from a restaurant called Perros at the corner of first street and Mission street; and now this would be too far to walk to for lunch, or maybe not. I also frequented a Chinese restaurant named "Lucky one" on Mission between 1st and 2nd streets which had great food too and was always busy.

This was my parents' first real Christmas and we celebrated it at Marc's parents' house, which was the tradition for every year since I met him. Sheila's husband Bob would be taking videos of the whole affair. After Christmas dinner of ham and turkey, everyone open their presents one by one. My dad did not care about the instructions, but just started ripping the paper off his presents and he got house slippers and he was totally delighted with them. He was like a little kid on his first Christmas. My mother was also the same and Marc had bought her a popcorn machine and she could not wait to get home and have Marc pop the corn in it for them. They were totally fascinated when Marc did, just like little kids. We made reservation at Bobby McGees for the New Years Eve party and overnight stay at a hotel close by, as we did not want to be drinking and driving. We fed mom and dad and got dressed to go to our party. I told mom that we would come back the next morning and they should be ready to go our GURUDWARA (our church). I always had this tradition that the first thing I did on New Year's Day was to go to my church. That way the year starts good with God in your heart. I had done this for years. When we got home, dad said that he did not want to go and to take mom with us. So Marc and I took mom and all three of us went to the Gurudwara. As we were coming out we saw Mickey who said hello to us. Boy, we had not seen him around for a while.

Dad had a habit of waking up in the middle of the night and come downstairs and sits on the carpet in the living room in the dark, praying or meditating. I had asked him if he would not do that and stay in his room until Marc and I got dressed to go to work. I usually would come down half dressed sometimes and did not have him sitting there, scaring me half to death. But he was also very stubborn and did what he wanted to do, or he forgot what I had asked him lovingly. One morning I was in a real hurry and snapped at him. Marc heard that and got pissed off at me for doing that. He said he would sleep at our new house in Hercules and we had a fight. I think he was just looking for a fight with me and this was happening a lot lately. I started to cry and it was all dads' fault in causing our fight; if he had just stayed in his room, this all would have never happened. I apologized to dad later. Mom tried to console me saying that Marc would be back and not to cry. Marc did come back the next morning which was a Saturday. We both apologized to each other and hugged and kissed and made up. He said it was very cold in our new house and he slept on the carpet with only one blanket, as the heat was not turned on there yet. I cooked breakfast for all of us and all was forgiven and forgotten. My parents left for India on January 30th, 1994. I did not know at the time that they would not be able to return again. We were going to miss them very much.

At work, the employees of all credit union in the area would meet for dinner at a restaurant named Gabianos, which was right next to the Port of San Francisco, and had a spectacular view of the Bay Bridge. I would meet Sandra, Andre, Andrew and their manager John at these meetings. We would have a great dinner, along with everyone from our branch, including Hope, our President who would give these long speeches along with other credit union Presidents. When it came time for the speeches, some of us would slip away and go home since we still had to go to work the next morning. My boss, Helen quit her job in April, as she was offered a position with the 911 operator, after passing their test. Our receptionist Julie had quit her job a month before and was already a 911-operator. They told me to take the test too. But after I took this test I did not pass.

CHAPTER 12 – OUR MOVE TO HERCULES

Marc and I settled down in our new home at 109 Pepperwood, in Hercules. We decorated it to our own individual tastes. Marc started his gardening project. He planted an orange tree in the front and also a lot of flowers in the spring. Also, we were planning another vacation to Hawaii in May, but since we had already gone to Maui and Kauai, we wanted to visit the Big Island this time. Our travel agent Kathy booked our trip for us and included a car rental, and Condo rental with our airline tickets. Our vacation week got approved at work. In the meantime my friend Ruth called me at the end of April, telling me that she got hired by a large bank called Providian, and they were looking for people who had intensive knowledge of the credit card disputes with VISA, and were paying good salaries. If I was looking to move to a better paying job, she would refer me to her boss, Mark. I told her to go ahead and refer me, as my salary at the credit union wasn't that good, and they kept piling more responsibilities and work on me. I was called for an interview with Mark and Providian's human services department, in Pleasanton. The bank had offices in the Embarcadero area of San Francisco and also four or five buildings in Pleasanton. My interview went well and they sent me for a drug test, which I passed. I was offered a position in their chargeback department by Mark the next day. I told Mark that I would have to give two weeks' notice at the credit union and the next week we were leaving for our vacation to the Big Island, in Hawaii. I was going to start my new job on May 30, 1994.

What a great way to celebrate my new job by going to Hawaii. After we landed on the Big Island we checked into our condo, which had a living room area with a small kitchenette stocked with all the utensils for cooking and dining area. Our bedroom opened up to a balcony which overlooked the ocean, with reclining chairs also. We had upgraded our car rental to a convertible mustang, and picked a hot pink color. We thought we were unique, but every other car we saw on the road was mustangs with all type of colors imaginable. We got in our car and investigated the area for activities and ended up discovering a nude beach, tucked away in a secluded area of the coast. Marc swam with these giant turtles, butt naked. After that first day at the beach, we would come by there almost daily and spend some time there and that is what Marc wanted to do for his birthday during the day and I took him to dinner that night. For my birthday on May 19th Marc cooked me breakfast first and then he took us shopping and bought me a beautiful dress and sandals to match. I was going to wear it for dinner that night. While we were shopping, we read in the newspaper that Jackie Kennedy had died from cancer. In the evenings we would go out to Luaus at different hotels. One day we spent the whole day driving all around the Island. Since we were located on the Kona side, we traveled through Hilo, where it was drizzling and had to put the top back on the car. We stopped at botanical gardens and also went to see the active volcano spewing smoke. We took a lot of pictures of our trip.

On the second to last day on the island, Marc wanted us to hike down to a "Green sand beach" which he had looked up on a map. We ate and took our drinks in our cooler and headed down to this beach. We parked our car and started walking on this long terrain of rocks. We saw no one all afternoon on this trail and we must have walked four to five miles and still no sign of a green sand beach. I was getting totally pissed off at Marc. My foot was bleeding from these flip flops I had on and it was so hot. On all sides there was a sheer drop down the cliffs to the ocean, which was lashing the shoreline. Finally after two or three hours of walking and carrying a heavy cooler, we saw a four wheel drive SUV coming past us. Marc waved the couple down and asked the guy about the beach. He told him that it was a mile or so down from where we were and they were headed there too, and drove away. I was very mad at Marc as he did not ask him to give us a ride too. We finally arrived at the edge of the last cliff and there it was a sheer drop down this cliff was a tiny little beach, as the tide was coming in. We saw tiny figures of a couple down there from the top. I could have killed Marc, as we wasted a whole day on a wild goose chase. I finally sat down on the cooler and opened up a cold beer and told Marc to go ahead to the beach as I would sit here and eat my sandwich and wait for him. He did not have the guts to do that. I did not know how that other couple got down there, but I for sure was not going to hurt myself going down that steep cliff. I had already hurt myself once in Hawaii and wasn't going to risk another injury or death if we fell down. After a little rest and refreshments we started our trek back to our car. The next day we pretty much relaxed at our condo by chilling out at the pool. Marc started to take his bathing suit off, thinking that he was at the nude beach and I had to yell at him, and he stopped; there were other families with children there. We ate a nice meal that evening and packed, as our flight was early in the morning the next day.

We finally arrived home and I had about a couple of days including the memorial day holiday to go back to the credit union and work the last four days before I went to my new job at Providian. Those four days were pure torture, as my manager was trying to ask me how to do this and that. They should have crossed trained another employee, when I used to suggest before, for times like this, and no one ever listened to my suggestions. Four days were not enough time for me to teach them my job, which took years for me to learn. I had to work the first three weeks at the Providian's Pleasanton location, where they were going to train me on their system called Total systems. There were two other employees named Jafar and Priscilla, who had no experience in VISA chargebacks. My friend Ruth had started working in mid-May. We were a close knit group and took our lunches together, along with Mark, our senior manager. At the end of three weeks, we packed up all our documents and moved to our office at 150 Spear Street, in the Embarcadero area of San Francisco. Our office was on the 8th floor. This was a very large building and occupied by our bank. Mark told us that he was in the process of hiring our immediate manager in a couple of months. I took charge, and with my contacts at VISA, ordered about five or six regulations books for both US and INTERNATIONAL disputes. With the help of Ruth we had our department running and also teaching Jafar and Priscilla. I would take the Bart train from the Richmond station; since that was the first station, we had ample parking and choice of seats on the train. Since Richmond station was in a bad neighborhood not many people would go that station. We, in San Francisco, processed the bank's secured card disputes and the Pleasanton office processed disputes for the bank's unsecured program. The customers at this bank were the worse from all the other banks I ever worked for. They were getting a second chance to rebuild their credit with Providian and some were destroying it even worst. They would eat at a restaurant and dispute their charge saying that food was not very good. We had to tell them that this was not a basis for a dispute and if they did not like the food they should have left and not kept eating it.

Marc's job at Courtaulds in Berkeley was moving to Mojave Desert. He had worked there since he was twenty one and they were offering him and all their long time employees' jobs there. I told him he could go there if he wanted to, but I was not moving out of the Bay Area. I knew his whole family lived here so he decided not to move. He started looking for jobs elsewhere. His plant was still open for a year or so and he was still employed. Some of his co workers had already moved to Mojave but they were still keeping the Berkeley plant open for a while.

In July we were introduced to our new manager, Anthony. He had come to us from Bank of America's merchant chargeback department in downtown San Francisco. In a couple of weeks Ruth and I realized that he did not have too much knowledge in the chargeback process. But he was our manager and we all kept working towards the success of our department. I mentioned to Mark, before Anthony came on board, that we should all go to the VISA chargeback seminar in November and he approved for all of us to go. By now VISA had new headquarters built in Foster City. They had a whole lot of new reason codes for travel and entertainment merchants, which we needed to learn. My friend Sandra called me saying that she wanted to get out of the credit union too, and if I could recommend her to my manager Mark and Anthony, which I did. She got called in for an interview with our HR department and within a couple of weeks she got hired for our department. Ruth also recommended her friend Margot, who also got hired. Our department was growing very quickly now we had six chargeback analysts and a new manager.

Billy called me and told me he was now in North Carolina, stationed at Fort Bragg there. There was talk of "Invasion of Haiti" in September and Billy's battalion was the first to go there. My poor son had just got out of boot camp and he was sent to war already. When I talked to Bill, they were waiting at the airfield to get their orders to go. They ended up waiting all night and got their orders late morning, the next day. I told Bill to be careful and if he wanted to call me collect from there, it would be okay. He sounded excited about getting into action, like he used to when he was little boy playing army with his brother and friends. God, he was only nineteen. In the beginning of October, I was outside the building smoking my cigarette and I heard and saw large jets screeching and flying pretty low in between the large skyscrapers and I thought "Oh my god the enemy was near" and they might start the bombing. I noticed that I was the only one panicking and no one the streets was the least bit affected by this. I asked the guard at our building about it and he told me it was THE BLUE ANGELS practicing for their show on the weekend. I was embarrassed at panicking before. At home I kept my television on the CNN station. Actually as soon as our troops landed there, the Haitian army surrendered right away. So there was no war, but Billy was stuck there for six months.

My doctor found out after my MRI that my left knee that had been bothering me for the last three years or so, was barely hanging in with one tendon and that I had to have surgery to rebuild it. My specialist who was going to perform the surgery had operated on some of the football players with the 49ers and was highly recommended by my doctor Wallach. When I fell down in Hawaii and broke my ribs on the left side in 1990, I must have shattered my knee too. My medical leave was approved and my surgery was set for December 1ˢᵗ. This was the year of El Nino and we had a lot of rain, practically every day. So after attending the VISA seminar in November, I went in for my surgery. They told me not to eat or drink after 8.00 pm the night before my surgery. I drank my last beer on November 30ᵗʰ. Marc drove me to Alta Bates Hospital, in Berkeley at 5.00 am. They were going to perform surgery in the morning and I would be able to go home that evening. Marc dropped me off for the surgery and hung around the hospital cafeteria for breakfast and lunch. I went in and changed into a hospital gown and they put an IV drip on my arm. The nurse asked me to count and I only go to maybe four or five and I was out like a light. When I woke up the doctor and nurses were hovering around me, they said the surgery was successful and if I need a BLOCK for the pain, and I would need it when the numbness went away. Marc was there also, and I needed to go to the bathroom, they helped me up and right away I felt the room spinning around me as I was dizzy. Slowly they helped me to the bathroom and I also wanted to vomit as my body had gone through trauma with a major surgery. After resting a little, they released me at 6.00 pm that evening. I was helped into Marc's truck by him and we drove home. We had to stop on the side of the road twice, so I could throw up, mostly nausea from all the medication they gave me through the IV. The next week was a very difficult and painful one for me, and a lot of work for Marc. The hospital sent a therapist to our house with a machine, which was strapped to my leg and kept it moving, to prevent blood clots. I did not like doing that, as pain was excruciating. Of course they gave me vicodin for the pain. Since Marc had to go to work, I slept in the extra bedroom and my bathroom was right across from it. That first night I had to go to the bathroom I got up slowly with my crutches to go. Marc heard me and sprang up out of the bed to help me. I told him to go back to bed as I could handle this myself. But it was a sweet gesture on his part. That weekend on the 9ᵗʰ was Providian's Christmas party, which I heard, was a gala event in San Francisco. Priscilla came by to see me on the weekend and brought me a big teddy bear. She lived in San Pablo, which was not far from our house.

In the middle of December Edwin called me and asked if he could fly down from Germany to spend Christmas with us. I told him of course, as I had not seen him in over five years now. I told him about my surgery but Marc would come to the airport to pick him up. He said he would call me back with his schedule on his flight number and the time of arrival. I was so overjoyed to hear that he was coming. My poor Bill was still stuck in Haiti. My two sons were my diamonds, which I told them every chance I got. Edwin finally called me saying that he would arrive on the 26ᵗʰ instead of Christmas Day, and I told him that the day he arrives would be my Christmas. Marc told me that I was going to the airport, even if he had to rent a wheelchair for me. That was so nice of him. He said that since I had not seen him for so long it was appropriate of me to go to the airport to meet him. I was so excited to see my grown up child now. I told Marc that I did not want to go to his mother's house for the Christmas Eve celebrations because of my leg which had not fully recovered and the painkillers made me drowsy. I had extended my leave from work for about three more weeks by my doctor's note. On the 26ᵗʰ Marc and I left for the airport with my wheelchair. Edwin's flight came in around late morning at San Francisco International airport and Marc wheeled me down to arrivals, and after a while when some of the passengers passed by, I saw my beautiful and handsome son in his dress Army uniform. He saw us and came over and we hugged each other. We had so much to talk about and catching up to do and we did that on our drive home. He told us that he would be getting out of Germany in the summer of 1995 and would come and stay with us much longer, before he goes to his next duty station. I told him all about Bill and wished that he was here with us. Due to El Nino, it rained every single day that Edwin was with us. We took him to pier 39, with me in a wheel chair. We ate there and spent time on the sights, of which one was hundreds of sea lions kicking back by the water front. We also made reservations to take Edwin to Bobby McGees for their New Year's Party. Even though my leg was still in bad shape, I was going to party; it is not every day that your young son comes to visit you. Party, we did and also danced our butt off. At one point Edwin comes back to our table with a gorgeous girl and asked if she could sit at our table, after introducing her to us. I asked him later if he had picked her up to dance with him, and he told me "No mom, she asked me to dance". Edwin was a great dancer, whereas Bill danced like a white boy. Marc got pretty drunk and after midnight he was practically jumping up and down instead of dancing. He said that he was doing the Russian dance. Of course I did not drink at all, as I was going to drive these two guys home. We partied late into the night and did not leave till the lounge closed. Edwin had about three weeks leave. I even took Marc and Edwin to the Gurudwara, my church, on January 1st, 1995 so we could start our year right. Marc was nursing a serious hangover and he also complained that his feet hurt; Edwin and I looked at each other and started to laugh. I told him how he was doing the Russian dance and stomping his feet on the hard floor. He could not remember that. No wonder his feet hurt. It rained the whole month of January that year. Marc went to work and Edwin and I hung around the house. Since my leg had not healed fully, I could not take Edwin to a whole lot of places and also it rained heavily day after day. One afternoon we decided to go shopping at Costco in Martinez, but due to flooding there the roads were shut down and we had to turn around and go home. Edwin told me that when he got ready to leave Germany later that year he was going to come and visit us for a whole month and in better weather. My boys were so into guns, even when they were little. Edwin sat in the living room reading books on guns while it poured outside and watched television. I cooked some nice meals for us and on the weekend we took him out to eat. He loved hanging out at Taco Bell. He told me that in Germany there were other fast food restaurants, except Taco Bell. As a matter of fact I took his picture outside the one in Hercules. Mina and Boyd came to see him at our place. Even though he loved his auntie Mina, he did not care much of the ever so superior Boyd. In a conversation he was having with Edwin, he put down his profession to be a soldier for his country. He was insinuating that people who join the services are less brainy, which was not true in this case as both my sons were more than brainy for the likes of Boyd. If we did not have soldiers defending our country, his sorry ass would be in a sling in time of need. After the end of three weeks I took him to the airport for his flight back to Germany. The flight was around 9.30 am but the commute traffic was so bad that he barely made it to the airport in San Francisco. He told me he could never live here because our traffic was ridiculous. I told him to call me collect when he reached his duty station in Germany, so I would know that he was safe. He promised he would. I gave him a goodbye hug and he boarded his flight. My heart was heavy to see him go. The thought that he would be back in the summer, kept me from not crying.

I went to work the next day on my new Vanpool, run by Quyen and his wife Tammy who also lived in Hercules. They came right outside my house to pick me up, which was good as I had to be careful on my left leg. Some of the other riders were Hari (south Indian), Mai (west bank), and two Fillipina ladies, Rachel and Elsiee, one Pakistani lady, Ameena. Quyen and Tammy are Vietnamese. I had signed up with them for one month to see how it would work for me. They would drop three of us at Fremont Street about three blocks walk to my work on Spear Street, and would pick us up at a designated place on Beale Street. The rest all worked at Bank of America building at the corner of Van Ness and Market. As my leg started healing I quit the vanpool as their hours were too long. I was the first one they picked and the last to be dropped off. I did not like the hours so I started taking Bart again.

The Forty Niners had won the second Superbowl in a row and there was a parade in the city and the players Steve Young and Jerry Rice were riding in an open motorcade. Thousands of people had jam packed the streets around the corner from our work. Ruth, Sandra, Margot and I all ran downstairs to see the parade, and when we came back to work after twenty minutes, our Manager Anthony reprimanded us. What a sourpuss.

Billy called me in the first week of March saying that he was getting out of Haiti and will come see me mid March. That was great news and I was very happy. I told him all about Edwin's visit with us earlier. I also told Bill that Edwin was coming back in August and it would be great if he could get leave and come back to see me then too, that way they could both see each other and I could have them with me together. Bill said he would try. He finally came over on March 15th on two weeks leave. He told us all about Haiti and about the poverty there and all the smell of burning bodies of dead people that he could not forget. They cremated the bodies outdoors. Of course we took Bill to Bobby McGees too. He always had a great time there before. We also took him to the Mustard festival in Napa. Dixie called saying she wanted to come visit Billy and I told her to come on down and gave her the directions to our place. She was living on her own in West Oakland. After an hour when she did not show up I got in the shower. I heard Marc saying that Dixie's car broke down and was by Denny's restaurant in San Pablo. I told him to tell her to stay there and I was going to drive down to help her car towed on my towing service. Five minutes when I came out of the shower, Billy told me that Marc had already left to go see Dixie at Denny's. This totally pissed me off. There was no call back from him or Dixie. He was gone for about five hours. This was totally unacceptable to me. What could he be doing with her for five hours? I was getting madder than hell. I knew Dixie was a user. I could not leave Bill by himself, or if we left, they might call. Bill was telling me not to fight with Marc, when he finally decided to come home. I told him are you kidding me; I was going to tear his head off. He saunters in looking drunk and when I asked him where was Dixie. He said she decided to be towed to her place as she had to go to work, and he had to take her there himself while the tow people towed her car. I was so mad and pushing and cussing Marc and told him he was the biggest liar and a cheat. That fucking bitch Dixie was ruining my relationship with Marc. Of course Marc had no excuse either, running after her like a dog in heat. That was it I did not want a man like him in my life. On top of all this that bitch had Billy mad at me too. Bill would not talk to me and of course I was not talking to Marc either. I had to take Bill to the airport the next morning. I was so angry that I could not sleep all night. Marc went to work and I drove Billy to the airport. He never talked to me all the way in the car or at the airport and I did not even get a hug from him. I told him to call me when he got back to Fort Bragg, North Carolina. No response from him and when the boarding was announced he just got up and left. I drove down to work crying. He never even called me back. I called Dixie at home, and she picked up the phone, I told her I thought she had to go to work and why she wasn't there. She mumbled something about being sick. I told her that if I ever saw her near Marc I would break her legs and more, and never to step in my house again and hung up. My friends Margot, Ruth and Sandra heard me talk to her, as I had explained to them what happened over the weekend, they all agreed with me.

The next few days went by with Marc and I was not talking to each other. He was trying to make up with me. I would never ever trust him ever again after what happened. He kept saying nothing happened between him and Dixie that night. I was not ready to hear his explanations' yet. Meera called me telling me that Dixie was not interested in Marc and she had a boyfriend who was young and black and his name was Maurice. I am sure Marc tried his best to get in her pants, and knowing Dixie, I was sure having a boyfriend would not have stopped her from using Marc to get what she wanted done for her.

After a major breakdown on my Ford Tempo car, I decided to buy a new car. I called my friend Sumita, who was working at Albany Ford, where I bought my Tempo, and she told me to come down and see her. I went there on a Saturday morning. She told me that she had a Mazada Protégé, which only had thirty seven thousand miles and was loaded with options, and the price was under 10k, but the color was black. I went for a test drive and I loved it as it had a one point eight engine. I told her that I would think and call her back. She told me that it might not be there if I waited. I started the process of buying it that morning and they used my Tempo as a down payment, and I drove away with my new car. When I parked my new car in the driveway, Marc comes out to look at the car and said "So you bought a new car?" and I said of course. He said how come I did not take him with me. I said why I would do that, as we are not talking to each other anymore, and I did not need his advice in what I needed to buy. Only time would erase some the distrust and anger I felt towards him.

After not hearing from Billy all summer, I got a call from Edwin from Germany and I told him about the whole fiasco with us and that if he talked to Billy to please ask him to call me. Edwin said "Mom don't worry", he would have him call me. He also told me that he would be coming to see us in a couple of months. This brought some happiness in my life. Slowly Marc and I started to make up. At Providian we got a new manager Michael H. who worked with VISA. Anthony had resigned (we all knew that he was fired) we were told by our new senior unit manager, Michael P. Anthony was going to stay on till the end of the November.

In May we decided to take a cheap vacation by flying to San Diego and staying at a Motel 6 and getting a rental car. The day we flew out of here, the weather in San Francisco was in the high eighties, which is pretty unusual. When we arrived in San Diego it was pretty chilly and foggy there. It was a mistake staying at Motel 6 as the rooms around us were rented to college age students who had very loud parties, which kept us awake. Marc also found out that drinking beer was not allowed at the beaches there, unlike at home. We tried to make the best of it and went to the San Diego Sea World one day, and a comedy shows another day and went to dinner and dance afterwards. Marc and I went to Nordstroms at the mall in downtown, and he bought me a couple of outfits and shoes for dressing up that night to go partying. That afternoon after we were returning from our shopping trip, the freeway was totally shut down.

Luckily our exit was just before the freeway closure. We got back to our motel and got dressed to go out for the night. Marc and I went out to the comedy show and dinner and dance afterwards. We had a great night out and returned to our motel. This time the freeway was wide open. The next morning at breakfast we bought a newspaper, where the headline was mentioning that some guy had stolen an Army tank and had run amuck in his neighborhood crushing cars and getting on the freeway, endangering people's lives. They showed the video of this on the television news, which finally ended up as the "THE SCARIEST POLICE CHASES". After one week we returned back home.

Marc found a new job at C.I.M., Inc. in Oakland in the month of August, since his old job in Berkeley was phased out. He was going start work in mid September. Edwin came home to visit us in September. He told me that Billy was in Zimbabwe, in Africa, that is why I did not hear from him. Marc took Edwin to the waterfall beach on the way to Point Reyes, since he had two weeks off to start his new job. The weather was perfect and warm and we also took him fishing in Marin at the Richardson's Bay on the weekend. We had or perfect spot there, where Marc and I fished all the time. The tide was out and we brought along our subway sandwiches and beer and soda along with three chairs and fishing equipment. We were catching fish and would let Edwin fish with my fishing pole. I know I was the happiest having my son with me and he was such a comedian. He took off his t-shirt and with a grin said I think I will work on my tan. His arms were tanned but his chest and shoulders were pale and in the shape of his t-shirt. At one point my pole bent in half. There was a big fish on. All three of us fought it for about forty five minutes and finally pulled it in. It was a very large leopard shark and was hooked in its fin. No wonder it was so hard to get him in. Unluckily, we did not bring our camera with us. Edwin was really excited that he had helped bring in this huge shark. I kept telling Marc that we should move from our spot as the tide was coming in fast and we would be trapped there. But he never listened to me and we had to waddle through pretty high water. I had tied my skirt way up to my waist so my clothes would not get wet. Edwin, who was six feet and three inches tall, was the only one safe in the water. As we carefully walked through the rising water, I suddenly screamed as my panties got wet; that was definitely not a good feeling. When Marc and Edwin found out why I screamed, they would not stop laughing, and that was very rude. All in all we had a great outing and adventure.

We all went out to party at Bobby McGees with Mary. Edwin and Mary were dancing together and I realized that they were coming on to each other. That was okay with me as Mary, even though much older than Edwin, was a good friend of mine. As the night wore on Mary was getting pretty drunk and when we left the club she started to follow us in her car. We were kind of worried about her driving at this point and when we got close to our house, there was two-way traffic and she started to drive on the oncoming traffic. I stopped my car and Edwin jumped out of my car and got behind the wheel in Mary's car and drove the rest of the way to our house. It was 2.30am in the morning already and we were all tired and wanted to go to sleep, and now we had to make coffee for Mary to sober her down, as she wanted to leave in her car. We could not let her drive drunk. I asked her to sleep at our place and when she sobered up she could go home. The night turned out to be a real fiasco. The sun came and after making sure Mary was okay we let her drive home.

We bought three tickets to see the CARLO SANTANA concert at the Concord Pavilion on September 16th evening. Marc's sister Sheila and her husband Bob also bought tickets for the same concert. We all met at the Pavilion and we all had great seats too. Marc told Edwin "you watch your mom go crazy when Carlo comes on the stage". I did not even need a drink as a motivation to start grooving to his music. We all had a great night out and Edwin enjoyed himself thoroughly. I bought us SANTANA tee shirts. On Edwin's 23rd birthday on September 28th, we took him to Gabiano restaurant for dinner and the next day we took off for Reno, Nevada in my Mazada, for the weekend. We had reservations for two rooms at the Reno Hilton hotel. We checked in and freshened up and took off for the gambling at the hotel. After dinner Edwin took off gambling by himself and Marc and I went to our room to go to sleep as we were very tired. On the next day, which was a Sunday we ate breakfast and checked out and drove to downtown Reno, where we parked our car and cruised around by foot, to different hotels to Gamble and shopped. We ate lunch at one of the outdoor barbecues. Late afternoon we headed home, as the traffic was going to be bad later on.

Edwin was stationed at Fort Carson in Colorado Springs, the same place where his dad was stationed when he was a year old. I took him to the airport for his flight that week and after seeing him off, I drove to work. I parked my car at one the parking lots there. When I walked to work on Spear Street, large trucks carrying movie equipment were parked in front of our building and catered lunch was being served to the movie production people. I asked someone as to what was going on and was told that they were filming a music video the whole day there. It was one of the girls from the group EN VOUGE who was going solo. They were playing the song loud while the girl was lip syncing and the camera was rolling. We could see all of this from our eighth floor. Since I did not have any lunch I was going to walk across the street to Rincon center, where there were several restaurants to choose from. Jafer came along with me. I went right up to the singer and asked her for her autograph signed to Edwin and Billy, but she ignored me and turned around to talk to her video director. I thought that was pretty rude. No wonder her video never took off and she is not a big star now. So I told Jafer that I was going to walk right through her video being filmed, on our way back from lunch, which I did, even though Jafer kept saying not to. When the video came out they had edited all the people off it. All in all it was a pretty exciting day. Edwin called me saying that he had reached there all right and would call and give me his phone number and address once he settled down. I told him to stay in touch with me and he promised he would. Billy had returned to Fort Bragg in North Carolina and was now talking to me. I was so happy that both my sons were back in the US. But in November Billy had to go to France for about six weeks. That took away his Thanksgiving and Christmas dinners as they were on a field trip there through Special Forces of the US Army. He got these rationed meals and had to sleep out in the freezing rains in tents. Edwin said he had met this girl he was seeing and was going to spend the holidays with her.

That summer Meera called me and told me that Dixie was getting married to a guy named Maurice, and was a few months pregnant with his baby. Meera was having the wedding at her and Boyd's house in San Francisco. She invited us to the wedding. Everyone was supposed to bring finger food for the event and asked me to bring one hundred samosas (Indian appetizers). I told her that these would cost me a hundred dollars as they were a dollar a piece and I could not afford it. I told her I would check around and if I could get it for half the price I would call her back. The next day she calls me at work and starts to argue with me saying that I promised I would bring them and now I was reneging on it. Boy, that got me furious with her, and I told her that I did not promise her anything. After another twenty minutes of arguing I hung up on her. First of all she calls me at work and argues with me and wastes my time at work, and then puts words in my mouth. I decided not to go to this wedding as I was pissed off at Meera and here was Dixie getting married, after the altercation I had with her in March and ruining my relationships with Marc and Billy. I heard that she had a boy in November, and they named him Malik.

In December my company had a Christmas party at the Steinhardt Aquarium in San Francisco. I heard that their party for 1994, which I missed due to my knee surgery, was absolutely fabulous. When Providian did these parties they were very upscale. This year Marc and I were definitely going and taking his sister Sheila and Bob with us. My friend Priscilla and her husband Romy were not going and she gave her invitation for Sheila and Bob and they had to wear their name tags. Each person was given two free alcoholic drinks and when some employees did not drink they gave us their tickets. The company had so many employees that no one knew who was who. The dress code was formal attire, men in suit and tie, and women in evening wear. I wore my fancy Indian outfit for the party. I was going to drive my Mazada and all four of us going there together. For weeks, Bob and Sheila were practicing to be Romy and Priscilla, which was so funny. There was a live band which would play the top-40 music. We arrived at the party and had a little trouble finding a parking spot. They had quite a spread of food. There was Chinese, Indian, Mexican and American food areas. The drinks were flowing. The company had a lot of cross dressers and few of them were dressed to the hilt with fishnet stockings and minis with perfect makeup on, that put the rest of us girls to shame. Ruth and her husband Michael, Sandra brought our old co-worker Cheryl who worked at Spectrum FCU, Margot and her boyfriend Richard, Jafer and his lady friend were some of the few friends were at the party. Our boss Anthony brought his partner and so did Michael H. The place was so big that we lost Bob and Sheila for while until we found them at one the bars telling lies to the bartender. Bob told him that he was the President of Providian and he would fix him up with a credit card, so they got extra strong drinks from him. Providian's CEO was and Indian named Shailesh. We all ate before the band arrived, and then the really party started. We danced till we dropped; especially Sheila. She was dancing with her brother Marc until he spun her around and she went flying on the floor landing on her butt on the newly polished floor, drunk as a skunk. She promptly got off the floor shook her dress and resumed dancing, even though everyone saw her fall. As the night wore on everyone was getting more intoxicated. Sheila kept saying how come no one wanted to buy her another drink. Mark and Bob kept telling her that she already had too much and we were leaving to go home. Finally we got her in the car and decided to take the Golden Gate Bridge through Marin County to the Richmond Bridge and on to Pinole. Just as we crossed the Golden Gate Bridge and got into Mill Valley, Bob said for me to pull over, and before I could, it was too late. Sheila had thrown up all over herself, and Bob and the back of my car. What a disaster this was Bob got Sheila out of the car. She had borrowed the dress and shoes she was wearing from her daughter Marie and they were all ruined now. Marc took out the fancy handkerchief from his suit pocket and the guys cleaned her up a little and told her to get in the car. She kept saying to leave her there to die. Marc picked her up and put her back in the car and we took off for home. We dropped Bob and Sheila off at their house in Pinole and went home. I could not believe how people drink to such excess and then throw up. I have drank too, and when I have had enough my body tells me to stop, and don't ever have to throw up. It was already around 2.30 am and we decided to go to sleep.

The next morning poor Marc had the task of cleaning up my car. It took him five hours to do it and he even sprayed air-freshners to eliminate the nasty smell in the car. Since it was a Saturday I did not get up till after noon, and poor Marc was already half way into the task of cleaning. I never thought my new car was ever going to be the same, but I was pleasantly surprised to see the result of Marc's hard work. Well the year was coming to an end and soon it would be 1996. Mary wanted us to party with her at Bobby McGees and we did just that Of course, she got pretty drunk again. Lately she was drinking way too much and Marc kept up with her. I don't know how she got home after her drinking sessions. She kept asking where her boyfriend Edwin was. Well we moved on to 1996.

I had a lot of female problems and ended up in emergency at least two or three times in the beginning of the year. My doctor referred me to a specialist who recommended surgery and on March 4th I had a hysterectomy at the Doctors Hospital in Pinole. My dad had surgery at the Army hospital in India on March 8th for something for his colon, just four days after mine, and mom told me that he was weak but doing alright. I always called them each week to see if they were doing alright. When I asked if they were coming back to the US they told me that since the travel was such a long one they did not have the strength for it. I also called my sons once a week, as Edwin was at Fort Carson, Colorado Springs and Billy was at Ft. Bragg, North Carolina

Marc and I were also in the process of buying a house of our own. We went to a house buying seminar held by an Indian lady named Asha. She had shown us a lot of houses for two months or so, and we finally settled on one that we liked. The lady was asking for 200K and we offered 190K. The bartering went on and on. Finally when she did not want to come down to our price, we told Asha to forget it on the deal. If you have ever bought a house for the first time, you know what stress it causes you and your family. I had just had surgery and was recuperating and off from work for six weeks, per my doctors orders and I could not go through this drama, as Marc and I were arguing and fighting about it. A week later Asha called us saying that the lady who was selling her house finally came down to our price but she had to take care of some of the things that had to be fixed before she could sell it. Her husband who was stationed at the Alameda Naval station was transferred to San Diego and they had to sell soon so they could buy their home there. We finally moved into our new home on June 22nd, 1996. It had four bedrooms and two and half baths. Since we were on top of the hill in Hercules, we can the San Pablo bay from the front of the house. We made one hell of an investment in the purchase of it. Now it is worth about 400K at least or maybe more. Marc's stepbrother Henry, and his sister Sheila and her husband Bob all helped us in the move. It would have been nice if my parents were able to see and stay at our new house.

Before my surgery in March, my doctor Wallach had prescribed some iron vitamins, as I was anemic. So, I kept taking even after my surgery as no one told me to stop. My whole body broke out with wound like welts, which did not hurt or itch, but looked horrible. I was referred to a specialist by my doctor, who in turn could not figure out what was wrong with me. To make long story short, I finally ended up with a third one, who was finally able to help me. He asked me what kind pills I was taking and I told him about my iron vitamins and also advil when I needed for pain now and then. He told me to stop taking any kind of medicine for one month, which I did. Slowly my skin started to clear up slowly. I guess I was getting some sort of adverse reaction from the vitamins.

Things at work in our department were not looking too good, as our manager Michael H. and our senior manager Michael P. had no idea about our chargeback procedures, even though Michael H. used to work for VISA dispute hotline. When we were actually processing our work things were different and he had no management experience to assist us. Our company was growing by leaps and bounds and our disputes were doubling and tripling, that the management needed to hire more qualified employees who were familiar with this sort of work. Margot's friend Grelyd, who worked merchant chargebacks at Wells Fargo along with Ruth, wanted to join our Bank. On my day off I went to my old job W.S.B.A. in Richmond to see all my old co-workers there and Grelyd was working there with Kinney and William. She told me she did not like working with Kinney and wanted to work for Providian. I told her to call us at work and maybe Margot could refer her to our H.R. I saw Tim, Debbie, Marylou and Gayle there and chatted with them. Tim was as usual smoking like a chimney in his office. These were times when some companies allowed smoking in the office but not in San Francisco, where I worked. Greyled joined Providian in March, 1996 and we would all go out to lunch together, which was fun. We also got Arnai and Paulette in our department. Now they had no experience at all in this field, and had to be trained, in taking calls from customers and processing their chargebacks and keeping up with the represtments from the merchant bank. Half the time I was pulled from one to the other to help in keeping our department running smoothly.

Edwin was getting pretty serious with the girl he had met in Colorado Springs, Kenya, who was black and it was no problem with me. He said that she was in the Army too as an M.P. (military police). I asked him to send me her picture and he said he would, but I never got them. I told Edwin to call his little brother Billy. And I would tell Billy to call Edwin whenever I talked to them as I wanted them to stay in touch with each other; but they said they would but never did. That was typical young men behavior. In the summer my company had a picnic party for us, the employees at MARINE WORLD AFRICA USA, in Vallejo. They actually shut down the park to the public for the party. Wow, that was POWER. The picnic was set for June, 1996. Billy called me in May, saying that his orders came in to go to Korea for one year in June, before his 21st birthday on June 10th and he would not return till May of 1997. This was not happy news for me, but he was in the Army and they could send him anywhere they wanted to. I made him call his brother and talk to him too, before he left for Korea. We went to my company picnic at the theme park. Our parking and entry were all free and so was the food. We had a great time at the picnic, where I met Ruth and Michael with their two children and also Margot and her boyfriend Richard. Later we also ran in to Greyled and her husband. The food was not that good catered through the park, and was only hot dogs, hamburgers and all kinds of salad side dishes but all beers and soft drinks was a better deal for Marc and I.

That summer we were invited to my nephew, Bobby's second wedding to Kawal, whom he had met through the family in Vancouver, Canada. Her family lived there. They got married there and had their reception in San Jose. The party was catered with Indian food. Marc and I had a great time eating great food and dancing away the night.

The weekend of Labor Day, we had our house warming. Marc barbequed and I also cooked and bought take out Indian food for about fifty family and friends. All my friends from work were also there. We had our music blasting and everyone was getting drunk and having a great time. Jafar's wife, Laurie made a batch of Margaritas, but forgot to put the lid on the mixer and the drinks flew all over the counters and some on the floor too. I guess she was too drunk anyway. Some of my friends brought side dishes and dessert cakes for the party. Everyone was dancing, laughing and having a great time. The last guests left in the wee hours of Monday, which was the Labor Day holiday. The house was trashed and now came the good part of picking and cleaning it up. It was a party to remember.

I finally got Edwin's girlfriend's picture and was very disappointed. He could have found a prettier girl; of course beauty is in the eye of the beholder. He called me to see if I received the pictures and told me that they were engaged and getting married in November. He asked me to talk to her over the telephone, which I did and she sounded nice. This was too overwhelming for me. I asked him to wait till next summer for two reasons, I was too broke due to us purchasing our house in the summer and would not have a good gift for them and also his brother Billy was overseas and wont be back till the summer of 1997 and he would like to be here when his older brother got married and be his best man. He would not hear of it and said they had made up their minds and now could not wait. I asked him if Kenya was pregnant, so they had to get married so fast. He said that was not the case. Their wedding was set for November 16. Even my friends were asking me what their hurry was. I think it was Kenya's decision and Edwin was following her wishes like a puppy dog. She had also hired a wedding planner and I didn't know where all this money was coming from. I am sure she was making Edwin spend his cash. We planned to fly to the wedding and stay at an Embassy Suites hotel for two nights and got a car rental. Edwin said that his dad was also coming, but his wife Robin could not come. I was going to wear my fancy Indian clothes and Marc was wearing the only suit he had, that I bought for him one Christmas. I made our reservations for our flight for November 15th, which I paid with my credit card and Marc, would pay for the hotel and car rental.

We arrived in Colorado Springs in the afternoon and Edwin and Kenya were there to meet us at the airport. It was very cold there. After renting our car we were to follow them to our hotel. I hugged my son and my future daughter-in-law. She was pretty tall (five foot eleven) and my son was six feet three. I was so happy to see my child and now he was getting married. They had told us that Kenya's mom and half sister would be coming for the wedding from Louisiana, but her dad, who was Jamaican, would not be able to come. When I asked them, they said since her sister was sick (she had siècle cell) her mom could not come for the wedding either. We followed them to our hotel, which was not very far from their apartment and after checking in and dropping our luggage we drove down with Edwin and Kenya to see their apartment. They had a dog, which was a boxer, in their two bedrooms and one bath place, which was a total mess. I already knew that my son was definitely not a neat freak like Billy, and found out that Kenya was the same way. Edwin said that they would take us back to our hotel as they had to pick up his dad at the airport and bring him back to the same hotel we were in as he was staying there too. He said we had to meet for wedding rehearsal and dinner at a restaurant that evening. He asked us if his dad could ride with us, since he did not have a car; I told him that would not be a problem. After the wedding rehearsal we all went to a restaurant they had picked for dinner. Ed paid for everyone's meal, including Edwin's best man and Kenya's maid-of-honor. The wedding was going to take place at this old castle in Manitou Springs, a suburb outside Colorado Springs. Edwin did volunteer work at their police department and had his own patrol car there. He wanted to keep up his police training, as he was looking for a career in this field after time came for him to leave the US Army. The next day which was the day of the wedding, it started to snow and Ed volunteered to drive our car rental to go to the wedding. It is tricky driving on snow and ice and Marc and even I did not have experience doing that. We arrived at the castle that afternoon all dressed up. Edwin was in one corner of the castle getting dressed in his Dress Greens army uniform and Kenya was in another corner and room getting ready in her wedding dress, helped by her maid of honor. Marc and I went out in the light snow and were taking pictures of the castle and he slipped on ice and fell down on his rump. He should have taken lessons from me, as I had the experience in it, while living in New Hampshire years ago. While inside, Edwin and his father were also taking pictures; my son looked so handsome. Soon, Kenya came down the stairs in her beautiful wedding dress and her long veil. We all had our pictures taken before the wedding. Edwin wanted to make sure that Marc, his step daddy, would walk down the aisle with his dad in the chapel after I was escorted in by two of Edwin's army buddies and seated me in the front aisle. Soon Edwin and Kenya were saying their "I dos" and the vows they had written for each other in front the army chaplain. It was like a fairy tale wedding. After the wedding and dinner, the party was on, as there was a DJ spinning the dance tunes and we were all dancing. We saw poor Ed sitting there with no partner. Marc told me to go ahead and ask him for a dance, so he would not feel left out. So I had a dance with my ex, and of course he was dancing like he was in the seventies and doing the John Travolta moves, which was hilarious. We were all drinking, except Ed who did not drink. I would step out on the balcony to smoke in the freezing cold outside. We all had a great time at the wedding, and we missed Billy there with us, as he was in Korea.

We got back to our hotel that evening and Marc and I went up to the bar to drink some more. The next day it was clear and very cold. Ed left for his flight back home to New Hampshire and Marc and I joined Edwin and Kenya to go shopping as our flight was not till later that afternoon. We returned home that night.

In December Providian had another Christmas party at the Steinhardt Aquarium and as usual it was a blast and Sheila and Bob came with us again, and this time I made sure they did not drink too much to ensure there was no repeat of the year before. Also this was the last year with Providian for our manager, Michael H. He was forced to resign, as obviously he was not doing his job that well. From what I heard, he was giving better raises to his friends in our unit and the rest of us were complaining about him. I still remember the look on his face, when Michael P called a meeting for our unit announcing that Michael H had resigned and was not able to say anything in his behalf. The Look was that of shock as he had been hit by a truck. It was a short and sweet meeting. Soon 1996 rolled into 1997 and we did not go anywhere for any New Year celebration.

At work I was telling Michael P, our senior unit manager, how I could show the company to retrieve some of the bank "right offs" through chargebacks. So in February of 1997 Michael P asked me how many people I needed to train in these chargebacks and I told him to give me at least three to four to begin with. Pretty soon we were bringing thousands of dollars back in expired, declined and no authorization chargebacks for the bank. After months of working hard on my project training and adding this new department as 'The Fraud Chargebacks", they told us we would be getting a new manager, who had no idea what we were doing. I felt belittled as they did not make me the manager of MY unit. The upper management's answer was that I did not have management experience. I had to grin and bear it when they presented our new manager Betty and our senior unit manager, David. Now they would not let me transfer back to the dispute unit either, as I had the knowledge in this and not Betty or David. I felt like a prisoner in this unit. Betty was a real puppet manager for the company and had no brains of her own and how could she be my manager. This was not fair and since this was my job I had to keep moving with it.

In May Marc and spent our birthday by staying the weekend at Best Western by the beach in Monterey. It is usually very cold and foggy there even in the summer, but for a change the temperature there was in the low nineties for the weekend. We stayed there for two nights and our room air conditioner was not working at full capacity. After we complained to the hotel, they sent someone over, but he could not fix it as it was an old unit and needed to be replaced. Well we had only one more night left and we kept our door open half way so we could get a sea breeze at night, as our room faced the ocean. The next morning we ate breakfast and left for home. We got home that afternoon.

The following week I got a phone call from Billy that he was back from Korea and at Fort Bragg, North Carolina and wanted to come home to me and Marc. I told him to come on down. He arrived the Friday before the Memorial Day weekend and the weather was very hot here. I went to pick him up at the airport. It was so nice see him after being gone out of the country for one year, and missing his brother's wedding too. That Saturday we took him fishing to our spot at Richardson's Bay and when we got home Marc had bought steaks, chicken and hotlinks to barbeque and I was inside cooking the baked potatoes and corn on the cob. I also made a salad for us to eat. Suddenly Marc yelled to me to bring him a bowl of milk. I asked him why he needed milk. He pointed towards the bushes in our backyard, and said that we had visitors. There were five little kittens peaking out at us, and when I put the bowl of milk down in front of them, they all converged on it. They looked so hungry. That milked must have helped a little as they all went back in hiding under the bushes. We felt their mother must be around somewhere. After we ate our dinner, we put some cooked, shredded chicken on a paper plate and those kittens cleaned that up too. The next day those kittens were waiting for us in the backyard, by the door looking for us to feed them again. They were all so cute. Two were black with a little brown and two were tiger stripes and one was a Siamese. The tiger stripes were a little aggressive than the others. Marc and I bought some cans of cat food for them. I had never had a cat before, and we even put a bowl of fresh water for them. The next day I was going to drive Billy to San Francisco to see his aunt Mina, but my car would not start, so I called Mina to see if she would drive down to our house to see Billy. She said she would bring Dixie and her baby son, Malik around too. They came by late afternoon and visited with us and we played with Malik. Around four thirty they were getting ready to leave, Marc and his step brother, Henry who worked with him at C.I.M, drove up. Henry was good with fixing cars and had my car running for me. That was great as I had to take Billy to the airport the next day. He had come in for a few days and had to get back to his unit in North Carolina. He said he would come back for a month in August. He wanted to bring his buddy, James with him if he could and I told him okay. James was with him in Korea for a year, also.

Marc and I had our hands full with these kittens abandoned by their mother in our yard, and we were going to trap them all and take them to our local animal shelter. Marc bought a trap from the hardware store. One of the tiger stripe kitten disappeared and now we had only four kittens left. He put the trap out with food in it and first one to get trapped was the second tiger stripe, so he took him to the shelter. In two days the Siamese kitten was trapped. It was the smallest one and had a really bad eye infection. Now she was gone. We tried to trap the other two which were black and brown, unsuccessfully for a week. They would sit by our back door and cry but would not go in the trap. After a while I would feel sorry for them and feed them. Slowly we felt that we had a readymade family now. I bought them kitty beds in the garage to sleep in as they could get in out of the garage through an opening, large enough for them. Now I could not wait to get home from work to see our kitties, I named Kikku and Maskoo. We thought we had a girl Kikku and a boy Maskoo. They would come running to us and meow to get their cat chow. Kikku was very approachable and I could pick her up but Maskoo did not want to be touched. Marc would pick up Kikku and hold her like a baby on his lap and watch television. She was daddy's girl. They would jump up on the kitchen counters if we were not watching. At night when we would sit in the family room to watch television, the cats would sleep on the love seat across from us. We broke down and bought them a four story cat-scratcher and put it in the family room. We also bought a whole bunch of kitty toys which kept them very busy playing. It is amazing how a pet like a child can pick up your spirits, as all they need is love and attention.

Providian was most famous for moving their employees work stations from one floor to another or to the next building, which was such a waste of time in my opinion, as our work was constantly disrupted. Our buildings on Spear Street were 150, 160 and 301. Then on Mission Street we had several floors at 201 where our CEO's office was located on the twenty third floors. We had one large department, whose main job was just moving us. Even though I was in a different department than my buddies in disputes, I was still on the eighth floor. One day there was a big commotion outside on Spear, and someone said that they were filming NASH BRIDGES for the whole day, across the street from us. Everyone was running out on their breaks to see the stars Don Johnson and Cheech Marin. All I had to do was turn my chair around and look out of the large glass windows and see them on the roof of a building across. I would have loved to have met them, but I am sure they had security guards around them to keep the general public at arm's length. It was an unusual and fun day.

Billy called me in July letting me know that he and his buddy James would be visiting us in the beginning of August. I went and bought new mattresses to replace the very old ones, so they would have a comfortable night of sleep while they were here. They were coming on a Saturday, so Marc and I went to pick them up at the airport in San Francisco. On our ride home from the airport, traffic was backed up due a baseball game that just let out. We got to talk to both the boys on our ride home. James was in the same unit as Billy and they became friends while they were both in Korea. I assigned them their rooms and after freshening up we ordered pizza for dinner. I had taken a few days off from work to take them around the city. I took them to my work and they met my friends. My friend Reena who was a little older than Billy had a crush on him and wanted to go out on a date with him. James was telling me if I could fix him up too. I also introduced them to my no-brainer boss, Betty who just ignored us. Then I had a friend at VISA, Carey, who was also our liaison at work, and wanted to meet Billy as I had shown her his pictures before. We made plans to meet at Bobby Mcgees in the Embassy Suites hotel in San Mateo. The one in San Ramon had closed in 1996. All my friends joined us at the Indian restaurant in the Rincon center for lunch. Reena joined us on our weekend trip to Reno by bus, as I did not want to drive. On the next weekend Ruth suggested that we go to this nightclub called "SOLUNA" in the city where they had Latino music. So Reena came as Billy's date. The club had a ten dollar cover charge and then there were not enough tables to sit at. I did not have that great a time there. Reena had the next week off so I left my car for Billy to drive them. I had joined Quyen's carpool since December of 1996. Quyen and his wife were both my neighbors since we bought our new house on Violet Road. He would pick me up first at my front door and drop me off in the evening, which was very convenient for me. Billy drove Reena and James to the beach on one day in the middle of the week. Reena practically spent that week at our house. Marc would get home before me from work, and would cook us great meals. On another weekend we drove all the way to San Mateo to meet my friend Carey from Visa at Bobby McGees, but she never showed up. We partied there and when we got home we had a message from Carey apologizing that she could not come as she had come down with the flu.

The last weekend of Billy and James with us on August 31st, Ruth wanted us to go to another fancier nightclub in the city. Marc and I did not want to go and said that Billy and James wanted to go, so she would have to pick them up. She called me and said that her best friend, Evelyn would pick them up, as she was already in the city at her mother's house. Ruth and her husband Michael had separated and had joint custody of their two children, a girl and a boy. I did not know Evelyn that well as she came to pick up the boys around 10.00 pm. We had fed them their dinner and they were dressed up to go party. Half an hour after they left, there was a news flash on the television that Princess Diana was in a horrific car crash in a tunnel in Paris, France. So after this, all programs were pre-empted to show about this accident. The princess and her fiancé Dodi Fayyed were being chased by the Papparazzi in their cars.

Their car speeds were well over 100 mph and impacted with a pillar in the tunnel on a curve. Only one person who was seated next to the driver had his seatbelt on. The driver and Dodi Fayyed died on impact but Princess Diana was terribly injured and died on her way to the hospital. This was a terrible tragedy. Your first thought goes out to her sons who were still too young to lose their mother. You never think that someone so famous, nice and well known would die so young, but death does not discriminate.

We went to sleep before Billy and James came home, as they had our spare key to the house. Billy and James told us what a fiasco the night before turned out for them. Ruth's friend was drunk and driving on the wrong side of the road first, and then once they reached San Francisco and met Ruth at this fancy nightclub where there cover charge was twenty dollars and the drinks at outrageous prices. They did not have enough money and had to go to the ATM; then were dumped by the girls at some side street and left them there. After walking around trying to get their bearing they did run into Ruth and her friend, who finally dropped them home. This got me so upset at Ruth. How could she treat my son like this? I let her have it when I talked to her, and of course she had a different version of the story. She said they told the guys they would pick them up. Oh well, Billy and James boarded their flight back to North Carolina the next week. By now James was calling me 'MOM' too and got a promise from me to fix him up with girl too. I told Billy to call me when arrived home. He did call and they arrived home safe and sound, which was a relief.

In October we were told that our unit at work was going to moving to the fourth floor of 160 Spear, the beginning of 1998. One side of the floor was reserved only for fraud related issues, and our senior unit manager, David's office was located there. Now we had a young girl named Sam in our unit also, who had a little knowledge of chargebacks. Sometimes a little knowledge can be dangerous. Every time I would tell everyone to do the chargebacks a certain way, she would do her own version which would end up in rejects by Visa the next day. These rejects cost the company five dollars each. Since I was not the manager I could not tell her that her way was incorrect. She would cozy up to Betty, who was a no-brainer already and get away with murder. It was hard for me to hide my frustration. When I would call Carey at VISA to verify my method, they still would not listen. I was sure Betty was not going to last long like this. Halloween was fast approaching and at work there was a contest, with the best decorated unit would win the first prize along with second and third prizes. I was not into the holiday mode as the work needed to be completed by the timeframes required for different reason codes, per VISA.

It was getting pretty cold and I would worry about our little kittens Kikku and Maskoo, as the heat was turned off in the house and since they slept in the garage it was still colder there. I had won a fifty dollar gift certificate for PetSmart from my work and went and bought a doghouse and placed their cat bed in it with a heating pad. They did not like the heating pad as it got too hot on their tush. The week of Halloween which was on a Friday, I came home on Tuesday from work and went to check our mail at the mailbox past our neighbor Brian and his mom's house, and I heard a MEOW which sounded like one of my cats and I looked around to see where it was coming from but could not see where. Brian's mother who was outside said that she had been hearing the meowing sound all afternoon, too. They had a large tree in front of their house and when I looked up, there was my Kikku up on the tree. I called her but it looked she was scared stiff on the tree limb, and possibly was not able to climb down by herself. I ran in the house and called the fire department if they could come down and help me, since they had tall ladders they might be able to help my kitty. They sent a fire engine and the guy looks up and said that was a large cat and their truck could not be positioned to get the ladder up. They did not even try anything and here we the tax payers pay their salaries. The guy told me I would be better off calling PG&E, our electric company since they have buckets on their trucks that go up. By this time Marc had come home too. We called PG&E and they did not have such trucks in our area, but would have one out tomorrow, Wednesday. It was also getting dark and my poor Kikku was crying up there and Maskoo was keeping it company on the ground. We had to eat and feed Maskoo and go to sleep since it was a work day. It got pretty windy and the tree branches were moving all around with my kitten crying no-stop. I had a feeling that Brian's dogs had chased her up there in the first place. I don't know how I was going to sleep to hear her crying all night, which made me cry too, as I considered her my little daughter. I left her a plate of food in the garage, in case she came down. The next day at work was all Halloween festivities, but my heart was with Kikku and Maskoo. When I got home she was still up in the tree; I called PG&E again and they gave me the run around again, that they could not get there again that evening. Marc and I tried to shake the tree, so she could get down, but she climbed further up, crying all the time. She got so scared that she peed. The fireman had said that when she gets hungry she would come down herself and that never happened as she had been there two days in a row without food or water. That night was a repetition of the night before. We heard Brian our neighbor mumble that he would have to shoot the cat if she did not quit crying, I went outside and yelled at him that I would have to call the cops, if he ever laid a hand on my cat, bad enough we had to hear his dogs bark constantly, keeping us awake almost every night since we moved into the house over a year now. That shut his mouth up. On Thursday someone at work told me to call a tree cutter in my neighborhood, and by charging me something they would be able to bring my cat down. I went home and called a guy from the yellow pages in my telephone book, located in Pinole. His wife said that her husband was not home yet, and if I gave her my phone number he would call me. I explained to her my situation, and she said they too loved cats and he would be able to help me and I could pay him whatever I could. After half an hour he called me back. He said he would be at our address on Friday morning, while we were at work, and bring my kitten down. I gave him my work phone, and asked him if he would call me when my cat is freed from the tree. I left extra food for Kikku in the garage again. At about 11.00 am I got the best call of my lifetime. He told me he got my kitten down and set her on the ground, and she sat there for a few moments and then bolted to our garage. That evening when I got home, guess who came to greet me at the front door, none other than my crying Kikku. She just came into my arms and I cuddled and loved her. I put her in her bed and caressed her until she fell asleep, and Maskoo came and lay down next to her to keep her sister warm. That was the best Halloween I ever had to see both my cats safe at home. It was as if the weight lifted off my heart. I told Marc that he could give out the candies to the kids, as I was going to stay with my cats.

In December we went to our Christmas party again, and this time it was at the downtown Marriott Hotel. Of course Sheila and Bob were also with us. I wore my fancy Indian outfit and everyone was dressed up to the nines. This year instead of the live band they created the winter night's theme. There were ballet dancers performing to the music in their double ballroom, while we all helped ourselves to the buffet laid out for us. The food was great and the drinks were unlimited. Providian must have spent a lot of money

on this get up. After dinner, the floor was cleared for dancing to the Deejay playing the top forty tunes.
We all had a blast as usual. Before going home we went up to the hotel's bar on the top floor, which had
an excellent and awesome view of the city.

It was a great way to end 1997 and move on to 1998.

CHAPTER 13 – THE END OF MY LIFE

The year 1998 started off good. At work our Fraud Chargeback department moved to the fourth floor of 160 Spear Street, next door to 150 Spear. The dispute department remained at the eighth floor of 150 Spear. I was the only person of our original group of disputes area to move. This meant that I would not see my old buddies for lunch every day, which was kind of sad but at least once or twice a week we would all go out to the Rincon center for lunch or meet at their building to eat my lunch. Our new senior unit manager was David. They finally advertised a job opening for our unit manager and I applied, since I was the one who formed this department. Our manager Betty was moved to another unit somewhere in the company. One side of our floor had fraud related groups and the other half was the call center for the Spanish speaking customers. It is here I met Carlo Santana's sister IRMA. I was showing all the tickets of my Carlo Santana concerts to another manager who was Irma's boss. He told me to come by his area and he would introduce me to Carlo's sister. I thought 'oh yes as if his sister would be working here of all places'. He finally introduced me to Irma, who seemed like a much laid back person, and it was no big deal that her brother was one of the hottest celebrities of the entire music business of America and the WORLD. I asked her since her brother was so rich, why would she be working anywhere for that matter. She told me that she had her own life and her brother had his and that her sons did jam with their uncle but she very rarely took part in his life. She gave me an address for his International fan club and for twenty five dollars I could become a lifetime member of his fan club, which I most certainly did.

One of my co-workers Dave, who was my kid's age, and whom I had originally trained told me the other girl Sam had also applied for our manager's position. Then another person Janet who was a favorite pet of David's had also applied for this position. Technically, the person with the most experience should get this position. In February, after everyone that applied had gone through the interview process, David called me in his office and told me that Janet was our new manager and I should support our group and his decision. I was totally shell shocked, but outwardly I told him that I would support our group and not necessarily his decision as it was not very fair to me. He said if I played by his rules, maybe I could move up too. I left his office training someone my job, when they had no previous management experience or work experience either. So this how it works in the corporate offices of America "it's not WHAT you know but WHO you know" that moves you up the ladder. I was happy that even Sam did not get this position either. I accepted it and some try to move on.

In December of 1997 we had got Kikku neutered knowing that she was a girl and wait to get Maskoo fixed later, thinking it was a boy cat. To our amazement one evening while we were watching television in our family room and had the door to the garage open to keep an eye on our cats, Marc yelled to another cat that was humping our Maskoo. We were totally shocked thinking our Maskoo boy got raped by another male cat and Marc told me to never mention it to another person, as we were ashamed of what happened here tonight. So I agreed to it, but three months later now our boy Maskoo was pregnant. It never occurred to us there are no GAY animals and Maskoo was a girl cat too. DDDUUUUHHHH. When we realized this I could not stop laughing.

Also in February when I called my mom in India, she told me that my father had been admitted in the Army Hospital in New Delhi from pneumonia, and he was very sick and wanted to see us and specially his son Harbhajan. She told us to come see our dad maybe for the last time. Even though I was very worried, mom was known to exaggerate things and situations. I called my brother in San Jose and told him about dad's condition. He said that because of his job he could not leave right away, but would go later to India. By March, dad was still in the hospital and mom told me tell our brother that dad wanted to see him for the last time, message was relayed to him by me. I was very hurt that he specially asked for his son and not his daughters. This is the Indian men's mentality. He had already given everything of his to my brother and we girls never ever got a cent from him. I did not care about the money, but my dad's health. Of course I could not go to India either, first of all, I did not have the money or the time off from work. On a Sunday morning of April 25th, my sister-in-law Amarjeet called to say that our dad had passed away. I started to scream and cry out loud. I would never see my dad again. I was totally inconsolable. We also got a call from Ninni and Goodi who were in New Delhi with mom, and they told us not to worry that he would see to it that dad gets a full Military Funeral. I called Edwin and Billy to let them know that their grandpa Kishan had passed away. He was two and a half months away from his 95th birthday on July 17th. I knew that my mom was totally devastated. I told her that I would visit her soon after the summer was over. Unknown to me even though Ninni took care of the funeral, he even pilfered the house of my dad's army uniforms and his medals from the Indian Army. My dad had retired as a Lt. Colonel from the army. He had fought many wars and had tons of medals. My son Edwin sent me flowers for his grandpa, here. There was a live flower arrangement of all sorts of white flowers and English Ivy. I thought that was so thoughtful of him. I, on the other hand could not send flowers from us to India. Ninni said he bought the biggest wreath of flowers from all of us, and we could send him money if we wanted to, and I did. I did not go to work for a week, as when someone so near to your heart dies there is no consolation.

That summer we did not go anywhere or do anything. I could not wait for the fall so Meera and I could fly to India to see our mother. In the meantime I called her every Friday after work. On the other hand Maskoo had her first litter of kittens in May, and she was a good mommy, but with five kittens and our two cats, we had to get rid of her kittens as soon as they were old enough. One day I came home from work and opened the door to the garage, and stepped in cat shit and it looked like the kittens had shit everywhere. When Marc came home I told him that the kittens had to go soon as I could not go through this at home every time. Yet, it never occurred to us to put a litter box there for them. Marc and I got into an argument and he started rounding up the kittens and putting them in the cage, except one black one we called Blackie. Then he leaves them in the cage crying in the farthest corner in our back yard all night. If you have ever lived in the Bay Area, it gets really cold outside at night even in the summer. Maskoo and Blackie were by her kittens in the cage in our back yard and Kikku ran away for a few days and we thought she was never coming back. In the morning Marc picked up the cage and the kittens were sliding in their own poopoo. He took the cage and let the kittens out far away in another neighborhood, on his way to work. How heartless of us. Now we had Maskoo and

Blackie and Kikku who returned after several days; and ever since Maskoo got pregnant Kikku and her were not getting along.

The things at my work escalated, and Marc told me to go see my Human Resources and demand an explanation of how Janet got the manager's job, when she had no management or work experience. When I did this no one had an answer for me and I felt that "I shook the beehive" and I was going to be stung. In my time of sorrow, I listened to Marc's bad advice. Everyone who was high enough in rank at my work was after my hide. The lady at our Human Resources, who was a blonde bimbo, could not explain anything to me, so yelled and intimidated me at our meeting, I knew this was totally wrong, so I reported her and the next day she was gone (FIREDDDDDDD) from PROVIDIAN. The battle raged on, as I would not quit my questioning. I knew that Janet and the very married with children David were having an affair after work. They did not know it but I had someone follow them. For that I think they did a credit check on me four times, and found nothing wrong. They were looking to fire me but could not. In the meantime, Janet became our senior unit manager, and another lady named Maria, who was Mexican, became our manager. I liked her better than Janet, who was a bitch and now mingling with Sam in our department. What got their goat at work that every month VISA would conduct a completion of a contest on line, and I alone would win it every time; and I would win all sorts of goodies from VISA, and my friend, Carey, there supported me a hundred percent too. She could spot talent when she saw it. On the other hand David would make my life hell at work, as I had the audacity to question his decision. When it came time for a yearly review he gave me a very small raise, when I was working hard at training everyone, and now my boss Maria. I felt like I was held hostage in that department and could not even move to another department. I really wanted to quit there and started applying at other places. I would come pretty close to these jobs but all of a sudden the company would not call me back again. I wondered what was in my credit report by PROVIDIAN; and thought I would investigate it soon.

Since there are reasons set by VISA to do these chargebacks, and Maria did not know much and to her it became a data-entry type of job. She would encourage us to go faster and faster to finish our reports. The next day all these chargebacks would be rejected by VISA, and it cost our company five dollars per reject by VISA. Together with the mental and physical stress my right arm was locking up. They sent me to our disability doctor in the city and they prescribed therapy for me for several weeks, so I could only work half a day and not get paid for my therapy time.

Meera invited us to her wedding to Boyd at the Gaylord Restaurant at Ghiradelli Square in San Francisco on August 15th, her birthday. She and Boyd had got engaged that summer and he gave her a twelve grand engagement ring of white gold and a great big rock. It was absolutely fabulous. We went to her wedding together with the rest of our family here. My niece Dimple was there too. We all had a great time at the wedding. They were married by Judge David, a mutual friend of ours. And two weeks later we took off to India to see mom. Also my son Edwin called me to let us know that his wife Kenya was expecting their first baby in April 1998. They already had adopted a new born girl Elleona who was born on November 5th 1997 and this would be my first biological grandchild. I was so happy, that they were finally having their own baby. This was great news for us.

In September 1998, and since February of 1978 of my last visit there, my sister Meera and I flew out by Singapore Airlines to see our mother. We flew to Hong Kong and then down to Singapore where we had a six to eight hour layover and then proceed to New Delhi the next day. By the time we reached Singapore I wanted to lie down and sleep and Meera told me about the transit hotel at the airport, where for a small fee I could rent a room for six hours to sleep. Meera said that she was going to wait for me at one of the chairs in the airport, as she was deep in conversation with another Indian lady, as she had slept on the plane here. When we finally arrived in New Delhi things had changed a lot in twenty years. We landed at the Indira Ghandi International airport which was huge, compared to the old Palam airport. When we went home to mom, we were totally shocked to see condition. Her hair had turned totally white, and she had lost tons of weight, since I saw her only four and a half years ago. We all hugged and cried to mourn our dad. Even though my mom and dad were years apart in age and had their ups and downs, my mother was lost without him; they were like two peas in a pod. We also noticed that Lali would not talk to us much. She would wake up late and have her breakfast in bed prepared by Nabu, our servant; go to the bathroom but never took a shower and get back in bed and watch a little television and go to sleep. She rarely talked even to mom and was of no help to her, but a burden for her to worry about. In the meantime Goodi and Ninni arrived with my aunt Harprastish from Chandigarh. We all took mom to my dad's bank and got his widow's pension put in her name which was still under dad's name. Mom did not have any money coming in as her tenants had stopped paying her and still living at her property. We were told we would have a court case against them to get them evicted. She had this started while we were there. We also took her to a lawyer, who like Meera, was a disciple of Guru Mai, in the US, to have her will written up, in which she wanted to leave everything to her four daughters. We encouraged her to include our brother too, and she did that on our saying. She also left Meera and me in charge of her will. Everything was to be divided in five parts and we were to provide for Lali, as she was mentally handicapped. We all agreed to this. In the two weeks I was there with mom we tried to do everything she wanted to do with us. Pretty soon it was time for me to leave, as I was still working. Meera stayed with her a little longer, as she did not work. I promised to stay in touch with her and try to come back next year again, and left back for the US after taking many group pictures.

I got back home and learned that Maskoo was pregnant again and ready to have her kittens. If only we could have caught her and got her fixed after her first litter, but she was very difficult to catch. She would climb up in the highest part of shelves in the garage. Marc even tried to drug her, so he could climb up the ladder and grab her, but she would wake up and try to claw him. The next day after my arrival she had her litter of four in our garage. In a week Marc was leaving to see his brother George and his sister-in-law Pam in Oregon. He was going to drive up there. I did not know how I was going to handle the cat fiasco in our home by myself. Kikku would run away from Maskoo and her kittens. Maskoo was also trying to get rid of Blackie as she had new kittens now. Marc left on a Sunday morning and said he would call me when he got up North. I made my dinner for that week and left for work on Monday. I was looking forward to coming home that evening and kick back and heat and eat my dinner, after feeding the cats. I get home and went to check in the garage. There were two large cat's beds; one for Kikku and one for Maskoo. Maskoo had arranged her new litter in Kikku's bed and she was in her bed and no Kikku around. This got me absolutely furious. I was tired and did not want this cat drama, so I yelled at Maskoo telling her to take her kittens out of Kikku's bed; as if she could understand what I was saying? She looked at me and just meowed for her food. I took matters into my own hands and picked all her kittens and threw them in our backyard in the cold and as an afterthought took out a blanket and threw it on them. That was terrible of me but my Kikku was still missing. Late that night she came home and I fed them all. So when Marc called me from Oregon that evening I let him have it as he was supposed to catch Maskoo and get rid of her while I was in India for two weeks. He yelled back at me saying he was not able to do this now that Maskoo was pregnant. Actually that was mean of me. When he returned I apologized to him. The next morning I caught all the kittens and left them at the humane society in Pinole.

Towards the end of October Kikku started to get very sick and would be short of breath and also she was losing her coat of hair a lot and quit eating or drinking. We decided to put her in the house at night with a litter box, keeping her away from Maskoo and Blackie. We would try to force her to eat maybe one or two bites and gave her milk to drink. On Monday November second when I got home, Marc said that Kikku was very sick and he would have to catch Kikku and put her in the cage and we had to take her to the emergency hospital for pets in Berkeley. We hurried up and drove her, while she cried like a little baby all the way. My heart was in my throat. By the time we got there and they were having us fill the paperwork, and I could not stop crying either, she was frothing at the mouth and could barely breathe. I yelled at the nurse to put her in an oxygen cage so she could at least breathe while we did the paperwork, so they took her in. The doctor came and talked to us saying that there could be any number of things wrong with her, she might even have asthma, and it would cost us anywhere from eight to fourteen hundred dollars and she could not guarantee that would live. So there and then since Marc was hungry and had not had his dinner, he told them to put her to sleep. I said no I would put the cost on my credit card, but he would not let me do that. If only I had been strong enough and put my foot down and quit crying so much, I would not have lost my Kikku. She was like a daughter to me and Marc was having them put her to sleep, as his stomach needed food. The doctor asked us if we wanted to see her one last time, first I said no, but changed my mind and told her yes. They brought her in the oxygen cage, she seemed to be breathing slightly better, but she turned away from me like saying "go away as you are leaving me here to die alone". I will never forget that last look she gave me. I bawled all the way home and when I opened the garage door, Maskoo and Blackie were in their beds and I cried and told them that Kikku had died and they could occupy her bed now. I called work and left a message for Maria that I could not come in to work as my Cat had died and I needed a few days of bereavement time. This was not an ordinary cat but my child, and Maria knew about how much I loved her. Marc also cried and before leaving for work next morning he wrote this poem for our Kikku:

I had a kitty; I loved so much   my other cats are just not the same

That now I cry, and miss her touch   they don't love me or meow my name

She came to us and stole our hearts   Life just isn't the same without my cat

It was not fair that we had to part   Am I to blame? Love you Kikku

I had lost two people I loved and yes Kikku was not just a cat but very special to us. Life went on without my father and Kikku. Of course we fed Maskoo and Blackie now, but it was not the same without my cat. We learned to accept Maskoo getting pregnant every six or seven months. 1998 turned to 1999 and Maskoo was pregnant.

Every once in while I would stop in at my old job at WSBA, at their new location and go see all my old friends there. I learned that Tim had cancer of the lungs, as he smoked so much and after going through Chemotherapy, he had got a clean bill of health now. And he looked at me and told me to quit smoking and I told him I would try but it was not easy as all smokers know how hard that was. I told him that I wanted to come back and work for them, and he said he would try to get me back. I was sick of working for Providian, where the left hand did not know what the right hand was doing. But we did attend our Christmas from Providian at the Marriott hotel in San Francisco, together with Sheila and Bob.

In 1999 Providian was sued by their customers' big time. Due to a computer glitch our customers got charged a 29.00 late fee, even when they were not actually late and instead of reversing these fees, the managers would not do so. In the early part of 1999 our company was on all three channels news (ABC, CBS, and NBC). The news cameras were always aimed at our company headquarters at 201 Mission Street. Providian had grown to a gigantic company in three or four years and things were not controlled very well at the headquarters; as all the departments were not in sync with each other; they were doing their own thing. I knew back then that they would fall big time soon, but not soon enough for me.

On April 23, Marc called me from bed in the morning, saying I was a grandma again, and that Maskoo had her kittens last night. January through April I would let Maskoo sleep on the couch in the living room, as she was our only cat left now. Sometime in February Blackie disappeared and never came home again. Since we had coyotes in our area, maybe one of them grabbed him at night; who knows what happened to him. We got up to see her kittens; one was a tiny orange ball of fluff that I started calling YODA as he was a boy and his brother Blackoo. Then there were two girls one gray colored with white patches, who reminded me of Kikku and we named her Patchee and finally the smallest totally grey runt named Betty. I told Marc we were going to keep at least two of them for ourselves. After having so many kittens in our garage, we were learning and placed a big litter box by the kittens. It is amazing as small as the kittens were they learned to go potty in there, instead of the floor. Maskoo was a good mother to them. Marc told me that it is better to bring the kittens in the house and away from their mother as soon as possible so they would get exposure to us. So, one evening he went and grabbed Yoda and brought him in the house and shut the door to the garage. Little Yoda was so terrified that he bit Marc's hand and Marc let go of him and he crawled under our television console and hid under it and did a poopoo, and when we got him out from under there he ran behind the refrigerator; he was a tiny terror so we put him back in the garage.

On the next day April 24th Edwin called to tell us that his son Efrem was born and they chose "Kishan" for his middle name after my dad. I was one proud grandmother and totally happy.

My dad had died exactly one year ago and now there was new life for me this year. I told Edwin to take pictures of both Elleona and Efrem and send them to me, which he did.

I would still call mom on every Friday to see how she was doing. She said that the case she had against her tenants had stalled as they had locked the house and disappeared. Lali was still the same, and gaining a lot of weight, as all she did was sleep. Mom said that she would take Nabu and his wife and kids and walk around a little in her neighborhood. I told her that I would try to come and see her soon as I could; maybe in the fall. That summer when we went to see my brother and his family, I was alarmed to see my niece Dimple; she had dropped a tremendous amount of weight. When I asked her, Amarjeet told me that she had pneumonia and had to be hospitalized and fed intravenously for a while. Dimple always loved the beaches around California and got a bad cold which turned worse. When I saw her in the latter part of 1998, at her brother Bobby and Kawal's wedding anniversary party, Marc had noticed that she was losing a lot of hair on her head and told me to look out for her. She had lost a little weight but she looked good. She was short and always very pudgy but now she looked good. But in the summer of 1999 she really looked anorexic. She showed me her arms to show where she was fed intravenously and had black marks; her arms looked skeletal. I told Amarjeet to fatten the girl up a little and she agreed. Something was very wrong with her that she did not want to discuss it. She had been working with Cisco Systems as an administrative assistant to one of the head person for that company. They gave her a couple of months off to recover. She told me that she would try to get me a job there too, as Bobby had joined the company on her recommendation too. I told her that I wanted her to get better first.

Since the kittens were getting bigger, Marc was going to trap at least two kittens, and we would keep two. Yoda went in the trap first but somehow did not set it off. Next, Patchee went in there and she came out unscathed. But when Blackoo got in it he got caught. So Marc took him to the animal shelter and on his label put down that he was a Ferrell cat. The next morning we had a change of heart to bring him back home, but too late, as they said, since he was a Ferrell cat, he was euphonized already. We felt so sad and guilty about that. Of course after a couple of months Maskoo was pregnant again that summer and was trying to get rid of Yoda, Patchee and Betty. When we put the food out for them she would hiss at her kittens and eat all the food and not let her babies have any. I told Marc that we definitely had to get rid of her. In Hercules, there is a park area, where there is a creek of water plus plenty of birds for her to catch and eat. She was a good huntress and if we left her there she could fend for herself. But this was not going to be easy for him to handle all alone. He said he would ask his step brother, Henry to help him.

In the fall we at work were told that a lot of us were moving to a location in Oakland. Our company had rented five or six floors from the Cal Fed Bank building on Broadway Street right outside the 12th street Bart station. Of course we did not like that but who were we to question the company decision. So the first week of September we were moved to our new location. In a way it worked out for me as Marc and his stepbrother Henry both worked in Oakland too. I started to drive my car in the carpool lane every morning, leaving with Marc and picking up Henry in Pinole and reaching my work before seven in the morning. I would let Marc drive my car to their work. He started work at seven and was tem minutes away from my work. Since they had half an hour for lunch and I had one hour. They would come back to pick me up in the afternoon at 4.00 pm. Life was good again. In October my friend Sandra quit Providian and gave her two week notice. Since she lived in the San Francisco, this was too long a commute for her. She said she was going to look for work in the city. I was worried for her as what if she was out of work too long, how she was going to pay her rent etcetera. She was out of work only a little over a month and found a job at a credit union in the city. Of course we always stayed in touch via telephone and email. Back in January I had bought a Dell Computer for ourselves which was the wave of the future. This year the Providian had their Christmas party at the Marriott hotel in Oakland which we all went to on December 7th.

Edwin called me saying that they had to take Efrem to his pediatrician as at six months he was not developing like other children of his age. There was something wrong with him as he would have seizures and scream in pain. My heart went into my mouth learning about this. Upon further diagnose, the doctors found out that he had a stroke before he was born and would never be normal and needed special care like all handicapped children do. I felt that I should not have pushed him and Kenya to have their own child. That is why Kenya wanted to adopt. I also learned that her half sister who lived with her mother in Louisiana, that we never met, had health issues like 'sickle cell' too. And this was passed on from mother to child and so on. She tried to put the blame on my son, Edwin. No one in our family ever had a problem like this. I tried to console my child and that he should do whatever the doctors told him for his son Efrem. I would come and visit him soon, sometime in 2000.

That summer on July 16th we heard on the news that the plane flown by John Kennedy Jr. and carrying his wife and her sister crashed near Massachusetts in the Atlantic Ocean and all three died. What a shame this was; ending the Camelot dream of that family.

In November and December when I would call Dimple in San Jose, I learned that she had gone back to her job at Cisco, but had a terrible car accident and her health condition was not getting any better. Also she had moved out of her parents' house and had bought a condo in her name in San Jose. She invited Marc and me to come spend the holidays with her and her new boyfriend named Doug. She had also invited Dixie and her husband. Since the holidays are big in Marc's family, we could not go and I told her that we would surely come visit her soon another time. Also in December we got Patchee and Betty neutered and Yoda in January of 2000. Catching them was another hurdle for Marc, and to this day the cats never forgave him for it.

Of course there was a big scare worldwide that as soon as the year 2000 hit our computers would shut down. All companies were bracing for Y2K preparedness for their systems. When the New Year rang in nothing happened to our computers, and everything moved along as it always did. People were getting paranoid for no reason at all.

Billy called me and said that he was getting married in November to Xandra, who had two children already. He had met her in the summer when he had to go to Maryland from work. She was working at a restaurant called HOOTERS. She was a pretty girl and since Bill had made up his mind he was going through with it with very little notice to us or Edwin. Xandra's parents lived in Maryland and after marrying Bill, she and her children Eric and Taylor were going to locate to Fort Bragg, North Carolina, where he was stationed since 1998. They got married by the justice of peace, with her parents and children present in Maryland. They rented a house in Fayetteville, North Carolina. I called and congratulated them over the telephone.

In March of 2000 when I called mom, she was saying that she had won the court case against her bad tenants and the court had authorized the locks to be removed by the tenants on my mother's property and she be reimbursed with back rent. She also told me not to tell this to my sister Meera yet. She told me to come home and take care of the house as she was not going to live forever. Two weeks later we learned that mom was very sick and asking for us to come and see her for the last time. I told her that we would definitely come in a couple of months, as I had no time off yet from work. I told her to get better soon and also told our servant Nabu to take extra care of her till we got there and he said he would. Now I had to worry about her, Dimple and Efrem. Life is not fair. To top that my ex-boss Tim was told all his cancer had come back and spread throughout his body and he had maybe a month or two live. My friend Ruth and I went to see him at his home in Moraga, with a fruit basket. He came out and greeted us and we sat with him and his family and talked of all the great times we had at WSBA.

Back in February Marc had bought a vacation package for us to go to Maui, Hawaii for our birthday week. Now with my mom being sick this did not seem possible. On May first when Meera called India, she found out that mom had stopped eating or drinking; even water and was deathly sick. So that Friday I called my travel agent to cancel our vacation package and buy my airline ticket to go to India and my sister Meera would pick it up in San Francisco at their agency. We were leaving that Sunday early morning hours by Singapore airlines. I also called my boss Maria that I needed an emergency leave for two weeks to see my mom and she approved it over the telephone. Now I called the Indian consulate for my entrance visa just before closing time on Friday. They told me that I would have to come back on Monday as they were closed on the weekends. I begged and pleaded with the guy that I needed this by Saturday as my flight was early Sunday morning. After promising him twice the money for the visa, he agreed and told me to come by on Saturday morning and he would personally come and take care of my visa. On Saturday I met the guy and after about half an hour I had my entry visa for India. I hurriedly packed whatever I needed and Marc and I left for the airport in my car. I was to meet my sister Meera at the Singapore airlines counter at the San Francisco International airport, and told me that she had my airline ticket. As soon as I paid the toll for the Bay Bridge my car died down the road just before the incline to the bridge. So I parked it on the side of the road, and luckily called the tow truck people on Marc's new cell phone I had just bought him for an early birthday present. When the tow truck people learned that the car was on the Bay Bridge property we would have to call Cal-Trans people to get us off their property first. In the mean time Marc told me to call Meera, who lived with her husband Boyd in San Francisco to come pick me up at the bridge, and he would take care of my car and have it towed home eventually. Boyd's answer to me was that I should take a cab. This totally annoyed us; as if the tables were turned Marc would readily help Meera. I called a cab company on the Marc's cell phone and they told me that they would send a cab from Oakland as soon as they could. It was just sprinkling when we left home, but by now it was raining hard. When the cab came I got in it and kissed Marc goodbye. I felt so bad leaving him with a broken down car not knowing how long it would take him to get home that night. He had to go to work the next morning too.

I let Meera and Boyd have it, when I got to the airport and had to pay seventy five dollars to the cab guy. I told my sister that I would remember this for a long time. We finally boarded our flight for India. This time I was going to rent a room at the Singapore airport to sleep in for at least four hours or so, as I wanted to be refreshed when we got home. We had to take mom to the hospital right away when we arrived there. She had not eaten or drank for almost a week and was totally dehydrated and week. They checked my mom in at the Military hospital and put her on an IV which gave her liquid nourishment right away. Meera, Lali and I stayed with mom till it was time for us to go home that night. The worst part was that it is not easy to catch a cab from there at night. We told our servant Nabu to get a cab from home and drive to the hospital to pick us up, which of course cost us twice as much. The next morning we showered and cleaned up and took a scooter rickshaw to the hospital. The nurse told us that they had done some tests on mom and we had to pick up the paperwork by walking down to another section of the hospital for it. When we were walking by, there was a crowd gathered across the street there. We asked Nabu to find out what was going on. Nabu pointed to the top of the other building, where a soldier had hung himself and committed suicide the night before and no one had even cut him down from the ropes yet. They were saying that the soldier had found out that he had AIDS. This was not a very good omen. Somehow the doctors could not tell us or pinpoint mom's ailment. She kept saying that her Uterus had fallen, which prevented her from going to the bathroom. Of course they had to do more tests. By the end of the first week the monsoon season had started early. One night when we were leaving the hospital, it was pouring so hard outside and the road had flooded. There were no street lights either and we had to walk in foot high water to get to the front gate of the hospital. I was freaking out as when it floods in the monsoon seasons, the snakes come out of their burros and would be floating in the water too. Luckily we saw a jeep coming towards us from with its headlights shining on us; we waved to it to see if they could drop us to the front gate, where we could call for a cab. There was a young girl in it with her driver and she said sure she wouldn't mind giving us a lift. After talking to her and explaining our situation to her about our mom and how we had to fly thousands of miles from the US to see our ailing mom, she told her driver to take us all the way home. We thanked her tremendously.

In the next few days mom got a little better and strong enough to sit on the balcony of her room at the hospital. Meera did her nails for her and I combed her hair and fixed it the way she wanted it. She would still have problems going to the bathroom though. The doctor discharged her that weekend, after a week in the hospital. We took her home and tried to make sure that she was eating right. Two days before I was to go home, she complained of pains in her stomach again. She was lying sick in her bed. Meera asked me to stay longer too; I wanted to, but I had only two week emergency leave. I also had to take my mom's doctors note to bring back to work. On May 19th, my birthday, I kissed my mother good bye. She lay in her bed and looked at me longingly, without saying anything. Meera told me to take a good look at her as this might be the last time I would see her. I told her no, she was going to get better and come back to the US again, and go fishing with Marc and me. Meera said she was going to stay on with her longer. With that thought I returned to California and home to Marc and my cats.

Marc told me he had great news for us. He and Henry finally trapped Maskoo in the garage and went to work. They were going to capture her on their return home. He said the mistake he made was that he did not leave food or water for her all day, and she was pregnant. When they got home Marc took the big fishnet he had in the garage and placed her in the cage and Henry helped him. He said that when he drove Maskoo to the park and let her out, she clawed him one last time and ran under the bushes. She had the look on her face, like what did I do wrong and why you guys getting rid of me? This was all so sad, she could have stayed with us forever, if we could have caught her and got her fixed, as we did for Kikku.

When I called my brother's house in San Jose on my return from India, I found out that Dimple had been released from the hospital to her parent's house, as she could not fend for herself anymore. My brother rented her condo out. That first weekend upon my return from India I talked to Amarjeet and she told me that Dimple was eating anything again. I asked her that I was going to buy her strawberry shortcake, which used to be her favorite, and feed it to her myself. So Marc and I left for San Jose to see my niece. What we saw there totally shocked us. Dimple was in her bed and had adult diapers on her, as she could not control her bowel movement. I brought a plate of cake upstairs to feed her as she was a skeleton of her old self. I shall always remember her beautiful laughter. She ate a few bites of the cake just for me; Amarjeet was happy to see that I finally got her eat a little, she would not for others. We sat by her and she told us her hospital stories. She said they had put her next to another person, who died the next day. She told them to move her out of that room as she was not terminally ill like the person who died in her room. She finally wanted to walk to the bathroom and with the help of walker and took tiny steps to get there. She said that she wanted to shave her legs but her mother would not let her. She said that she could not let her boyfriend Doug see with hair on her legs. I told her that she was beautiful the way she was, and did not need to shave at all. We sat with her for about an hour or so and went downstairs to talk to my brother and Amarjeet and Bobby and his wife Kawal. I asked them what was wrong with her, and they told me that since she used to drink a lot, her liver was failing. Now this was a total lie, as I knew she could not drink like that at all. I used go out to party with her and I knew her very well. Someone there was not telling us the truth. After that we drove back home. I told them that I would come see her again in a couple of weekends. We learned that she was back in the hospital again. She had worked for

Cisco systems for a couple of years and never had any health insurance. This was costing my brother a lot of money, I knew.

Marc and I had bought tickets to go see the OJAYS and the WHISPERS at the chronicle pavilion on June 17th, which was a Saturday but my brother called me that afternoon saying that Dimple had passed away in the hospital. We were all crying over the telephone. He told me to go ahead and go to our concert, and there was nothing we could do now to bring her back. He said that the funeral would be in a couple of weeks and he would inform us of it and wanted us to come to it. We fed our kittens Yoda, Patchee and Betty and left for the concert. The next morning Marc woke up before me, to feed the cats their breakfast. He said all three kittens ate, but that night Betty never came home. Yoda and Patchee would be mean to Betty, since she was the littlest one, so she would wander out across the street to other neighborhoods. I am sure Betty got grabbed by a coyote too.

We attended Dimple's funeral after two weeks and hundreds of our friends and family were there. Meera was still in India with our mom and our brother had called her and gave her the bad news of Dimple's death. Meera's husband rode with us to San Jose. There was Dimple's favorite music being played and you could see her in the open casket laying there. I started to cry thinking why was she not getting up and going to the beach with us. She loved the beaches of California so much. All through the prayer ceremony for an hour or so I could not stop crying for my beautiful niece. My brother and his family were totally devastated and walking around like zombies. At the end of the ceremony her casket was taken to the area for her cremation. Some of our cousins from my dad's side were crying out so loud and beating their chests. Dimple's boyfriend Doug was there too, but no one paid any attention to him at all. He thought that my brother would let him stay at Dimple's condo for a while. I think he was in it for the ride only. On the other hand when I called my old job WSBA and I talked to my friend Danny; he told me that Tim, my old boss, had passed away in May sometime. I felt heartbroken at all this negative news. When I called Edwin and Billy I told them all about Dimple's funeral, and told them how much I cried and never wanted to go to another funeral. I made them promise that they would take care of themselves just for me, and they were my diamonds and I would not want anything to happen to them. They made this promise to me.

When I called Meera in India to see what was happening with mom, she told me that she had taken mom to a private doctor. When he took X-rays of mom, he saw a mass of something on her upper intestine that met her stomach. He said he could not do a biopsy in her frail condition to see if it was cancerous or not. He was going to wait and see what else he could do find out what this mass was. Meera said that this doctor scolded her for not bringing her in to him earlier. Mom was again in a lot of agony and pain. I prayed and prayed that she would get better, if she ate little by little. Meera said that she had to return to the US, as she had a work assignment here. She was to arrange flowers for someone's wedding here and then she would return to India.

When I came home that afternoon, I realized that I had not seen my sons in a while. What if something bad happens I might not see them again?   Since at my work, I had a sabbatical of six weeks off after working there for six years, I decided I was going to take that and go see my boys. When I called Edwin, whom I last saw was in 1996 at his wedding, he was very happy to hear his mama was coming to see him and his children. So was Billy, who last visited me in 1997. So I took two weeks in July and the whole of August off to visit them. First I flew off on July 15th to see Edwin in Colorado Springs for a week. His wife Kenya had got out of the Army when they adopted little Elleona in 1997 and was working for a school of handicapped children and totally quit work when Efrem was born. My poor son was working two jobs to put food on the table. He was already in the US Army as a M.P. and worked evenings and weekends at the Manitou Springs police department. He took the week off for his mom. When I got off the plane my son and his family met me at the airport, with Elleona holding a homemade sign saying 'WELCOME TO COLORADO SPRINGS GRANDMA'. We all group hugged and I could not stop kissing my grandchildren. We stopped at an Italian restaurant to eat and Edwin would not let me pay the bill. He said that this was his treat. We drove to their three bedrooms and two bath houses. The main floor covered the living room, dining and kitchen areas. Next to the dining room were a few steps down to their den and one bathroom. On the third level were the three bedrooms and one bathroom. One bedroom in the back was the children's playroom. Edwin and Kenya slept in the master bedroom with a crib for Efrem. Elleona had her own bedroom with double bunk bed. They put me in Elleona's room and she would sleep with her parents. They had a backyard through a sliding door in the dining and kitchen area, where I was to step out and smoke. The weather there was very hot in the summer. Edwin was very proud to show me his vegetable garden, where he was growing corn and some other vegetables. I hate to say that Kenya, even though a good mom, was not the cleanest person in the kitchen. I told them that I was going to cook them an Indian meal that night, but they did not have nice pots to cook in.   We all drove down to Sears and I purchased a whole set of good pans, then we went and bought the groceries to cook my meal with. I remember buying a bottle of Zinfandel wine for this occasion. It took me an hour and half to cook chicken curry, potatoes and cauliflower vegetables (Indian style) and lentils. We bought frozen Naans as bread and plain yogurt to go with the spicy food. Their refrigerator's frozen section was totally crammed with things sitting in there for I don't know how long, but I was not going to say anything about that. We feasted that night and I poured three glasses of wine for us to toast our meal. Edwin looked at me and said, "WE DON'T DRINK MOM". I said for him and Kenya at least take a sip only and they were adamant about not drinking at all, so I had to drink all three glasses myself. I was happy to see my son and his family enjoying their meal. We put the leftovers in the refrigerator for dinner the next night.

The next six days we did a lot of stuff together. They took me to a minor league baseball game, we went to the zoo one day, also we took a train ride all the up to PIKES PEAK. Edwin told me to wear jeans and not shorts as up there they still had snow, and gets very cold. I am glad he told me that. The train tickets cost him over a hundred dollars, and he would not let me buy them. I did not want him to spend all his money on his mama. The train goes slowly uphill and the views from it are spectacular. Once we reached the top we had to put our jackets on. There was ice and snow up there and you get very light headed, almost like you had been drinking alcohol. We lunched up there and bought a few souvenirs and headed back down on the train. The children were so well behaved; of course Efrem cried a little as he was just a baby. I noticed while holding him my arms his little body was so rigid, as he is always waiting for his next seizure. He had a lot of strength in his little body. After our train ride they took me to a dinner theatre which was expensive again, and as usual, and they would not let me pay. On the way down, Edwin showed me his cop car at the Manitou Springs P.D., which was a suburb outside Colorado Springs, The next day it was Elleona's violin lesson and she was dressed like a little ballerina going to her class. We also went to Efrem's therapy class. He would ride on a horse with the instructor and they placed him on a large colored ball and rolled him around on the carpet, to loosen rigidity in the body. I also noticed Kenya showing this catalogue of things for a handicapped child and all these things cost hundreds of dollars, and Edwin got this helpless look on his face, how can I buy all these things. I did not understand why she would not go back to work at the handicapped children's school, to help out financially. My son could not do all this on his own. Of course at home Elleona would not stop following me into the bathroom too. She would say "But grandma, why can't I come in the bathroom with you?" I would tell her that grandmas need some alone time too; to that she would say, "But Why?" She was so cute and smart at two years old as she would dress herself and pick out an outfit for her brother too. My son had done well with his children. In the evening he would sit on his recliner in the den with both his kids in his arms and when I asked him to give me one of them his reply was "I am okay, Mom."

On the second day of my visit, when I woke up, I stepped out in the front yard to smoke, and I heard voices around the corner of their house. It was Kenya talking to a Hispanic guy and girl, who were their neighbors' maybe. When they saw me they stopped their conversation. Then Kenya was introducing me to the guy and his sister, she said. The guy was also in the army. Then on another morning I woke up and asked Edwin, who was cooking breakfast for me, where Kenya was. He hesitated and said she must have gone on an errand and will be back soon. There was something going on that I could not place my finger on. How could she go on an errand when both cars were in the driveway? I decided not to butt in their affairs. Of course even though Edwin was off from work for a week, he did have to go to his daily work outs required by the army very early in the mornings. We all took our daily showers, except Kenya. I never saw her get in the shower once, while I was there. How could she not shower in this heat here, I did not know. On the night before my flight, Edwin told me that he had to go his post for a meeting and that Kenya would drive me to the airport. That was a total disappointment to me. I wanted to hug my child goodbye. He said that he would try to swing by the airport if he could. The next morning we put my suitcases in their new van and loaded up the kids and left for the airport. I told Kenya to take me to the departures straight and there was no need for her spends money on parking, with kids and all. I hugged and kissed them all and said my goodbyes and walked into the airport to check my bags. After checking my bags I was walking up to my gate, when Edwin ran up to me from behind. I was so glad to see him before I left. He told me that he was very happy I came for a visit. I think he wanted to say something else, but did not. He hugged me goodbye as I boarded my flight. Sadness came over me as I left him standing there.

I arrived back in San Francisco and Marc came to pick me at the airport. I told him all about my trip to Colorado Springs and the fun I had there with my son and his family. We stopped at a store in Pinole, to purchase my lotto tickets; we were behind a guy's work truck with a trailer hitched to it. He stopped at a stop sign and I was driving right behind him, and instead of moving forward, he started backing into my car, without looking to see who was behind him. I honked and yelled at him, but he scraped the front end of my car. The guy stepped out of his truck and looked drunk; Marc got out and yelled at him and all he could say that he was sorry. We took his name, address, phone number and his insurance information. The next Monday I called my insurance lady and told her what had happened to my car. Since this was positively the guy's fault his insurance company was going to pay to the body damage to my car. For which I got estimates, and had the damage repaired before I had to leave for North Carolina to see Billy and his family the next weekend.

Meera called me saying that she had come back from India in the beginning of July, as she had a work engagement here for two weeks. She was going to fly back to India on July thirty first and I was leaving on the twenty ninth to see Billy. Since I had a lot of mileage on my United Mileage card, I purchased my airline ticket through that. I had to fly from San Francisco airport to Denver, Colorado and change planes from there to Raleigh-Durham airport in North Carolina. Bill and Xandra were to pick me up there. When I disembarked at Denver, my flight was totally delayed for hours. There were a few false starts but we were at the Denver airport almost all night. I called Bill on his cell phone to let him know about the delay. After maybe six or seven hours, we finally boarded our flight for North Carolina. We landed there around noon the next morning. Billy and Xandra and her kids came to pick me up. I was meeting Xandra for the first time and she was dressed in short shorts and a tank top. Right away they both grabbed my two suitcases from me. We all hugged each other and proceeded to the airport parking lot. Xandra's daughter Taylor who was four years old suddenly started crying that she had to pee and was told to go there in the parking lot. I guess when you have to go, you have to go. It was a little over an hour drive to their home in Fayetteville. On the way back, we had to pick up her son Erik, who was seven, from school. We went to their house and they were renting; it was a one level home, with three bedrooms and two baths. They also had a dog named JESUS, who I heard was Billy's baby. After situating in their home, Billy said that we were to meet another couple at a pizza restaurant to celebrate Eric and Taylor's birthday party. Taylor had turned four on July 24th and Eric had turned seven on July 29th. I had not slept all night and was very tired but went along with my son's plans. We all ate at the pizza place and I chipped in bought two of the three pizzas for all of us. We all had a great time. On the way back we had to stop at a pet store to buy the kids two hamsters that were promised to them. I asked if they could wait and buy these after I left there, but NOOOOOO they had buy them, now. These kids were a handful and I knew I would have trouble with mice running around the house with a dog loose too. I was absolutely right on that count. Since Billy and Xandra both did not have time off from their work I, the grandma had to deal with them. Taylor tried to take her hamster out of its cage in the car itself and was yelled at by her mom.

That night we came home and told Bill and Xandra that I was going to take a shower and retire for the night. They put me in the bunk bed in Taylor's room. As soon I get out of the shower and all clean the dog jumps on me and drools on me. So much for cleanliness. This was going to be a long week. Luckily they had central air-conditioning in the house which helped with soaring temperatures there. When I woke up the next morning, I was going to cook breakfast for all of us. Xandra and her friend were in the dining room having coffee. The kids had finished the leftover pizza but one piece which they saved for me. I was really hungry and that one piece would not do. I looked in the fridge for eggs or bread or butter, but nothing at all in there. There were no canned goods or even potatoes or onions in the house. I asked Xandra if she could take me grocery shopping so I could at least buy the basics for the house. She said Bill was going to do this when he came home from work that afternoon. What was I going to eat? I thought if you knew your mother-in-law was coming to visit you for the first time wouldn't you buy the basics? After this Xandra left with her girlfriend and her daughter Taylor was left with me. I was totally pissed off and told Billy this, as I was left all alone with no food at all. Bill apologized and took me shopping at the PX, where we bought everything for the meal I was going to cook them Indian style that evening. After picking up and eating a burger I proceeded to cook them a meal I had promised them. Bill invited some friends of his for this occasion as he was proud of his mama; but I did not know that they were going to bring their big dog for this occasion. For my safety they put both dogs in his backyard, which was nothing but muddy. I had bought beer for the guys and wine for us gals. Everybody enjoyed the sumptuous meal I had cooked for all of us. I had been drinking my wine while I was cooking. Unlike at Edwin's house, Bill's house had people coming in and out as Xandra was a socialite that brought Bill's character out too. I liked that about her as I was the same way. I was brought up in a household, where we could expect extra guests at a minute's notice. Unlike Edwin (who was suppressed by his wife), Billy was brought out by his extrovert wife, who brought out the best in him. That night we had a party of all parties. After that, everything went downhill. Bill would go to work in the morning and return at three or four in the afternoon and Xandra would leave at five or six to go to her waitressing job in the evening; she would sleep late every morning. Every evening Taylor would cry for her mom who was not there. But my son was already a great father to them. He would bathe them, feed them and put them to bed every night, aside from checking Erik's homework. I was soooo proud of my sons as both Edwin and Billy were the GREATEST fathers of all times in my book. My children had gone through hell and back with their parents broken marriage and done very well for their own lives. I was the proudest mom in the world. For the rest of the week I was there, I ended up babysitting the kids. The kids made the poor hamsters' lives hell. Every now and then they would take them out of the cage. Taylor's pet was squeezed and tormented by her. Then she dropped it and it disappeared somewhere under the bed and the dog was chasing it all over the house; she finally found it and I made her put back in its cage. If they were not playing with their pets they would knock all my clean clothes on the floor and jump up and down on my suitcases. I could not wait to go home.

On the last day of my trip there, Billy answered his telephone on the afternoon of August 4th. I heard him say that he would let me know. I asked him if that was Marc and he said yes. He told me to sit down before talking to him, and Marc told me that my mom had passed away. I felt like a brick had hit me. I just sat there and not a tear would come to my eyes. I guess I was shocked, as I thought she would make it through somehow. Marc said that Amarjeet had called him from San Jose, as they had talked to Meera in India. Meera told them that she was still at the airport and mom passed away then in her own bed. Lali told her mom wait Meera is on her way from the airport and she replied to her, "I can't wait, as THEY have come to get me". This sentence of her made me believe in "AFTER LIFE". My son Billy hugged me and said that he was really sorry. Together we called Edwin to let him know that their grandma had passed away. I packed my stuff as Bill was to take me to the airport. Taylor had come down with a fever that day and by that evening her temperature got pretty high. We put her to bed, and of course Xandra was not home but at work. She should have stayed with her as she kept asking for her mommy. I finally went to bed and when I woke up I got dressed to go. Bill said that after I went to bed, he had to take Taylor to the emergency room at the hospital, and did not come home till after 2.00 am. By morning her temperature was normal, and of course Xandra had left to run some chores. I guess she was not going to say goodbye to me. Bill got dressed and just when we were leaving for the airport; he got a call from Xandra who wanted to say goodbye to me. She said she was sorry to hear about my mom. This sounded so impersonal, after all my mom was Billy's grandmother too. We took off for the airport, which was over an hour's drive. We had to take the kids with us, of course. Once we got there, I told Bill to take off with the kids and he did not have wait with me there. Taylor was still not out of the woods with her fever. He said that he wanted to wait with me. Of course, wait we did. This time around they had the United Airlines Pilots' STRIKE. After an hour or longer I told Bill to take off as I did not know how long my wait was going to be. He hugged me goodbye and they left. Eventually we were told that our flight was postponed to early next morning and the airlines would put us up at the hotel at the airport for the night. Finally our flight took off that next morning and I had called Marc about my delay. He came to pick me up at the airport that evening. Marc took me camping, which I had promised him on the rest of my sabbatical. But we had to cut that short as every night there would be bears right outside our campsite. This happened three nights in a row and that was enough to get back home. On the other had when I talked to Edwin he told me that he took his family camping too in the same area where we had taken our train ride to Pikes Peak. In his conversation to me he said, "I am getting old". I told him old at 27? I told him if he was old, I guess I must be way over the hill. Marc said look what he had to look forward to, as he was working two jobs and did not have any fun or go on a vacation as Kenya refused to get a job.

What a year this had been, I had lost my old boss Tim in May, my niece and my cat in June and finally my mom in August. Meera, Goodi and Ninni took care of mom's funeral. Meera told me that she was going to stay in India to take care of mom's financial obligations and also stay at mom's house to show occupation, as she was afraid Ninni and Goodi were waiting for her to leave and take over the house and sell it for their own profit, as they did not care about mom's will or wishes anyway. Meera was going to sell the house and divide the profits five ways so we would each profit from it. Selling a house in India is not that easy, as we all found out and a speedy transaction. We found out that the house was worth at least a few million US dollars, and now mom's neighbor, Dr. Roshan Lal was trying to block the sale, as they wanted to buy it at a lot less money themselves. After being in India for several months, Meera was tired of being away from her husband here. She asked her husband to join her there and help her with the sale of the home. She also looked for a nice and safe apartment for Lali and moved her to it. I wish I could have been there to help her, but could not because of my job. This had not been a good year.

When I called my work mid-August, I was told that now Providian was moving us all from Oakland to Pleasanton, which is forty five miles away from home. I started going to job fairs and applying for jobs, as I knew that Providian was not going to last much longer, the way they were spending and running their business practices. Even our CEO Shailesh had sold all his stock and resigned from the company about a year ago. Again I would have other banks so interested in me and finally I would not hear from them. I called the credit reporting agencies to see what was on my report. One guy told me that it did not look good that my own company had done four credit checks on me back in 1998. I knew that was it, so I told the guy what had happened to me and I wanted this off my record. He told me to send this to him in writing and he would take this off. So that is how they were holding me hostage at Providian.

Come September they moved us to Pleasanton, and now I had a new manager named Janie, who again was a puppet manager of our company. Our Christmas party was to be held on Friday December 7th at the Oakland Marriott. I took that day off and stayed home just to sleep in so I could party that night all rested. I checked on my cats Yoda and Patchee and fed them in the garage that morning. After a while when I looked out in our backyard, I saw a grey tail and thought it was Patchee, so I opened the sliding glass door to let her in. That was not my cat, but a kitten which was white and grey who ran inside. Every time I would put it outside, he would run back in. I asked him where his mommy was and he just meowed. So I thought maybe it was a homeless cat. I picked him up and showed him to Yoda and Patchee who did not like having him in the house. It was so cold outside I did not have the heart to throw the kitten out. So I named it BOOBOO kitty. When Marc came home from work that afternoon I showed our new kitten. For some reason this was an intelligent cat and must belong to someone. That night we left BooBoo Kitty in the house and our Yodee and Patchee in the garage and took off for our Christmas Party with Sheila and Bob of course. In the next few days no one claimed the kitten around our neighborhood so we kept it with us. That little kitten was constantly in our feet. When you thought you lost it downstairs he would come running upstairs to you. Marc and I thought we would take him fishing with us, so Marc told him to get in the cage, and in a minute he was there in it and not scared of it like our other cats were. We took some snacks and toys for him to play with. Once we got to our spot by Point Malate we put the cage close to our chairs and opened it for BooBoo to get out. He ran out investigating things around for a while we had poles in the water. Then he heard the swwooossshhh of the water and got scared and ran back into his cage and fell asleep on his blankie. He had us smiling and laughing at times too. Of all the pain of the year 2000 I had gone through, here springs a little cute kitten in our lives. On Christmas Eve we took him with us to Marc's parent's house and also brought a litter box with us to place in their garage, in case he wanted to go to the bathroom. He was all over the Christmas gifts wrapped up in the house and everyone enjoyed his company. Best of all, when Marc sat down on the couch in our house to watch television, he would jump up sit by him and smell his farts. We grew so attached to him. Of course Yoda and Patchee hated him, so one day when he was in our backyard, Patchee cornered him ready in the attack mode. He darted back in the house. Patchee would climb the tree in our backyard and glare at him through the windows.

On a Sunday morning after BooBoo was with us for over a month, there was a knock on our door and there were two boys outside our door asking me if we had their cat and I told him no. The teenage boy said that his grandfather, who lived across from us, said that we had their kitten. Marc had gone grocery shopping and all the time I was having this conversation with the boys, BooBoo ran upstairs and was hiding from them. I told the kid why did he wait this long to claim their cat and asked them if they wanted to sell him to us. He said he would take a thousand dollars and I told him to take a hike and he could talk to my husband when he got home. Clearly BooBoo did not want to go with them; maybe they had been mistreating him. When Marc came home and parked his truck, the kids came back asking him for their cat back. I could hear a heated argument going on outside, and Marc asked me where BooBoo was and I told him he was upstairs hiding from those kids. We finally ended up giving BooBoo back to them. We felt so sad; I had already bought him a bed and a lot of toys. We will never know his fate, as the kids were taking the kitten back up North where they lived.

In the meantime in January 2001, I stopped at our local Luckys store on my way home from work to pick up a few groceries. I was in an asile when a girl asked me if I wanted an account with DOWNEY. I thought she said if I needed the downey fabric softner and I said no. She finally explained that she was with DOWNEY SAVINGS AND LOAN bank inside the store. I got talking to her and said I really needed a job close to home in banking. She told me that they had a position open in their branch for a Customer Sales Manager, and come talk to her manager. I followed her and she introduced me to Gaddy her manager, who in turn gave me an application to fill out. I told her I would complete it and drop it by their branch the next day, if that was okay with her. So the next evening I dropped off my completed application with Gaddy. She said that job was in retail banking, which I did not know at all. She told me that was okay, as there is extensive training by their bank, if I was hired. A week later I got a call from her boss Darney on my cell phone. I told him I would have to call him back on my break, as I was at work and he said fine. I took my break that afternoon and walked and sat in my car and called Darney on my cell phone. He actually did my interview over the telephone for fifteen minutes, and explained my job and offered it to me for 35.8k annually and I accepted it and told him that I would have to give a two week notice to my present job at Providian, and would start with them around the fifteenth of February. I was supposed to go by my new bank, DOWNEY on the weekend and sign some more papers with my boss Gaddy. I was so happy to be free of Providian finally, where I only made 29K annually. I could not wait to tell the good news to Marc. The next day I gave my written resignation to my boss Janie, letting her know that January 31st would be my last day with them. After that I felt like I was floating in the air and saying my goodbyes to all my friends there and Carey at Visa too. She said that she would come by my work and take me out to lunch, which was fine with me. We made a lunch date on the last week I was there, and Carey would drive down from Foster City where Visa headquarters are located, and call me and we would have lunch at Chillis across the street from us. I told Janie about my lunch plan and told her that I would take a later lunch that day. She was so jealous and said that I should go at my regular time, noon. I told her that I would take my lunch only when Carey from VISA got here, CAPISE? I was leaving the company anyway and I would do what suited me. What was she going to do? FIRE ME?

I met Carey around two in the afternoon and we went to lunch. She brought me a lot of gifts from Visa to take to my new job. We promised that we would stay in touch. I had already gone with my friends Ruth, Margot, and Grelyd for lunch and they were all very happy for me.

Meera called me from India and told me that she ended up selling the house to Dr. Roshan Lal, anyway. We would each get 120K at least. I trusted her to do the right thing. Goodi and Ninni took their money split, without paying taxes and the four of us had to split our money on our and their taxes too. She opened up four accounts, one each for her, my brother and me and a separate account for Lali. We had to send her all kinds of signed paperwork, letting her work on opening our accounts, on our behalf. This all was taking too long and tedious for all of us that I got into an argument with Boyd over the telephone and had to slam it to end our argument. Meera and Boyd were totally alike; they were always right on everything and would have the last word. I was sick of all this family drama.

Finally, 2001 was my Breakthrough year. After taking it easy for two weeks I reported to my new job, just five minutes away by car from home. I called Edwin and Billy also about my new job and they were very happy for their Mom. My boss and coworkers were all very nice and helpful to me. Aside from my boss, Gaddy, we had two or three tellers. In the absence of Gaddy, I was second in charge of my branch and my title was Customer Sales Manager. Here I met my customers in person, unlike at my old job, where I talked to them over the telephone. We hired one more teller, Manzar, who is Iranian and was coming out of a bad marriage. She had a little girl who was taken care of by her mother, and they lived in Hercules too. The other two tellers were Larisha, who introduced me to this job, and Nisha. The first two weeks I was to be at the branch and observe and learn my job from my boss and then in March, I was to travel to Los Gatos for one week training at one of their older branch there. The bank paid for all my travel expenses and put us at the Los Gatos Lodge for my stay. The new teller Manzar was also going for this training the same week as me.

I drove down there and checked in on a Sunday evening, and went for my class the rest of the week. Our trainer's name was Scott. In the evenings we would all go out to dinner together at Downtown restaurants. I would call Marc and my boys at the end of the day. On one such evenings Edwin asked to borrow some money from me since his house payments were behind. This was the first time ever he asked me for money. I told him that when I got home I would mail him a check, by cashing in my old retirement plan which I still had at Spectrum credit union. But he said he wanted that money wired to his bank, or they would foreclose on his house. I asked him why did he wait this long to ask me. He said that he thought he could handle it, but things got out of hand. Why was that bitch Kenya not working and helping my son; I was furious at her. I told him that I would wire his bank the 3.5K when I got home, which I did as soon as I could. Edwin called me and he was very thankful to me and that "MOM YOU SAVED MY LIFE" is what he uttered. I told him not to worry, he was my sweet son and I would do ANYTHING to help him or Billy, as they meant a lot to me. Now that I was making so much more, money would never be the issue. Aside from my salary, we got quarterly bonuses too for selling our bank products to our customers. So in April I got my quarterly bonus, I went and bought a burgundy leather couch recliner for twenty five hundred dollars cash and added a side chair and a special order burgundy color coffee table to go with the couch for our living room. I went back for weeks more of training in Los Gatos in April and again in May. Edwin said he was doing better now and Billy said that he would be going to Ghana (Africa) in May for a tour for three months with the special forces of the Army. I kept encouraging Edwin and Billy to call each other and stay in touch and hoped they did. Family is very important is what I always instilled in my children.

The week of our birthday in May, I was in Los Gatos for a week of training and asked Marc to drive down there to be with me on his birthday, May 15th, which fell on a Wednesday and take the next day off from work. So he came down to see me there and we all treated him to a fancy dinner at a brewery at downtown location. He got to meet my instructor and other co- workers with the bank. He stayed that night with me and left after I drove off to my training, the next morning. I finally returned back home on a Friday afternoon, and had to work the next two days, as our in-store bank was open seven days a week. On Sunday which was my birthday on the 19th my boss gave me Sunday and Monday off. Marc took me out to a fancy Indian restaurant in Mill Valley. We had a great time there. Since Marc had to go to work that Monday, we got home early after eating. On the twentieth of May Edwin called me and I really let him have it. I told him that he never called me on Mother's day or my birthday and there was no excuse for this. Of course Billy was not in the country and was in Ghana, I could understand why HE did not call. I was so mad at him about this. What he said to me next totally floored me. He said that no there was no excuse for him not calling me, but Kenya left me. That hit me like a ton of bricks, and my anger turned into concern for my child. I asked him where the kids were and he said with him. I told him not to let the kids get away from him as this was called DESERTION. He said that he had to go to work and could not take of the kids too. I told him to send them to grandchildren, and maybe get a nanny for them here. He sounded bummed out, but in my heart of hearts I was glad that ugly bitch had gone and now I will set my handsome son, with some of my good girlfriends. Why did he not understand that he could have any girl he wanted? I think that Kenya bitch had some sort of spell on my son. On the other hand I was doing well at my job and finally got to meet our senior managers Darney, JC and JM who had come up north to participate in the Hercules Annual Cultural festival where we had our Downey booth too, to trump up more business for our bank. This festival was for two days June 1st and 2nd. Edwin called me at work asked if I could send him another seven hundred dollars to get his car fixed. Kenya had taken the brand new van that Edwin had purchased and left with him an old Ford Escort. I wired him eight hundred dollars right away from my bank. I told him to go buy himself and the kids a nice meal for the extra hundred. He said to me again, "Mom you saved my Life". I told him, "This was only money, and I would climb mountains for him or Bill". After the Hercules festival our senior managers wanted to take us all out to Outback steak house, and since I did not eat steak, I opted out, as Marc wanted me to come home also. I had been at the bank for ten hours already and was ready to go home to Marc and my kitties, Yoda and Patchee. The only problem that I had working at the bank is that my boss Gaddy would have me working almost fifty hours per week and she had every excuse in the book not to come to work; either her car broke down or she was too sick to come in. Being close to home now did not matter as I would leave at nine in the morning and would not get home till eight at night almost every day. Also my breaks and lunch were cut short due to customers coming in and the tellers' needing an override from me. I still kept hanging in there, and sold checking accounts to all my friends and family members so our Branch would be the best among the other three branches one in Napa, one in Antioch and the 3rd in San Ramon. The results were WE were the best branch among four branches. Our bonuses would be great in July.

I would call Edwin and leave messages for him to call me back but there was no call back from him. I was so worried about him. Around the 15th of June (five days after Billy's 26th birthday), Edwin called me and told me that he was on a police call and had to break up a fight with his partner; there were fifteen big guys drunk and fighting (Edwin was six foot three and 155 pounds) and he got hit in the head in a scuffle and had to go to the hospital to get everything checked out as a precaution. He said he was alright and I asked him where my grandchildren were, and he replied they were with Kenya; he flew them out to the state of Washington and Kenya took them at the airport and he could not even go to the house where she was staying. I told him he was stupid to think that HEFFA was going to give him a break. So the eight hundred dollars I sent him were not to pay for his car but fly the kids to that bitch, Kenya or give her the money to buy back her affection. This got me mad at Edwin; yet he was my child and I had to take care of him no matter what happened here. Kenya most probably took the money also from him. If there was EVIL in the world, it was Kenya the bitch. She was putting my son through so much torture, I could not bear it. I told Edwin to come home to me and I would get him a job as police officer here in Hercules, as there were job openings here. I even sent him police officer job applications. Then on June 27th Edwin called me again at work. The good news was that he got the job as a Deputy Sherriff in the DOUGLAS COUNTY, the largest county in COLORADO. He said, "I need a thousand dollars to get my car fixed so I could drive to my new job near DENVER, which was an hour's drive from Colorado Springs, and he was going to be making 44k annually." I told him that in the early part of July, I would be getting a good bonus from my bank if he could wait for that. He said he could not, so I told him to call his dad in New Hampshire, as he wanted to help him too. Billy's wife Xandra told me that Ed wanted to help Edwin. This was the wrong thing to say to him as he said his dad had not even recognized his children as his own as they were BLACK. I told him that was not true. He said that June 27th was his last day in the US ARMY and now he would be a civilian fighting crime with the Douglas County. That was the last I talked to him. I told him if his father could not help him to call me back and I would think of something else. Since he did not call, I kept leaving him message after message, but he would not call me back. On Sunday July 1st I called Ed in New Hampshire to see if Edwin had called him, and he said that he did. He had asked Edwin to give the phone number of the Ford car repair place and he would charge the cost of it on his credit card. Which he did and got his car repaired to go to his new job. I took a sigh of relief and knew he was just mad at me for not giving him the money like I did before. Despite that I kept leaving him messages on his phone over and over again, and even on the 4th of July. Since Marc and I were off that Wednesday Marc and I went fishing to Richardson's Bay in Mill Valley and tried calling him on my cell phone, but no response. I was so worried about my child.

I went back to work on the 5th and 6th of July and then my boss gave me the next three days off as I had been working so many hours already at the branch. On Saturday the 7th, Marc and I were invited to my co-worker's daughter's birthday party at a Chinese restaurant in Antioch. They had so many food choices there and after we ate they had a DJ for dancing. We had a great time at the party. The next day on the 8th Marc and I went fishing at our spot in Benecia. At the end of the afternoon I put my pole in the shallow water as we caught only small striped bass. The tide was going out real fast and their two people in a kayak going by us. All of a sudden my pole bent down real low and if I had not caught it when I did, it would have gone in the water. I had caught something real big. I fought it for about twenty minutes or so and landed a huge striped bass. Marc was whooping it up and the kayakers were clapping for me. I told Marc I wanted to let him go, as it was so beautiful a fish and too big for the two of us to eat. But Marc was having a hissy fit and said that he had spent so much money on bait and he wanted to keep my fish. We took it to the bait store and had it weighed and measured. It was eight pounds and thirty inches long and had our picture taken with it. Marc took it out in the back lawn and cleaned it and wrapped it in aluminum foil and put it in the freezer. Of course there was no message on my phone machine from Edwin. I tried to call him and got his answering machine and left him a message about my fish. No call back from him. The next day was Monday and Marc went to work and I was going to just hang around the house and do housework and personal things for myself.

Around 10.00 am I was sitting by the window and plucking my eyebrows when my phone rang. When I picked up the phone it was Larisha from my work. She asked me how was I doing on my day off and I told her that I was enjoying it. She said that by the way, either my daughter-in-law or my sister-in-law called at work looking for me and she told them to leave me a message on my cell phone, something about a death in the family. She asked me to check my cell phone message like she had showed me how to. By this time I got very nervous and my blood ran cold. I turned on my phone and heard Xandra's message all crying to call her back. By now I thought something had happened to Billy in Ghana and I could not stop shaking and screaming. When I called her back my first question was "What happened to Billy? Is he okay?" To that she said that he was okay and he was on the other line and wanted to speak to me. Bill got on the phone and he was crying and said, "MOM, EDWIN SHOT HIMSELF" I started screaming as my life had ended. All I wanted to do at that moment was to die; how was I going to live without my beautiful son? Bill kept crying on the phone "Mom, I need you too". Bill said that he was coming home on the first flight he could get from Ghana. I was inconsolable and asked the Lord, "WHY MY CHILD LORD? I was supposed to die before Edwin. He was only 28 yrs old." Larisha called me back from work and I cried and cried and said that I was going to jump out of the window. She said not to do anything like that, as that would only hurt me and not kill me. I called Marc at his work and left a message on his boss's answering machine. Within fifteen minutes Marc called me and said that he was on his way home and to hang in there. Everything seemed to blurr from that moment on and I think Marie, Marc's niece was the first to show up here with a bouquet of yellow roses, followed by my boss Gaddy. I kept crying and punching the walls in my house. Marc showed up after that and we were all gathered in our living room and everyone trying to console me. Gaddy told me to take as much time I needed off from work. After an hour Gaddy left and so did Marie. I called my brother in San Jose and Meera in India about the death of my child. My brother said he and Amarjeet would come and keep me company the next day.

I made several calls to everyone that was connected to Edwin in Colorado Springs. First he went to his new job in Douglas County, where he had started his work on the 2nd of July. The lady there told me that he came in to work both 2nd and 3rd for his orientation and pick out his benefits and sign papers for his medical plan. She said when she asked him if he would have any beneficiaries on the Plan and he smiled and said no. He was to return back to work on 8th and had 4th, 5th, 6th and 7th off due to the fourth of July holiday. When he did not come in and they called his home and left several messages with no response from him, they asked the Colorado Springs Police department to check on him. That is when they found him dead in the house, lying there with his brains blown all over the walls, with his gun and telephone in his left hand and maggots and flies all over his body. Two bullet holes in the ceiling and one in him. They could not find the shell casings to the fired bullets. His gun still had seven bullets in the casing and one in the chamber (where did the 3rd bullet come from). He was shot in the evening of the 3rd when he got home from work and was still in his police uniform and died on the 4th of July as the police report indicated. My poor child was lying dead for five days without anyone knowing what happened to him and his body was decomposing rapidly in the heat of the summer. The front was locked shut with no dead bolt from inside. The floor fan was knocked face down on the ground and still running and all his change knocked down too. This indicated to me that there could have been a struggle there and he did not know what hit him. Yet the coroner's report had ruled it a suicide..........no way. The coroner's report also indicated a blood alcohol level of........ ; but Edwin did not drink alcohol as I remember from the year before and me trying to have him take a sip of my wine glass and he would not. The police report did not indicate that there were these empty booze bottles in his room. They found a supposed suicide note that said was downstairs on the dining room which said "I leave........and......to take care of my belongings". So in other words he wrote this note, which was his handwriting, left it on the dining room downstairs and went upstairs to shoot him. When I talked to the lady at his job, she told me they were shocked that Edwin had committed suicide, as he passed all their psychological tests with flying colors and he was their top candidate for the Deputy Sherriff's job. She did tell me that Kenya called his job too after his death and had no emotions in her voice, showing that she was the least bit concerned about it. Kenya called here too and Marc gave me the telephone and I called her every nasty name in the book and told her never to call me again and hope the same would happen to her one day too.

Edwin's funeral was set for July 15th in Keene, N.H. by his father Ed who organized it. He was already cremated in Denver, as his body had decomposed considerably. His ashes would be flown to Keene for his funeral. Bill had come back to the US already and was in Keene with his wife Xandra and her kids. He said he and his dad were going to pick me up at the Bradley airport in Connecticut, when my flight arrived there. On the plane ride I thought, just a year ago exactly, I was going to visit him in Colorado Springs and now I was flying to his funeral. Billy and Ed picked me up at the airport and we had over an hour drive back to Keene. Ed told me that he had picked a plot for Edwin next to Kay, his dead grandmother. On my drive I could not let go of my only son Billy. We got to Ed's apartment in Keene, where he lived with his daughter Carla. Billy had told me on our car ride that Robin had left Ed a few years ago. I was going to sleep on the couch in his living room and Ed was going to sleep on the floor in Carla's room and he gave his bedroom to Billy and Xandra and her kids. Since Ed had asthma we could go on the balcony outside his room to smoke. Xandra and I both smoked there. I could see my son, Edwin among the clouds smiling down at me. That evening there was a WAKE at the funeral house. All of Ed's family and friends were present and I just moved around like a Zombie looking at this jar, which contained my son's ashes. The next day on the 15th the funeral service was held in the same Catholic Church, where Edwin used to sing hymns when he was a baby and people would turn around and look at him and smile; now that beautiful child of mine was gone. After the service at the church, the whole police department of Keene had turned out to escort us to the burial plot, with a gun salute. After we got to the burial site, I almost lost it and Billy and Xandra had to hold me up through the ceremony there. After that we moved for the refreshments in a hall in the backside of the church. I met Robin there with a bunch of her girlfriends there. I just stuck close to Billy and Xandra. Finally when this was all over I flew back home to California promising Ed that I would send him a check for half the funeral of our son, a promise I kept. I got back to work and tried to immerse myself in my job. All my customers were so sympathetic to me.

I felt that talking about my son helped me heal slowly. There was one customer of mine who was black who told me that Kenya could have put a spell on him. When I explained to her that Kenya's mother was from Louisiana and her dad was Jamaican, she told me that there was a lot of Vodoo down South. In one instance to control your man, the woman puts a little pee in the man's coffee. Even though I had not heard of this, I somehow believed it. If you ever looked at Kenya's ugly face you would wonder what my handsome son saw in her, unless he was controlled by her. My customer said that is how she maybe had placed the gun to his head and fired it. I kept calling the Colorado Springs Police department to have them send me a police report and they would send it but never did.

My boss Gaddy and her husband were planning a vacation to Paris on September 21st, for three weeks, and asked me if I could handle the branch by myself, and I told her yes and that she could take her vacation. She had given me almost two weeks off too. In August I received an envelope from the WHITE HOUSE in Washington DC, which contained a certificate signed by our president George W. Bush. It reads. "The United States of America honors the memory of EDWIN V. BUDD. This Certificate is awarded by a grateful Nation in recognition of devoted and selfless consecration for the service of our country in the Armed Forces of the United States". I display it in honor of my brave son, in our living room. From now on I did not complain about how many hours I worked at the branch and try to keep my mind off my grief by working overtime.

One morning in September Marc called me from work and told me to put on our television. I just woke up and had to get ready for work. He insisted I turn on the television on any channel, what I saw on the 11th of September that morning knocked my socks off. It was like a horror movie and how the terrorists were blowing up the skyscrapers for real in New York City. The planes had crashed into these buildings and thousands were dead or trapped. They shut all airports in America down and no planes were landing or flying out. What a disaster that day was in the lives of people who had lived to see it. There was total chaos in our nation and these suicide bombers had created this mess for us. I went to work that day and it was the topic for weeks and months to come. I asked my boss if they are halting all flights how was she going on her vacation now. She said when the flights resumed she was leaving and not scared of the flight getting blown up. She was a weird one, I guess. What we heard was, that the only flight they let out that day was that of OSAMA-BIN-LADIN's family that was flown to Saudi Arabia. Was he not the guy that had created this chaos? Well Gaddy was right all flights resumed and she went on her vacation to France on the 21st. I worked for three weeks straight for ten hours a day without a break. I asked our senior manager Darney if I could take September 31st, a Sunday, off as we were going to a concert by EARTH, WIND AND FIRE at the Concord pavilion and he gave it to me; this was to celebrate my dead son Edwin's 29th birthday. Marc and I went to this great concert and had fun.

When Gaddy returned from her trip, I had to keep working the fourth week too, as she had gotten sick. I knew she was taking advantage of my grief for my son. Inside our ATM room door she would keep everyone's work schedule and the hours that we had all worked. She had inflated her hours, when we all knew she did not work, so I changed her hours on the sheet. When she got back finally, after a week she noticed the schedule sheet and from that day on she was after my life and picking on me at work every day. I was not her friend anymore. From the looks of it she was finding ways to get rid of me. I started looking for work at other banks, just in case.

In November since our branch was the best, we got a big bonus plus Darney was going to give us an outing at Hearst Castle, in San Simeon, Gaddy drove us all in a rented SUV to Hearst Castle and Darney was going drive down and meet us there from southern California. Marc and I had already gone there about a year ago and enjoyed it. To tell you the truth I did not want to go but being second in charge I had to go. We arrived there after about four hours or so and waited for Darney to meet us. He barely got there for us to take the last tour of the day. After that he wanted to take us for dinner and asked me if I knew where a good place to eat would be, since I had spent the weekend there a year ago. I took them to this fancy dining area of the hotel we stayed at. This is where Gaddy started putting me down in front Darney and all our tellers. I had worked my butt off to help her and she was turning on me. There and then I decided I was going leave this bank. So the next month in the latter part of December I applied with Bank of America through a friend of mine, who was a manager of the Bank of America branch in Pinole. One day when our senior manager JC came by and asked me how long would I be grieving my son? That did it, I knew I was going to get out of this job for sure. What a heartless thing for him to say to me. Goodbye DOWNEY SAVINGS AND LOAN.

THE YEAR 2002

The year began with my wanting to change my job as a Customer Service Sales manager at Downey Saving. My manager and I were having some differences at work. She would dump all the work on me and she would have every excuse in world not to come in to work. Since my son died in 2001 she would take advantage of the state of my sorrow. I was spending fifty hours per week at the branch without any breaks and sometimes my lunch was also cut short by assisting a customer. I decided I did not want to work more than forty hours. My friend Asha, the realtor who sold us our house introduced me to a Pakistani lady who was the branch manager of Bank of America in Pinole, who in turn gave me instructions on how to apply for a job with her bank. I did a telephone interview with one of their job recruiter to get an assessment after a written test at their center in Concord and I got the go ahead letting me know that I was hired as a Personal Banker with Bank of America. On a Friday when I was going to give my manager my two week notice, she had called in our senior manager who said that they were letting me go on all made up charges by her. Nobody ever asked her work ethics at all, who was always gone from the job. Oh well I told them that I too was giving them notice that I was quitting, since I had another job. The senior manager asked how long I was going to mourn my son's death. He had died not even a year. I told him maybe one day he could find that out himself, as he had children too. That was so cold of him.

In February I finally received a copy of the police report filed by Colorado Springs P.D. on my son Edwin's death, after requesting it several times since his death in July 4, 2001. They had told me that he had committed suicide by shooting himself. I received the Coroner's report and the police report. I am going to put a copy of each in my book for my readers to decide if this was a suicide or a homicide? As when I read them both the incidents in one do not confirm the other. According to the police report the gun and the telephone were both by his left hand and my son was right handed. There was a sign of a struggle in his bedroom as the floor fan stand was knocked on the floor and still running and all his change knocked on the ground. He was found pushed back in his bed with his legs dangling to the ground. His brains splattered on the walls. I am also including his supposed suicide note, even though it was his handwriting, it did not read like one. It seemed he was forced to scribble something saying "I Edwin Budd, am assigning-------------- and -------------- to take care of my belongings" and signed by him. Also there were two bullet holes right above him on the ceiling and one in him. His gun that has a clip of ten bullets still had seven and one in the chamber, altogether eight still in his gun. After lying dead for five days his body was decomposing with maggots on him and flies all buzzing around. They never found the shells of the bullets fired according to the report. Also the front door was pre locked from the inside and slammed shut and no security lock on the inside which he always did. His hands were never dusted for gun powder residue. This is the same police department that botched the investigation of the little girl, Ramsay murder in December of 1996. I realized right away this was no suicide but a homicide. So I called the district attorney's office in Colorado Springs and explained my version of what could have happened, to a lady named Laura, who answered the call. I also told her that the police report did not collaborate with the Coroner's report, which said that my son had had an alcohol level of---------. I told her that my son did not drink alcohol, as I had offered him a glass of wine the year before when I went to visit him and his wife Kenya, and he told me "Mom we don't drink" and he wouldn't even take a sip. Even if he had been drinking, why did not police report say that there were empty alcohol bottles in his room? They had described the room to detail in their report. This lady Laura sounded very agitated when she answered me saying "Do you know that a police officer can shoot with either hand? No we will not re-open this case without substantial new information on this case". I told her the fact that they can shoot with both hands, I would use my correct hand to commit suicide. She hung up on me. I called my son's police department where he worked in Manitou Springs and talked to his boss there and he suggested that I could hire a private investigator, and referred the name of an ex-police officer from LAPD who lived in Colorado now. I talked to him and sent a thousand dollar deposit to have him investigate my son's murder. To make a long story short, he took my money and did nothing. When I called him he told me he was working on it and did uncover a few things, one of which was that if you argue with the Coroner's office they threw you out of the office. He said that he was working on two other cases in which a lady cop's death by two bullets in the head was also ruled as a suicide by the same Coroners' office. To this day nothing was ever done and the investigator took my money and never called me back. My heart breaks when think about my son Edwin who died at twenty eight years old.

In late March my only son, Billy was shipped out to Afghanistan for six months. Since he is my only child, I tried to fax letters to Senator Feinstein's office to stop this action by the US Army for two reasons, he had not even had a full year to grieve for his only brother, Edwin and also there is a law in the military saying that the surviving sibling not be placed in harm's way. Her office referred me to this other office and they in turn shoved me to yet another and by that time, it was too late. He was on his way to war in this foreign land, leaving his wife Xandra and her children. This was so difficult for me and his wife too.

I started my new job the first week of March at the Bank of America branch in El Sobrante. Of course they sent me to their training center on Van Ness Street in San Francisco for three days per week and the other two days learning at my branch for about a month or so. I would be opening all types' accounts for walk in customers, including loans they were applying for. I had to work one Saturday per month only and got a Friday off in substitution. This was a better deal here and also got my full breaks and lunch too. The branch was a very busy one and the day would just fly by. There were a lot of North Indian customers at the branch and our branches' largest account was with our GURUDWARA (sikh church) in El Sobrante. I assisted the non-English speaking customers in Punjabi. Since we had safe deposit boxes at the branch I had to assist these customers too. Since we had merchant accounts had to have their point of sale machines installed at their facilities. The rest of the bank operations were similar. In May we had a barbeque party at our house and invited some of my co-workers from work along with my family and other friends. All of us had a good time and great food.

Marc's company C.I.M. was moving to Houston, Texas and he had to look work if he wanted to stay in California. He was successful in getting a job with BP Lubricants in Richmond. Mid August I was laid off due to bank cuts and my last day was August 12th and Marc's first day at his new job was August 15th. I had to look for work all over again. I was the happiest mom when Billy returned to his family in September. I talked to him on the telephone and he told me thanks for sending him and the other soldiers there, CARE packages I kept sending throughout the six months he was deployed there. I told him if he was coming to visit me in California; he said he would try next year.

This year we went to several concerts. In the beginning of August we went to see AL GREEN concert opened by the WHISPERS. On September 22nd we went to see LUTHER VANDROSS. Before I left for India on October 4th we all went to see THE CARLO SANTANA concert. Sheila and Bob also came with us for this concert.

I decided to fly to India to visit my sister Lali, who was living in an apartment by herself in New Delhi, India, since my parents died. Since I was not working now, I thought would be good time to visit her. Lali was taken care of by someone or the other in our family but now she was on her own. Her drinking (alcohol) problem over several years has ruined her brain function. She is like a little lost child trying to manage life on her own. She does not know how to handle her finances or even balance a checkbook. She keeps saying she has no money. Meera had set up her account, so she would get a certain amount each month in her checking for her monthly expenses. She never became a US citizen while she lived in the United States for over twenty years; as she was too busy drinking. Her children don't care for her, as she was never there for them when they were little kids. Goodi and Ninni also came down from Chandigarh and picked me up at the airport and brought me to Lali's apartment, which was infested by cockroaches. I could not think about opening my suitcases there. Even though her apartment had two bedrooms with two baths and living room and large kitchen was very nice and she had a servant to clean and cook for her, I could not live among roaches. Since I was here for two weeks, I decided we were live in class, at the Ashok Hotel. We all drove down there and I booked one suite for Lali and I and another for Goodi and Ninni and their granddaughter, Bonbon who was with them. They all had asked me to bring things for them, which I gave them after opening my suitcases. I cleaned up and we all went down for some lunch in the hotel's dining area. Goodi and Ninni were leaving back for Chandigarh the next morning. We all had breakfast in my suite and had them checked out of their suite and they left to go home. I made them a promise that I would come visit them in Chandigarh the next weekend. I took Lali to the dentist as her teeth were bothering her. The dentists recommended that she took the remaining teeth out on the top and have a denture put in its place. After discussing this with Lali, we decided to have this procedure done for her. I had a taxi waiting and soon as the procedure was completed at the dentist's office I took her back to the hotel and put her in bed with a painkiller. She slept through the day and had some juice and some soup that evening. We were to go back to the dentist to get her dentures put in her mouth. Per doctors orders she was to rest in bed a lot. I decided to go to my bank, while Lali rested and withdrew money to pay my hotel every two or three days so the full payment would not come at one time. I also stopped and did some shopping for myself. It took a few days for Lali to recover slightly but she still could not eat solid foods. She ate a lot of daal soup. This was my major concern as I wanted to take care of her medical needs. We also went to pay her phone and electric bills, as she would not be able to do this after her dental procedure. That Sunday after five days I rented a car and had the driver drive us to Chandigarh. While I was there Ninni did nothing but berate my parents over and over again. My maternal aunt Harprastish (my mother's sister) was also at their house. Her house was a little further down there. I told Ninni to shut up and stop trashing my dead parents, since they were not here to defend themselves and I did not come to visit them to hear his trash. I had already spent so much money on them, and instead of being grateful all I could hear was him running his mouth. At one point I started to cry as I missed my son and parents. There and then I decided I was never going to come see these moochers again. If it was not for my mother they would not be able to get this fancy house they were building, which they showed me. Lali and I drove down to New Delhi the next day with our driver. I had only five more days left to return to United States. Lali was acting up as she wished I could take her back with me. When I was in the shower she would order beer through room service, and drinking when I came out. I did not mind her drinking one or two at the most, but she would keep drinking if I let her. My last night there, I had to take her to her apartment, as my flight was leaving early in the morning. I promised I would come back to visit again next year. This was one of the hardest things I had to do. I returned home and Marc and my kitties were happy to see me back.

THE YEAR 2003

The year started off on a good note. My neighbor Tammy gave me the telephone number of a temp agency in Concord, for whom she was working too for a year now. She was laid off by Bank of America after working for them for over twenty years. She said the temp agency places you in county jobs all over the Contra Costa County. I thought it would not hurt to check them out. I called to a lady named Paula, who set up an appointment for me to visit their office. When I went there she signed me up and two days later sent me to a pre-school location in San Pablo, where I did clerical work for the facility's principal, Pam. This place was Pre-Start place for pre-kindergartners. I worked there replacing a clerk who was a permanent clerk on disability medical leave. I worked there for a month and a half. Everyone loved me there, and said that they rather have me than their permanent employee who was almost eighty and who could not work fast enough for Pam's liking. But when she was scheduled to return back to work, I lost mine. Pam bought me a pizza lunch for my last day there which was very sweet of her. I notified Paula at my temp agency, and asked her to look for another assignment for me. She said she would and contact me about it. In the beginning of March she told me she had another position as a clerk in Martinez for the Appeals Unit with the county. I started working there. Their main and permanent clerk is Gris, who showed me the ropes at their office. After two weeks there, they told our office was going to move to a location in Concord. My main jobs were answering the telephone and help pack and label file cabinets to be moved to our new location in Concord.

Also I got a telephone call from Billy saying that he was leaving for Afghanistan on March 24th for another stint there. This was not fair to him as he had been there just six months ago, and now I could not see him again for six months or even talk to him via telephone. This war was getting on the nerves of all the loved ones whose family member was deployed in this useless war. I said my goodbye to him and also that he should take care of him and come home safe and sound, which he promised me. My heart was with my only child.

On April 7th our office moved to Concord after my three weeks in Martinez. I actually liked our new office, where I had my own cubicle with my desk. There were a lot of places for lunch here, also a Metro Café in our building which served breakfast and hot and cold sandwiches and soup. This was very convenient to us. There were other offices in the building. In our section we had three departments, Appeals, Quality Control and Payroll. Once a month the judges from Sacramento to hear the appeals of who were denied for Medical, Food Stamps, General Assistance, etc. There was a lot of work to be processed daily, which I liked, as the time there would fly by fast. I asked my supervisor Scot if it was okay if I took a week vacation in May as Marc and I were going to Maui, Hawaii again. He said that would be alright with him. So Marc and I spent a week in Maui and we stayed in the Royal Laihana hotel again and had a great time. On my birthday I wanted to take a ride on the submarine, which dove under three thousand feet, which was great to see the fish up close. I bought some souvenirs for my coworkers.

On the first weekend of June, Hercules has a Culture festival every year and this year there was a group called THE DAZZ BAND as their headliner and we went to it and danced our buns off. Sheila and Bob were there with us too. We all had so much fun at the festival. I was going to be at my temp job until I found something permanent in banking. My friend Gris told me how I could be earning a lot if I became a permanent at my job by taking the county tests. I did just that and I would pass the written exam every six months but could not pass the typing, as I would get too nervous. I was placed on a list for six months, but no one called me for a job. But I stayed with them as I loved my job and all people I worked for.

In August my friend, Charmaine called me saying that her younger daughter Michelle, who was pregnant with her first child and her navy husband were stationed in Monterey and she wanted for us to come visit them there. Monterey is about two hour drive from our house, so we left on a Saturday morning and stayed that night at a motel there. We all went out to dinner at the Fish House the restaurant by the water, which has great views. We spent the whole day and evening with them, chatting about old times, and returned home on Sunday.

I took Marc to India for two weeks in the beginning of September. We stayed at the Ashok hotel, like I did in 2002. Since I had an account in my bank in New Delhi, I paid for the hotel with Indian rupees in my account there. Lali would come by the hotel and we would go do things with her and she seemed very happy with us. We also took a trip to Agra by car to see the TAJ MAHAL, one of the Seven Wonders of the World. We had a tour guide who took us to different places and events in New Delhi. We also went for walks in the Nehru Park, across the hotel, where Marc took a cutting of a Plumeria tree, so we could take it back home and plant it there. Marc also wanted to go to a plant nursery, where he found a seventeen diamond ring in the dirt and gave it to me to wear. That was a great find. Of course we spent a couple of days shopping there. I also took out twenty grand in dollars back home so I could pay off all my credit cards and the rest in my savings. We wanted to take a side trip to Goa, in south India, but we ran out of time. We returned home after two weeks with a big jet lag. I don't think Marc really liked India, as it was too crowded for his liking. He said "India is a place with weird smells and weirder men."

In September Bill got back home to North Carolina, and I took a breath of relief. I told him to visit me and he said that he could not pull the kids (Xandra's children from previous relationships) out of school. Well I asked him to come by himself as I needed to see him again too. Somehow we both got into an argument over the telephone. I talked to Dixie about Billy and Xandra's issue, as he could not come or go anywhere without her. I told her to keep this to herself and she promised she would. But one day when the bitch was drunk, she called Billy and told him made up stories about them and said I was worried that Xandra was going to do the same to Billy as Kenya had done to Edwin. I never said that. Billy called me all mad saying that I had said things about Xandra that he did not like. After trying to explain that I had not said what Dixie had told him, but he would not buy it. This all happened just before Thanksgiving holiday. I told Billy that if he did not believe me, I would not bother with him. As I hung up I cried so much, how Bill could do this to me as he was all the family I had. That bitch Dixie ruined my relationship with my only son, like she did back in 1995. I called her and chewed her out. I did not call or talk to Billy for more than two months, as I was very hurt by the whole situation.

In October we went to see another Carlo Santana concert and had a great time as usual.

THE YEAR 2004

At the end of January, I received an email from Billy's wife Xandra, saying that Billy was leaving for a third tour to Afghanistan in March and she wanted us to make up. She said that she knew that Billy loved me and was just as stubborn as me, and she did not want him going to the war zone feeling the way he did right now. She said he missed me in his life too, so if I could break the ice and either email or call him. I did call him, as I missed him too and we talked for a while on the telephone and he promised to come by after his six month tour in Afghanistan. I felt a heavy load lifting off my heart, now that my son and I were on talking terms. He left for Afghanistan in the beginning of May as his tour was shortened by two months.

Marc and I went to Fiji Islands for ten days in mid May, so we could spend our birthdays there. We arrived there on May 15th which was Marc's birthday. They are sixteen hours ahead of our time in California. It was pretty hot there and half of the locals there were Indian people who had settled there a long time ago. The other half was Islanders who were black and very tall, and their greetings were BULA. Our taxi drivers were Indian too and I could speak Punjabi and Hindi with them. It was like I was in India but in an Island setting. There were three big islands and we stayed at one call Nadi (pronounced Nandi); and of course Fiji consists of hundreds of islands both big and some very small. We went snorkeling and picnicking on this one island, which took only fifteen minutes to walk all the way around it. Since I don't snorkel, all I had to do was wear some reef shoes and walk into the water and be surrounded by hundreds of different colored fish. Marc also found a giant clam shell that is twenty inches in circumference, which we brought home. The day we arrived at our hotel, Sheraton, two hundred people from all parts of Australia had also checked in our hotel. They were there for a Honda Convention. We made friends with some of them. One guy John and his wife, Kathy were our buddies there. John took Marc for a long swim to a platform way out in the water, where they could rest and swim back. When Marc was climbing up the platform he hurt his foot by scraping against something sharp like a rusted nail or something. He returned with blood pouring out his wound and we had to apply an antibiotic and put a band aid on it. We also would go downtown to eat and do our shopping. The streets there and all the vendors reminded me of streets in India. We also went to Raymond Burr's orchid garden in the hills there. On our way there the driver of our van stopped at his village, where the locals had handmade jewelry and pottery to sell and we bought some. One lady who was the head of the village took us on a tour of our village. I realized that they had very large barbeque pits, so asked her why they were so large she said in the old days the locals used to capture people off shipwrecks and cook them on these pits and eat them. Then she asked us if we wanted to donate some money to their church. Marc and I looked at each other and I know I was scared. So if we did not give her money, were they going to cook us on those pits? We told her we did not bring any extra money with us on this tour. We finally got back on the van and took off for the gardens, which were awesome. They had all types of orchids growing outside in the garden.

Well our vacation finally came to an end and we did not meet another American except one couple on the day we were leaving. Since Marc was admiring John's Honda baseball hat, he gave it to him for his birthday present. That was very sweet of him. Also my friend Aruni, who lived in New Zealand now, called us a couple of times and asked us to go see her there. We told her now we did not have any time left and had to return home; maybe on our next trip. We got back home and our kitties Yodee and Patchee were so happy to see us. Whenever we went on vacation Marc's Sister Sheila would take care of our cats and our fish in our fish tank and feed them.

When we got home, Sheila and Bob had bought tickets for the four of us to see Carlo Santana concert at the Warfield theatre in San Francisco on June 22nd. That was one awesome concert as usual.

On October 2nd I flew back to India again to see Lali. Meera knew that I was going there as she called me at work to find out which airline and what time I would arrive there. I gave her the information. I also told her not to mention about this to Goodi and her husband Ninni, as they would show up at the hotel to mooch off me. She said she would not let them know. When I arrived at the Ashok hotel and checked in at 3.00 am. I got washed up and slept for a few hours and called Lali at her house. She told me that Goodi and Ninni were on their way to her place from Chandigarh where they lived. I asked her if she told them, and she said no, and they already knew my airline flight number and time of arrival. The only person I gave that information was to Meera. This got me so angry. I told Lali not to let them know that I was already here. We would play the waiting game and told the front desk to not let anyone know that I was checked in at the hotel. I hid in the hotel for a couple of days, hoping that Goodi and Ninni would go away and I could go see Lali, but every time I called her phone Goodi or Ninni would pick up the phone and I had to hang up. The third day I finally called another lady who knew Lali to call her find out how long they were going to stay there and for Lali to call me when they left. Lali told her that they were leaving the next day. So I wasted three and a half days on waiting for them to leave. I was so angry at Meera for doing this to me. Lali and I tried to make the best of our time together. I even took her to get an affidavit from the local office authorizing me to process her paperwork on her behalf and to have her green card re-instated and appeal her case to return to the USA. As soon as I got back home I was going to process her paperwork. With that promise and a little shopping I returned home. This time I had flown to Taipei, Taiwan, on to Bangkok, Thailand on to New Delhi, India. My return was from New Delhi to Bangkok to Taipei to San Francisco. I returned on October 19th, 2004. Just two and a half months later on December 26th, 2004 a large Tsunami wiped out Southeast Asian countries.

I came back from India and filed Lali's application to the Immigration office through an agency of non-profit lawyers who could help people like me. The lady told me that since I was her sister, the process could take up to ten years. If Lali had any children here, the process could be quick as a couple of months only. I called Dixie to see if she could petition for her mom to be with me here and I would take the full financial responsibility for her. She told me that she would talk to her husband Maurice and get back to me. When she did not call me back, I called her again, and her answer was that she thought that her mom was not mentally capable to be here and NO she is not ready to petition for her at this time. I thought what a bitch she really was and told her so. I knew both her and Meera who never ever call her were waiting for her to die so they could get her portion of the money, mom left for her. I told her to tell Meera that she is the one who called Goodi and Ninni about my trip to India when I told her not to. I told her that I have no more relationship with her or her mom Meera and never to call me again. I have not spoken to them over five years now and don't intend to either in the near future. My life is better without having their dramas in my life.

Bill had returned from Afghanistan and both he and his wife Xandra came to visit us for a week. I was so happy. I asked for a few days off from work to be with them. I even took them to my work to meet all my friends there. We did a lot of lunches and other things with them. I was just so happy to see my only son, and the fact that he had survived three tours in Afghanistan. He posted some of his videos from there on my computer so I could see what a miserable desert it was there.

THE YEAR 2005

I was doing very well and much happier that my son Billy had put in to transfer to another unit which was in Oahu, Hawaii. I could not wait to go visit him there. He told me he will know for sure in April or early May for sure if they were going to Hawaii. So, in April, I called him and he told me that they would be going to be moving there in June. I told Marc that this year let us move our vacation from May to June so we could go to Hawaii to see Bill there. In the beginning of April I had same procedure that Lali had in 2002 with my dentist. I had them remove all my top teeth and had a plate put in. I was out of work for a week, and it was a painful procedure. We also booked our vacation through the internet for one week in mid June to Honolulu. Our hotel was Outrigger on the beach on Kali road. Somehow Billy still did not have his transfer papers by the time we were to go to Waikiki beach. We flew down there for a week. Our room was not the greatest but we spent more time outdoors on the beach or our hotel's swimming pool. We went to Hanama Bay, one of best snorkeling resort, for the whole day. We also drove all around the Island of Oahu, going to the North Shore, stopping at the Schofield barracks, where Billy was to be stationed later. I asked the guard if we could drive around the barracks, as my son was coming there in two weeks. I also asked him if I could take a picture and he yelled "NO PICTURES ma'am", but after checking our drivers' licenses and searching our car he let us in. What was I thinking? This was a MILITARY base and we were at war in Iraq and Afghanistan and of course I could NOT take pictures there.

Afterwards we kept driving past beaches on the North Shore and stopping at most of them and taking pictures of the breathtaking views on the way. We stopped at a restaurant for lunch and shopping at the adjoining jewelry store. Marc bought me pair of black pearl earrings made from compressed black lava; as the lady said that brings you luck. We finally arrived back at our hotel in the evening driving through some residential areas in the West of the Island and passing Diamond Head. We had dinner that night and went to bed. Most of the days we would eat breakfast buffet at our hotel, which was one of the best restaurant in the area, and go lay by the pool, working on our tans. One night walking up the main drag we discovered the street named after the guy who sang "Tiny Bubbles" Don Ho. We also ate at the Cheesecake Factory which is chain that has restaurants in the Bay Area too. Also on the main drag were stores for every designer you could think of. I bought my perfume at CHANNEL. If I had the money, I would live in Hawaii as it is truly a paradise. How lucky for the people who live there. Our vacation finally came to an end and we had to fly back and return to our home in Hercules.

I called Billy in North Carolina told him about our trip. On July 15th Billy and his stepdaughter Taylor, who was now nine, flew in to San Francisco to spend a few days with us, on their way to their new home in Oahu. I had last seen her when she was only four in the year 2000. His wife Xandra and her son Erik were to join them after a week in Hawaii. They were going to rent their home in Fayettville, North Carolina and their dog Dred, a black Mastiff had to stay in quarantine for six months in Maryland, with her parents Raymond and Bernadina, before he could be shipped out to Hawaii. We took Bill and Taylor around to different places like the Pleasanton Fair, Marine World Africa USA, Pier 39 etc. by taking the Larkspur Ferry to San Francisco. They finally flew out to Hawaii after three or four days, as I drove them to the airport.

As soon as Bill and Taylor left, Marc gutted our guest half bathroom and redid it with granite tiles on the floor, painted it, and put a new vanity and toilet in it. The end product was great. It took him two or three months to work on it on the weekends only.

In August, we at the county had to take training on a new system that the Contra Costa County was going to convert to. It was a four day mandatory training. Also my boss Scot said that if I wanted to stay working there, I had to switch to another temp agency and we had four choices, and I picked TEAMPERSONA. The temp agency that I worked for BARRETT BUSINESS BUREAU's contract was not renewed by the county. This was sad as I liked my temp agency, and my contact there, Noel.

I stayed in touch with Billy and his family in Hawaii, and they said they loved it there. We made plans to see them soon as March 2006 to visit them there. Most precious were the pictures he sent me of their Christmas decorations in their home there. It was so Island……. I sent him some bling bling jewelry a 22karat gold chain with big SIKH locket called the KHANDA for his Christmas gift and the kids got money from us. Bill said that he loved his gift and the kids were very happy getting MULA. He even sent me pictures of him wearing it. He said that his dog Dred had to stay in quarantine till the end of March 2006, and Xandra had bought him another female Black Mastiff named Kimba. The year 2005 ended on a good note.

THE YEAR 2006

This year our weather in the Bay Area had a weird weather pattern. When it rained in January through March we had Icy rains and Hail storms. This was coming in from the Artic and not Hawaii. I hated the freezing cold weather. Also, my boss Scot was retiring at the end of January, together with Eleanor, who was one of the new Appeals officers. So they were going to have a retirement party for them which was arranged by Ralph, who was Scot's boss. After finding a replacement for Scot, Yrma who was one of our Appeals Officer was chosen, through interview, to replace. We all rejoiced at that, as she was a COOL boss, and we all loved her. I had asked her that since Scot had Okayed my vacation in March and May if it would be okay with her. She confirmed it for me.

Since I had a free airline ticket through my UNITED MILEAGE PLUS, I booked that but Marc had to purchase his ticket to fly out there. Billy had booked us at the HALE KOA hotel which was for military personnel and their families only, and had the largest property of ANY hotel on the Waikiki beach. The cost of our room was only 118.00 per night, which compared to the Hilton next to our hotel that charged upwards of 400.00 per night or more was so cheap. We were on the 12th floor with an awesome view of the ocean. Marc and I could not get the same flight, and he had to leave earlier in the morning flight. I had the flight much later that arrived that night. Bob drove Marc to the airport in the morning and I drove and parked my car at the PSA parking lot and took their shuttle to the airport. The weather was so cold that I left our heater and the cats' heater on. Once I got to the airport, I called Sheila and told her about our heaters. She said that she was on her way back from visiting her daughter Marie who lived with her significant other Larry and their boy Dakota's house in Sacramento and was getting pelted with a hailstorm and icy conditions. She said that she would go by the next morning to feed Yodee and Patchee in the morning along with our fish in the fish tank and leave their heater on, if it was still cold. I told her not to mention this to Marc who would chew my ass out. These cats were my children and I could not let them suffer just because I was in Hawaii. Sheila is a great sister-in-law to me and promised me that she would not utter a word to Marc.

When I arrived on the Island, Marc and Billy came to pick me up at the airport. Billy and Xandra had said we could use one of their cars, but when Billy picked up Marc at the airport in the afternoon, he took him to his place in the North Shore. Bill and Xandra left him alone in their living room with their dog Kimba, who is about two hundred pounds. Kimba pinned Marc down on their living room leather couch and drooled all over him for about twenty minutes to half an hour in that heat there. Finally when Bill and Xandra emerged from their bedroom he drove Marc down to the HALE KOA hotel down south to check into the hotel, under his name and when Billy tried to drive back home his car a FORD BRONCO like the one OJ Simpson had and drove the L.A. streets on a police chase in 1994, had broke down and he had to walk all the way back to the hotel and pick up his other car a DODGE RAM truck that they had leant us. To make a long story short, we had to rent a car after all. After they picked me up and told me their story, we arrived at our hotel where Bill dropped us off with the promise that he would drive us to car rental place the next day. The next day Billy came by to see us and we all ate a big breakfast at the Hilton Hotel next door and then drove down to the car rental place, where we could pick up a car. After picking up a car we followed Billy and his Buddy who was a good car mechanic too to fix his Ford Bronco and pick it up. We then drove to his house up North. He showed us around his neighborhood including his house, which had three bedrooms and two baths with a living, dining nook and a kitchen; in the pantry were the washer and dryer. Their yard was just a mud hole, waiting to have the grass planted there. They also had good schools nearby for the kids. I guess their living quarters were pretty adequate. All the houses on their street were pretty similar and they had a lot of friends that lived there. Xandra was now working too at Billy's base at their offices.

The next day a Sunday, Bill called us saying that they were all at Hanama Bay and to come to join them there. You had to be at the parking lot before 8.00 am for any parking, and we had just got up and still had to bathe and eat our breakfast. We told them to come down to the hotel's swimming pool afterwards, as we would not find any parking there now. We did our stuff and they all came and joined us at the pool. They had brought another couple, Paul and Charlene and their two kids too. We spent the whole day there and at one point walked the beach for a while. That evening we all cleaned up and walked to the Cheesecake Factory to eat dinner. After eating they picked up their car and drove home. The next day we met them at their house and drove down to the beaches up North, which looked pretty rough. The kids and Marc got in the Ocean to swim and Bill kept watch on the kids. Xandra and I were sat by talking. At one point I had to yell to Marc to get out of the water as there were large rocks and the surf was kind of pushing him towards them. I asked Bill why he was not swimming and he told me that it might not be safe and he was a better swimmer anyway. With that point in mind everyone got out and we drove around to other beaches there and finally ended up at our hotel's pool.

We had a great one week with my son and his family and they were very happy and lucky to be in Hawaii. As all great vacations end, it was time for us to leave. Marc left next Saturday very early in the morning driving our rental car to the airport and returning it there. I was leaving that evening. It really started raining hard and non-stop all day Saturday and our plans to meet at the pool were canceled. I spent the whole day by myself at the hotel trapped by the torrential rain. I packed up my stuff and waited for Billy and Xandra to come down and eat at Bubba Gumps restaurant and drive to the airport. I had to fly back through LAX, where I had a layover for a few hours and then boarded my flight for SAN FRANCISCO. I called Marc and he was already home by picking up my car at the PSA parking lot. I had called Sheila to turn the heaters at home off as Marc would find out about them. He came to pick me up at the airport that morning. It was nice to see Yodee and Patchee again. I called Bill to let him know that I had arrived home safe and sound.

Since we had never been to Las Vegas, I found a great deal on the internet for two people to fly and stay three days and two nights at the CEASAR'S PALACE for the price of 880 dollars in the week of May for our birthdays; and we split the cost in half. So we finally got to VEGAS baby. The weather there was in the hundreds and we spent a lot of time at one of their swimming pool eating, drinking and having fun. For the first time in my life I ate a lobster sandwich. We caught a comedy show at Harrahs and could not get the tickets to see Celine Dion show, so ended up in line to go to PURE nightclub for an hour or so. That was a complete let down. There was nowhere to sit and we just walked out of there. Too soon we had to head home. We decided to do more the next time we came to VEGAS.

THE YEAR 2007

Marc and I went to Cabo San Lucas in Mexico in May for ten days for our birthdays. We had ten blissful days in the sun. We stayed at Pueblo Bonito Blanco hotel. We took in snorkeling and fishing trips on the boat. One day we walked downtown to do our shopping and mingling with the sightseers there. The best part of our trip was that the flight there took less than four hours each way. We spent a lot of time at the swimming pool, drinking Margaritas and getting our tans perfected and making a lot of friends there. One of the head waitress there named Julia became our buddy. The day we went fishing we brought back some fish and she had the cook serve it us for dinner that evening. On my birthday Marc bought me the most expensive dinner of lobster, which was yummy.

In September we went see my son, Billy and his family in Waikkii beach, Oahu. He reserved our room at the military hotel, Halle Koa, which has the largest property on the beach. It also has an adjacent parking in a very large covered parking lot, which can be accessed via electronic badge for the hotel guests. The rooms were only 118.00 per day compared to 300.00 to 500.00 per day in the Hilton hotel next door. The views were so fantastic from our top floor room, facing downtown with the view of the ocean too. My son lived in the Army housing on the North Shore which was less than half an hour from our hotel at non commute hours. The reason we could not stay with Billy was that they have two very large BLACK MASTIFF male and female dogs that are scary and big droolers. They drool over all their leather furniture. We just wanted our own space. Also, since the hotel had two large swimming pools and easy access to the world famous WAIKKII beach. It has several restaurants and a military PX on its premises. Therefore Billy and Xandra could come and join us at the swimming pool. Of course they always came down with their friends and their families in a large posse, other military families in their neighborhood. At the end of the day, we would all walk downtown to go eat at the Cheesecake Factory restaurant or other hotel restaurants there. Since Marc or I were paying for the meals, our bill was large and expensive. Of course Billy paid for a few meals too.

We spent one whole day at the HANAMA BAY, which is the largest enclosed reef for snorkeling. The fish are protected there and all you have to do is walk into the water and there are thousands of fish, both small and large swimming around you. We watch a video first explaining the reef; then, either you walks down the cliff pathway or you get on their trolley car by purchasing all day ride tickets. There is no alcohol or cigarettes allowed there. If you want to drink or smoke you have to go out in the parking lot. Knowing Marc he did sneak in a few beers in our cooler but I would go out to the parking lot to smoke. There is a cafeteria, where you can buy lunches. We had an absolutely great day there.

Billy also took his step children Eric and Taylor with us to these man-made lagoons for the whole day. They are right outside this fancy hotel. They have canoe rentals which can be utilized. Bill rented one and we all had a blast on it. On our last there we all went out to eat at Bubba Gumps and said our good byes, as we left early the next morning in our rental car to go back home.

At work I knew I was going to lose my temp job at the Appeals Unit due to the budget cuts of our state. My supervisor, Yrma extended my contract up to the end of 2007 and then again up to February 15th, 2008. After this I guess her hands were tied, which was a shame as I knew my job inside out and loved it.

THE YEAR 2008

I was laid off from one of the best jobs I had for five years, where I was a temp clerk at the APPEALS UNIT (for social services of Contra Costa County) due to budget cuts in mid February. I signed up for unemployment and was looking for a job actively. In January my sister Goodi called and kept leaving message after message from her house in Chandigarh, India asking me to call back and wouldn't leave her phone number. I finally left a new answering message telling her to leave me her phone number. When I finally connected with her, she was crying and saying that her bastard husband Ninni passed away. I asked her why she was crying. She should be celebrating that the bastard who made her and my parents life miserable for forty years had finally kicked the bucket and she was finally free from his tyranny. I asked her what she wanted me to do. This was best news of 2008 for me. At the end of my call to her, I got her laughing. My aunt Harprastish passed away on January 13th. She was my mother's younger sister. I guess whatever goes around does come around. They all thought they were going to live forever hoarding money, and it was okay to rein tyranny on others around them. God's house does justice, eventually.

Marc started to redo his bathroom, in our master bedroom, with the help of his friend, Fred. They started the project at the end of February and finally finished in September, since they could only work on it on the weekends. The final result was fabulous, with Italian tile in the shower area, new floor, new vanity and new toilet. It looks gorgeous.

My temp agency got me another job at the social services office in Hercules with the help of Mitch, one of the Appeals Officer at the appeals unit. I worked in Hercules from April 8th to May 27th. On May 27th I slipped and fell down at work, hurting the back of my head really bad, aside from the bruises on my arms, as I tried to break my fall. My supervisor sent me to my temp agency, which in turn sent me to their doctor. The doctor checked me and after some tests, I was free to go back to work. I came back to my temp agency and was told that my supervisor told me to take the rest of the day off and go home to rest in bed and call the agency the next morning. I felt alright and even their doctor told me I could go back to work, but they still sent me home. Instead of going home, I drove down to Concord, to see if my old friends at the appeals unit wanted to go to lunch with me. When I told them what had happened, Mitch said it was wrong of them to tell me to go to sleep to someone who had a head injury; that could have put me in a coma. I had a big lump on the right hand side of my head and even though it hurt, we all went out to eat at a fish and chips restaurant there. When I called my temp agency that evening to see when I could return to work, they told me that my position at the county was terminated per my supervisor. This was totally not legal for them to eliminate my position because I fell down, which was not my fault. That could have happened to anyone there, and I had the whole office there as a witness to what happened. This made me very angry. I called one friend of mine, who went to law classes, and she told me that I could sue them, and asked me if I wanted to take the name of her lawyer friend. All I wanted was to go to work and not sue anyone. So I told my friend to hang on to that idea, as I was not sure what I wanted to do. I tried to work with my agency, but the lady there got very rude to me and started making stuff like I was late everyday, etc. I finally called my supervisor and told her I was coming down to pick up my stuff that I had left at my work station and she told me that I could. My temp agency called to say that I could not go there and they would go and pick up my belongings and I come down to the agency to collect them. This got me totally mad. How would she know where everything was at my desk? I did not get ALL my things back anyway. I should have sued all of them, but instead, I wanted to stay positive and look for work.

I did get another temporary position through a temp agency, in Vallejo at First Bank. I worked there for about a month in the fall.

In august my son Billy and his wife Xandra stopped by on their way back from San Antonio, Texas to Hawaii. They were going to move to Texas in November, which would be Bill's new duty station. They were looking to buy a house there and narrowed it down to two houses and put in a bid for it, which was a foreclosure. Xandra was three months pregnant with my grandchild. We were all excited about that. They said that they would find the sex of the baby after a couple of months, and if it was a boy they would keep him, but if it was a girl, I could have her. So we made this deal.

THE YEAR 2009

I worked at the Credit Union, in San Francisco for ten and a half months. My granddaughter, Isabella Parshan Budd was born on March 30th. In May, I took three days off for Marc and me to fly to Las Vegas for a mini Vacation for our birthdays and stayed at the Ceasars Palace hotel again and had a great time. We saw the CHER show on 5/20/09, which was great. We also saw the KOOL AND THE GANG show. Went to San Antonio, Texas, where my son Billy is stationed since 11/2008. He bought a great big house there, which is his second house purchase. He also has a house in Fayetteville, North Carolina which is rented. It was great to be with my only son and his family for a week and seeing my granddaughter BELLA (I call her my diamond queen) for the first time. She is absolutely gorgeous. I also got to hug CARLO SANTANA at the Mariachi festival at the HP pavilion in San Jose, California on September 27th. I was at the right place at the right time and he was performing at this event. This was my fondest wish and it finally came true. I asked him if he could come to my book signing and he agreed to it, time permitting.

Marc's stepdad Hank passed away at 85 years of age on 12/30/09. This was the sadness my year ended with.

I got laid off from my work at San Francisco FCU on 12/31/09.

COLORADO SPRINGS POLICE DEPARTMENT

CONTINUATION/SUPPLEMENTAL REPORT

CASE REPORT NUMBER
01-22864

OFFENSE	STATUTE NUMBER	UCR RECLASSIFICATION TO:	UCR CODE
DEATH OF UNDETERMINED ORIGIN			

VICTIM'S NAME (LAST, FIRST MIDDLE)	DATE OF THIS REPORT
BUDD, EDWIN VICTOR	07-12-01

ARRESTEE NAME (LAST, FIRST MIDDLE)	RES ADD:	RACE	SEX	AGE	DOB
	CITY & STATE:				
ARRESTEE NAME (LAST, FIRST MIDDLE)	RES ADD:	RACE	SEX	AGE	DOB
	CITY & STATE:				

PATROL/NH   NAMED JUVENILE VICTIM/SUSPECT? NO

OFFICER J. R. LEDBETTER/1866P

LOCATION OF OCCURRENCE: 2640 Maroon Bell Avenue

ZONE: 4   SECTOR: 7   AREA: 6

OTHER OFFICERS INVOLVED

Officer Mark Watson/9613P and Sgt. R. Konz/093P

OFFICER'S STATEMENT

On 07/12/01, I, Officer J. R. 'Ledbetter/1866P, conducted follow-up with the El Paso County Coroner's Office. I contacted JEFF CAQUELIN and was told that Mr. EDWIN VICTOR BUDD had a bullet wound to the right parietal side of his head. Jeff also said there was no exit wound, and a bullet was not recovered. Mr. Caquelin also said that the Coroner's Office does not typically do a gunshot residue kit (GSR) on their victims and that a GSR was not done on Mr. Budd.

It was recorded earlier that I could not find a shell casing in the bedroom where Mr. Budd's body was lying. I asked Jeff Caquelin of the Coroner's Office if they had retrieved a spent shell casing from the blanket that was used to hoist Mr. Budd's body into the body bag. Mr. Caquelin said they did not find a spent shell casing.

I asked Mr. Caquelin if the wound to Mr. Budd's head was consistent with the two bullet holes found in the ceiling of the bedroom where Mr. Budd's body was lying. Mr. Caquelin said they are not—if in, fact, they were bullet holes—and that oftentimes in suicide cases the victims test fire the weapons they are planning to use on themselves.

The gun that was recovered on the scene, a Glock Twenty-two 40-caliber, was recovered by me and placed into evidence by me at the Falcon Substation.

I was able to notify, through a supervisor, MARK ROSE of his friend Mark Budd's death; however, I was unable to find MOLLY FRASIER, whom Mr. Budd had listed in his Last Will.

No further by this officer.

UCR DISPOSITION	OFFICER NAME/NUMBER	SUPERVISOR	DATE	PAGE 1
OPEN	J.R. LEDBETTER/1866P	SGT.C HUTCHESON/372P	15-Jul-01	OF 1

RECORDS & ID

		CASE REPORT NUMBER
		01-22864

OFFENSE	STATUTE NUMBER	UCR RECLASSIFICATION TO:	UCR CODE
DEATH OF UNDETERMINED ORIGIN			

VICTIM'S NAME (LAST, FIRST MIDDLE)			DATE OF THIS REPORT		
BUDD, EDWIN VICTOR			07/08/01		

ARRESTEE NAME (LAST, FIRST MIDDLE)	RES ADD:	RACE	SEX	AGE	DOB
	CITY & STATE:				
ARRESTEE NAME (LAST, FIRST MIDDLE)	RES ADD:	RACE	SEX	AGE	DOB
	CITY & STATE:				

Patrol/pav   **Zone: 4   Sector: 7   Area: 6**

Named Juvenile: NO

Officer J. R. Ledbetter, 1866P

LOCATION OF OCCURRENCF

2640 Maroon Bells Avenue

VICTIM INFORMATION

Name: **Budd, Edwin Victor**

DOB: **09/28/72**

OFFICER'S STATEMENT

Once the Fire Department had used their ladder to find Mr. Budd's body on the upper level floor of 2640 Maroon Bells Drive, the screen was cut out of the east window in the north bedroom, in order for me to gain access into the home. Once I got inside the house, I went immediately downstairs and unlocked the door to let the rest of the Officers in. I noticed that the front door was locked by the handle only, and not the deadbolt.

SCENE DESCRIPTION

2640 Maroon Bells Avenue is a single-family dwelling, with the front door facing south. Mr. Budd's body was found on the upper level floor in the southeast bedroom. The southeast bedroom has a bed where Mr. Budd's body was lying, in the southeast corner. The door into the bedroom is in the northwest corner. A TV with stand and VCR was located on the north wall near the door. Also observed in the room was a fan that had been knocked over, and the cover was off, but it was still running. Loose change was also on the floor near the fan in the northeast corner, scattered about. In the southwest corner of the bedroom, there is a door going into a bathroom. Mr. Budd's body was lying along the wide part of the bed, with his head facing the south wall and his feet towards the northeast corner. On the bed with Mr. Budd's body were two cordless telephones, a black Glock 22 .40 caliber handgun, a bullet resistant vest, a BDU uniform, and a police officer's uniform. The two cordless telephones were located near Mr. Budd's left hand, which was on the left side of his body, lying on the bed. The Glock 22 was also located near Mr. Budd's left hand. Mr. Budd's feet were uncrossed and dangling at the knee to the ground. Both of Mr. Budd's hands were to his side. In the ceiling of the bedroom where Mr. Budd's body was found were two holes, possibly made from a bullet. Also, a live round .40 caliber ammunition was found under the bed where Mr. Budd's body was.

OFFICER'S STATEMENT (CONTINUED)

Pictures were taken of the scene and placed into evidence at the Falcon Substation. Also, I recovered the Glock 22 .40 caliber from the bed where Mr. Budd was lying. The serial number is DHHH16. The magazine was in the gun, and when removed had seven rounds in it, with a capacity of ten. Also, around was found in the chamber. The ammunition in the gun, as well as the bullet found under the bed, were all Federal .40 caliber hollow points.

The kitchen of 2640 Maroon Bells Avenue is located on the main level, and is directly across from the front door. On the kitchen table was a note signed by Mr. Budd, indicating that his belongings be left with a **Mark Rose** and a **Molly Frasier**. Mr. Budd signed the note, and there was no further.

After further investigation, it was found that Mark Rose is a soldier with the United States Army, stationed at Fort Carson. It was also found that Mr. Budd had just gotten out of the United States Army, and had been a MP with them until recently. Mark Rose's sergeant, **Sgt. Thornton**, also stationed at Fort Carson, United States Army, said that Mr. Budd's wife **Kenya** left him three to six months ago, and took his two kids.

Upon talking with neighbors, I found that approximately a week ago, a moving van was in front of 2640 Maroon Bells Avenue, and there were people removing furniture from it. I noticed that inside the house, most of the rooms were empty.

Coroner **Chris Herndon** responded and took possession of Mr. Budd's body. Deputy Coroner Herndon estimated the time of death as being three to four days expired. Ms. Herndon took possession of the note left by Mr. Budd, as well as the keys to the residence. Officers recovered the Glock 22 and placed it into evidence at the Falcon Substation on 07/08/01. Officers also recovered a Manitou Springs Reserve Officer uniform with badge, and several training manuals for the Douglas County Sheriff's Department. The Manitou Springs Police Department Reserves uniform was picked up a Manitou Springs Sergeant.

No further.

UCR DISPOSITION	OFFICER NAME/NUMBER	SUPERVISOR	DATE	PAGE 3
OPEN	J. LEDBETTER, 1866P	SGT.C HUTCHISON, 372P	10-Jul-01	OF 3

RECORDS & ID

NAME: BUDD, Edwin   ID: EL PASO

Date of Birth: 09/28/1972   Age: 28   AUT NO: 01A-298

AUT DATE: 07/09/2001

Sex: M   Ht: 73 ½"   Wt: 157 ½ lbs.   BEGAN: 7:55 AM

ENDED: 8:24 AM

MD: David L. Bowerman, M.D.   DATE OF DEATH: 07/04/2001

TIME OF DEATH: Unknown

Authorized by: El Paso County Coroner

FINAL DIAGNOSIS:

1. Gunshot wound, head, penetrating, self-inflicted. (The direction of fire is right to left and slightly

    downward. The range of fire is close contact.)

2. Advancing decomposition.

3. Acute alcoholism.

OPINION: Death is due to the self-inflicted gunshot wound of the head.

MANNER OF DEATH: Suicide

TOXICOLOGY:

Blood alcohol = 127 mg/dl

Drugs of abuse (blood) = Negative

GC/MS analysis of blood (AR) revealed the presence of caffeine; no other drugs detected.

"INSERT ARTWORK HERE"

David L. Bowerman, M.D.

DLB/gds

October 5, 2001

SCENE INVESTIGATION: The decedent was last seen by Douglas County Sheriffs officers on July 3, 2001, and found by Colorado Springs Police Department on July 8, 2001 at 11:15 AM.

The decedent had just begun work at a Douglas County Deputy Sheriff and July 8, 2001, would have been his third day. When he didn't report for work or answer his telephone his supervisor requested that Colorado Springs Police Department do a welfare check. They entered the locked house through a window and found the decedent in his bedroom. A note was noted on the kitchen table which is apparently of suicidal type. The decedent's wife had recently moved out and taken his children out of state. On <u>July 3, 2001 a moving van</u> showed up and took most of the furniture out of the house. The weapon is a Glock 40 caliber and ammunition is 40 caliber hollow point. There are seven rounds in the magazine, one in the chamber, and one live round was found under the bed. There are no suspicions of foul play. The decedent is identified via his Colorado driver's license.

GROSS EXAMINATION

<u>**EXTERNAL EXAMINATION:**</u> The body arrives in the El Paso County morgue surrounded by the usual blue plastic body bag. The coroner's tag has the name "Edwin Budd," and the autopsy number "01A-298." The individual contained within the body bag is surrounded by a beige-color comforter and is clothed in a white T-shirt with a cartoon-type figure with the inscription "<u>Yoda</u>" over the left front portion of the upper chest. Abundant maggot teaming is noted over the skin of the face and the anterior portion of the shirt. A second white T-shirt is identified beneath the outer T-shirt with the "<u>Yoda</u>" label. The lower trunk and extremities are marked by navy blue shorts with a trademark on the lateral aspect of the left pant leg "Hoyas." Beneath the outer navy blue trunks is white brief-type cotton underwear in the appropriate position with urine-staining. The feet are marked by tennis shoes which are black and white and are appropriately tied and laced. The soles of the shoes are moderately heavily worn. The shoes have the label "Reebok / Size 11." The socks are stained with postmortem decomposition fluids. The unstained portions of the socks are clean. The left wrist is marked by a watch with a stainless steel and yellow metallic watchband. The watch has the trademark "Bulova." The left hand is devoid of ornamentation as is the right hand. The same is true for the neck and the ears. Glasses are still attached to the front of the face with correction in the right lens. The body is accompanied by a Sheriff's deputy-type uniform with a leather belt marked by a velcro attachment. The left front pocket is marked by three copper-colored discs with the number "019" and some change. The left back pocket is empty. The right

back pocket is marked by blood-soaked paper. The right front pocket is marked by "Dentine Ice" gum. The label is "Hercules." The blouse portion of the grayish-blue uniform has the label "Flying Cross / All Weather Deluxe" *[inaudible]* and has the shoulder patch "Douglas County Sheriff." The badge is inscribed "Douglas County Deputy Sheriff." A black pen is noted in the left front pocket of the blouse. A list of telephone numbers is also noted. Above the right pocket is the name "E. Budd" and a metallic star. Beneath this hooked to the flap of the right front pocket is the tag inscribed "Douglas County Sheriff's Office Deputy / 019 / Edwin J. Budd."

This is the unembalmed body of a well-nourished, well-developed, approximately 30 year old white man in the advancing state of postmortem decomposition characterized by diffuse maggot infestation concentrated around the head and neck region. The obvious marbling is noted over the anterior chest and right inguinal region with minimal bloating and diffuse skin slip of the lateral aspects of the trunk and extremities.

Radiograph identifies a projectile three projectile fragments in the left posterior cranial cavity. A gunshot wound of entrance is identified in the right temporoparietal region at a point 70 ½ inches from the tip of the right heel, 4 inches to the right of the midline of the forehead, and < 1 inch from the top of the head. The shaved preparation reveals grayish-black discoloration of the inferior border of the gaping gunshot wound. The wound is altered by prominent maggot infestation. Palpation of the right parietal bone reveals a bevel which is inward. The projectile fragments are identified by x-ray of the skull. No exit wound is identified. The defect is 3 x 7 cm and stellate. The surrounding skin is grayish-black. The subjacent galea and skull bone are marked by grayish-black fouling over the medial aspect. The defect within the parietal bone is irregular and 30 x 8 mm.

Palpation of the scalp reveals bogginess over the mid right posterior occipital region. The hair is short, crewcut, and black with beginning bifrontal alopecia. The skin of the face is grayish-green with prominent skin slip over the forehead. The left and right upper and lower eyelids are discolored grayish-green due to the early advancing postmortem decomposition. The corneas are cloudy. The pupils are regular and round. The irides are brown. The sclerae are white to gray. The bulbar and palpebral conjunctivae are devoid of petechiae and ecchymoses. The bridge of the nose is non-crepitant. The septum is non-perforate. Left and right external nares are marked by maggots. The right and left external ears are grayish. The right earlobe is devoid of perforation. The left external ear is leathery tan-brown and the left earlobe is non-perforate. The external auditory canals are patent. The cheeks are not unusual. The mouth is open. The tongue is not protuberant at this stage of decomposition. The vermilion borders of the lips are not unusual. The frenula are devoid of hemorrhage but are grayish-black. Teeth are natural and in fair repair. The tongue is recessed behind the closely approximated jaw. The buccal mucosa is mottled tan to grayish-black.

The skin of the neck is marked by the usual redundant skin folds. The chest is minimally crepitant associated with the postmortem gas production. Nipples are not unusual. The hair distribution is that of an adult man. The umbilicus is inverted. The anterior abdominal wall is protuberant and tympanitic. No scars are identified on the skin surface of the abdomen. The pubic hair is dark brown, curly, and thick. The penis is circumcised. The shaft is distended with gas. The same is true to a lesser extent for the scrotum. Testes are scrotal bilaterally.

The right and left lower extremities are flexed and externally rotated. The medial aspects of the thighs are studded with greenish-gray marbling and prominent skin slip. The right thigh, knee, and lower leg are not further remarkable. Prominent marbling of the venous pattern of both lower extremities at the ankle and foot level is noted. Toenails are long and well-manicured. The nailbeds are reddish-purple. The plantar aspect of the right foot is clean and minimally callused.

The left thigh, knee, lower leg, ankle, foot, and toenails are similar to those noted on the right.

The left axilla is marked by silky dark brown hair The upper arm and elbow are not unusual. The antecubital fossa is devoid of needle puncture wounds, tattooing, and scarring. The volar aspect of the left wrist is devoid of scars. The back of the hand and fingers are marked by early mummification and leathery mottled tan to orange-red skin over the digits. The distal portions of the digits are bluish-black and cyanotic. The nailbeds are mottled gray to orange-red.

The right axilla is marked by silky dark brown hair. The lateral aspect of the middle one-third of the right upper arm is marked by a professional multicolored tattoo which is 14 x 10 cm with a serpent-like configuration. The antecubital fossa is devoid of needle puncture wounds, tattooing, and scarring. The elbow is unremarkable. The forearm is unremarkable. The volar aspect of the right wrist is not unusual. The distal portions of the digits of the right hand are similar to those noted on the left. The palm of the right hand and thumb is not unusual.

The postauricular regions are marked by blackish-gray discoloration. The same is true for the back of the neck. The entire posterior thorax is discolored tan to greenish-black in a V-shaped configuration over the midportion of the upper posterior thorax. Skin slip with vesicle formation is noted over the midportion of the back and the lateral aspects. The skin of the buttocks is devoid of livor. The anorectal region is marked by abundant smearing with tan-brown feces. The anal region is devoid of trauma. No hemorrhoids. The perineal body is not unusual. Posterior thighs and lower legs are unremarkable.

The urinary bladder is empty. For toxicologic analysis, 20 cc of bloody fluid are collected from the left pectoral pool. No vitreous humor is available.

DLB:gds

CPSIA information can be obtained
at www.ICGtesting.com
Printed in the USA
LVHW061105280622
722282LV00012B/231